MW00695473

HOW TO THINK LIKE
A POET

For Asa

HOW TO THINK LIKE A POET

The Poets That Made Our World
and Why We Need Them

DAI GEORGE

BLOOMSBURY CONTINUUM
LONDON · OXFORD · NEW YORK · NEW DELHI · SYDNEY

BLOOMSBURY CONTINUUM
Bloomsbury Publishing Plc
50 Bedford Square, London, WC1B 3DP, UK
29 Earlsfort Terrace, Dublin 2, Ireland

BLOOMSBURY, BLOOMSBURY CONTINUUM and the Diana logo are trademarks
of Bloomsbury Publishing Plc

First published in Great Britain 2024

A catalogue record for this book is available from the British Library

Library of Congress Cataloguing-in-Publication data has been applied for

ISBN: HB: 978-1-3994-0830-1; TPB: 978-1-3994-0829-5; eBook: 978-1-3994-0828-8;
ePDF: 978-1-3994-0825-7

2 4 6 8 10 9 7 5 3 1

Typeset by Deanta Global Publishing Services, Chennai, India
Printed and bound in Great Britain by CPI Group (UK) Ltd, Croydon CR0 4YY

To find out more about our authors and books visit www.bloomsbury.com
and sign up for our newsletters

CONTENTS

INTRODUCTION

Poetry is the art of thinking. At one level, this might sound obvious. Pretty much everything requires thought, so in a sense poetry is no different from any other type of human endeavour, from moving an arm to sending a spaceship into orbit. But there's a difference between these other activities, important as they are, and the strange cognitive encounter that takes place when someone reads or writes a poem. You could say that movement and aeronautics – or cookery, politics, caregiving, chess – are the products of thought rather than a record of thinking itself. They take the messy impulses of the brain and convert them into something else: something useful and external.

Poetry, meanwhile, brings us as close as we can get to the unmediated sound of the human mind in action. It lets us eavesdrop on all the inklings, tangents, flashes of insight, shouts of joy or grief and complicated, half-formed notions that it would be almost impossible to capture if we didn't have this art form. Each poem is a public rendering of the mental drama that whirrs away behind the scenes throughout one's life. It can be about anything and go anywhere. All that matters is that it hits on something striking or beautiful and worth setting down for its own sake. The American poet John Ashbery put it nicely. 'I don't look on poems as closed works,' he said. 'I feel they're probably going on all the time in my head and I occasionally snip off a length.'

This book is an attempt to get to grips with this rich and mysterious subject. What do poets think about? Or, to put a different spin on the same question, what kinds of thinking

1

count as 'poetic'? I want to trace how these ideas have evolved down the centuries, in step with broader shifts in literary taste. At the same time, I hope it will be a thought-provoking romp through the history of poetry, introducing some key figures who have contributed to the current state of the art. From age to age, there's never been anything that you could describe as a poetic consensus. In general, poets are an argumentative species, addicted to manifestoes and theories, constantly defining themselves against what's come before. (I'm allowed to say this because I'm a poet, and I can hardly agree with myself from one day to the next.) But we're also a broad and ever-expanding church. We argue because it matters – because we care.

To take just one example, the Ashbery quote above – which comes from a 1984 interview – would have been met with bafflement or staunch disagreement in almost any other era. Ashbery's relaxed approach to composition, which suggests that a poem is no different from any other thought that might cross the poet's mind before or after writing it, might seem ridiculously cavalier. Where does that leave truth, beauty, wisdom or any of the other lofty things we might hope to find in a poem? For the English Romantic poet John Keats, poetry was something far more exalted. Writing to his publisher John Taylor in 1818, he argued that it 'should strike the Reader as a wording of his own highest thoughts, and appear almost a remembrance'.

The Keats view of poetry, if we can call it that, has deeper roots than the Ashbery view and still proves enduring today. People tend to think that poems are high, moving, powerful forms of speech, not just snippets of inner monologue. How else to make sense of the fact that we reach for them at weddings and funerals? Yet part of my purpose in writing this book is to affirm both perspectives, Keats's and Ashbery's. On the one hand, poetry is unique and sacred; on the other, it's entirely routine. It touches on both our deepest emotions and the most ephemeral scraps of consciousness. In this, I'm a greedy omnivore – I want it all. Poems tell stories, make us laugh, set riddles and pass down advice. They're usually written in lines of verse but not always. In umpteen different forms, they woo lovers, remember the dead and cry out to God. One of the less appealing traits of contemporary poets is to forget this ragbag history and carry on like this thing we do is just a slightly confusing branch of modern art: something akin to a foreign language that requires the reader to master complex rules and academic jargon. I've lost count of the number of times that someone has confided in me that they wish they could get into poetry, but they just don't understand it.

Unapologetically, then, this book tries to make poetry a vibrant, inviting subject that has no entry requirements. Moreover, I hope to place the genre in historical context, to celebrate its mutating forms and purposes down the years. This isn't a transparent or simple thing to do, however. Any history will be contested, and will be shaped by the background and beliefs of the person writing it. Famously, of course, history also gets written by the winners, and for too long in poetry – scratch that; for too long in all of art – the winners have reflected the dominant classes in society. They have been straight, white, male and affluent. When those powerful figures are grouped together into a list of poets to be read and studied, then they form what's known as a 'canon'. (Think a hall of fame with added scholarly heft.) Over time the canon solidifies, its membership becomes one in, one out, and before you know it, these are the only names you can find in the poetry section of bookshops.

That is the flipside of the positive story I alluded to above. Poetry has always been a wonderfully varied art form, more interwoven with human life than its high-and-mighty reputation would suggest. Yet at the same time, for many hundreds of years it's been wielded as an instrument

3

of (quote-unquote) civilization. The western poetry canon has formed the backbone of school curricula across the globe, riding roughshod over local traditions. Even today, by quoting the right classical poets or airily intoning a Shakespeare sonnet, one can boast of one's intelligence and social credentials. You don't have to look far, certainly in the upper echelons of British life, to find examples of that breezy, swaggering character type rising to the top of the pile.

The next 24 chapters take us from ancient Greece to the present day. They introduce the lives and works of poets from modern-day China, Iran, Italy, Japan, India, Chile and Martinique, alongside a wider range of poets from Britain and the USA. Partly this concentration on English-language poetry is because I'm a product of the anglophone canon. (No doubt someone in Brazil or France writing on the same theme would come up with a very different set of selections and insights.) My attempts to read poetry originally written in other languages are often only possible at all thanks to the miracles of translation. I've tried to give credit wherever possible to the individual translators who've brought these texts within my reach. Indeed, it's been one of the great pleasures of writing this book to step outside my comfort zone and finally discard that old chestnut (usually attributed to Robert Frost) that 'poetry is what gets lost in translation'.

This book isn't an attempt to destroy the western poetry canon or pretend it doesn't exist – an exercise that would be neither honest nor desirable, in my view. It does, however, try to make a new pass at that canon, and to scrutinize how these things come about in the first place. Where it studies female poets or poets of colour – writers who have been woefully underserved in traditional poetic histories – it does so in the firm belief that these particular poets are every bit the equal of Homer, Shakespeare or Wordsworth. Tokenism is an ugly trait, occasionally present in well-meaning histories and anthologies, but more often mischievously ascribed to any effort to make culture more equitable. I've tried to write an authentic account of the canon that nevertheless helps us to understand why that canon is creaking at the edges, in desperate need of renovation. But I'll be the first to admit that more remains to be done if we're to refocus the historical lens and make poetry truly representative.

All the same, I wonder whether the book's transatlantic bias might reflect the very distribution of cultural capital I've been discussing. For several hundred years at least, Britain and the USA have been geopolitical giants – many would say tyrants – amassing wealth, power and literal or figurative empires. These historical forces have had a direct bearing on the types of poetry published, studied and preserved across the world. Scholars are slowly starting to reckon with that power imbalance, and to excavate the marginalized craft traditions that have survived in the wake of European and American imperialism. In later chapters, the story will tilt towards poets whose work wrestles with the legacies of slavery and empire, several of whom played vital roles in their nations' postcolonial destinies.

Tragically, though, we can only assume that much great poetry has been forever lost to these historical ructions. For that reason, perhaps the biggest gap in the book, to my mind, is not a missing chapter on Virgil or Gertrude Stein – glaring as those omissions may be – but, rather, a scruffier, more open-ended chapter titled 'How to Think Like Anon'. Anon (short for 'anonymous') accounts for the great 90 per cent of the poetry iceberg that lies beneath the waterline. Some fraction of that number may be visible, in the shape of folk ballads, slave songs, sagas and nursery rhymes that were passed from mouth to mouth for decades before getting set down, at some point, in print or ink. But much of it lies too deep to be recovered. Anon is the great disruptor and democrat in poetry's history. And, as Virginia Woolf once said in *A Room of One's Own*, 'I would venture to guess that Anon, who wrote so many poems without signing them, was often a woman.'

Each chapter, as well as being an introduction to a particular poet's thought and work, is an experiment in biography. Often it will start in the middle of the story, with a historical flashpoint or passage of writing that illuminates the originality of that poet's thinking, before working backwards and forwards to flesh out the details of their life. This zigzagging method seems more suited to a wayward art than any simple cradle-to-grave approach, though no doubt it leaves much out. The aim in each case is to present a thumbnail sketch, fractured along the fault lines of the poet's mind. Throughout, I'm indebted to the experts who have written more dutiful and exhaustive biographies, many of whom are thanked through direct citations in the text.

The lives of poets don't always make for edifying reading. At the benign end of the spectrum, they can be cads, spongers and terrible spouses. One thinks here of Lady Caroline Lamb's famous line about her lover, the poet Lord Byron, that he was 'mad, bad, and dangerous to know'. Thankfully, these days we have a more understanding view of madness, an affliction that poets have always been strangely susceptible to – something that might be connected with how they think unusually and metaphorically about the world, with a peculiar intensity. Beyond the scope of Lady Lamb's formula, we meet artists whose selfishness or proximity to power tips over into worse types of complicity or abuse. More often, though, the lives of poets are just plain dull, characterized by desk-bound, cerebral occupations, perpetual money troubles and the wearying pursuit of patronage.

Such are the pitfalls of writing the biographies of poets. To some extent, I've had to reckon with them, though time and again I was pulled in the opposite direction, to marvel at how fascinating these figures were, how complex, and how revealing of the times in which they lived. Dante, for instance, played a pivotal part in a civil war that convulsed Italy around the turn of the fourteenth century. He was rewarded for his efforts with exile from his home city of Florence, an event that shaped the writing of his masterpiece, *The Divine Comedy.* Not the first poet in this book to experience banishment, he inspired a great English poet writing almost 400 years later. When John Milton found himself in the thick of a civil war, and likewise facing harsh consequences once the political tides turned, he drew on *The Divine Comedy* as he shaped his own epic, *Paradise Lost.*

These political dramas are far from a coincidence. One of the most telling themes that emerged while I was writing this book is the propensity poets have for positions of minor public office. For centuries, they've been at power's elbow, reflecting, cajoling and interrogating it from the sidelines. Poets, it turns out, make handy functionaries and civil servants, finding in those vocations a way of funding and enabling their life of the mind. This certainly puts a fresh spin on Percy Bysshe Shelley's claim that 'poets are the unacknowledged legislators of the world' – but it's a bargain that comes fraught with danger, not least because poets are also allergic to speaking clearly and directly. If you want to pledge your allegiance, then for heaven's sake don't do it in a poem. Even the most apparently straightforward and sycophantic verse is liable to shoot off in unexpected directions. Ambiguity is baked into the genre's bones.

Ultimately, this characteristic is the one common denominator that I can detect in poetry across the ages. More than any formal or visual pattern, the quality that connects poems of all kinds is their resistance to one-dimensional interpretation. Poems work in three dimensions, multiplying rather than consolidating the available meanings. A poem can brilliantly condense meaning, but that's not quite the same thing as simplifying it; in fact, one could argue that it's the opposite. By compressing many meanings into a limited space and paying close attention to sound and rhythm, the poet creates new linguistic vibrations – frequencies they may not be wholly in control of, despite their best efforts.

For the finest thinking on poetry and ambiguity, we can return to Keats. When I cited him earlier, I set him up as an old-fashioned counterpoint to the suave modernity of John Ashbery. Often, though, this lower-middle-class son of a stable manager, who died of tuberculosis at the tender age of 25, articulated a vision that catapulted poetry into new territory. Ideas dart across the surface of his letters, pushing back against the stuffy consensus that poetry should be a tool of education and moral improvement. 'We hate poetry that has a palpable design on us,' he wrote to John Reynolds in 1818, 'and if we do not agree, seems to put its hand in its breeches pocket.' In that image of poetry glowering at the reader, with a 'hand in its breeches pocket', Keats skewers a long tradition of schoolmasters who approached the genre in the same domineering spirit. He saw poetry as a medium of discovery, not instruction – an art whose sympathies lay decisively on the side of the student, not the teacher.

More radical still was a theory he struck upon in an 1817 Christmas letter to his brothers George and Tom Keats. The insight comes tumbling out in the middle of a paragraph filling them in about his recent hobnobbing about town. It's fun to read the bits of this letter where Keats sounds like any other clever and opinionated 22-year-old, gabbing about the meaning of art and life, wrinkling his nose at the pretentions of new acquaintances ('they have a mannerism in their very eating & drinking, in their mere handling a Decanter'). Before you know it, though, as he recounts his walk home from the panto with his good friends Charles Wentworth Dilke and Charles Armitage Brown, the conversation takes a turn for the extraordinary. 'I had not a dispute but a disquisition with Dilke, on various subjects,' Keats reports, teeing up a reflection that would reverberate through literary history:

> several things dovetailed in my mind, & at once it struck me, what quality went to form a Man of Achievement especially in Literature & which Shakespeare possessed so enormously – I mean *Negative Capability*, that is when man is capable of being in uncertainties, Mysteries, doubts, without any irritable reaching after fact & reason.

Cast aside that routinely gendered 'Man of Achievement'. What matters here is the entirely new concept Keats coins in *Negative Capability*. Usually we're conditioned to think of capability as a positive attribute: a sign of competence or strength that enables people to do things. If you're capable at maths, you can do sums. If you're capable at aeronautics, you can send a rocket into space.

Negative capability, on the other hand, is a faculty that has no recognizable output. The alchemy is all in the mind of the person who has it, producing phenomena ('uncertainties, Mysteries, doubts') that many people would be inclined to dismiss as weaknesses. In his letter to George and Tom, Keats is generous enough to extend negative capability to all branches of human 'Achievement', especially in literature, but to my mind it applies with unique force to poetry. When someone encounters a passage of Emily Dickinson or Claudia Rankine that supercharges their awareness of language and the world, I'm convinced that they've been made capable in a new manner – made capable, that is, to see, feel and undergo the complexities of life in a way that not even the most perceptive novel or play could replicate. (This isn't a value judgement: novels and plays are good at doing plenty of things that poems are bad at.) Thinking like a poet means embracing illogic and inefficiency. It means thinking exorbitantly, metaphorically, imagistically, yet also with a degree of precision that defeats any sensible paraphrase. It's the art of both/and, not either/or.

Apart from anything else, Keats's letter sums up why I've built a life around poetry, and why I keep coming back to it for nourishment. I started writing this book a year after I published my second volume of poems, *Karaoke King*. For various reasons, that project ended up taking it out of me. I was anxious about the ideas I was exploring in the collection, anxious about how they'd land in a fraught political and literary climate. I'd started reading myself with that schoolmasterly rigidness that Keats identifies, a hand in the proverbial pocket of my breeches, as if a poem could only be interpreted in one way and I was getting it wrong.

Now that the dust has settled, I feel proud of that book. Amazingly, though – to me, at any rate – I see that I haven't written a single poem in the three years between sending *Karaoke King* into the world and completing this book. I'll save the ins and outs of that tale for another day. For now, it's enough to say that the process of reading and writing about great poets from the past has been regenerative. By spending time with them, I've reacquainted myself with the gift of negative capability. Over and again, their poems exceed my expectations and wriggle free of any 'palpable design' I may have for them. I hope that you find similar riches here, and likewise feel inspired to read, to write and, crucially, to think with renewed energy.

1

How to Think Like Homer

The western poetry canon begins with rage. Not with love, devotion, homesickness or nature, but incandescent fury. It's the type of anger that uproots people from their homes, clads them in armour, sends them overseas in ships. The men who succumb to it – and it is always men – become different versions of themselves. They suppress pity, forgetting what it is to offer care or consolation. They drive themselves onwards to be still more angry, until their pride is satisfied or somebody ends up dead. Anger becomes a force with its own logic and momentum. The fire fuels itself.

'Wrath' is the first word of Peter Green's excellent modern translation of Homer's *Iliad*. The poem opens in the manner of all Greek epics, with a plea to the Muse, the goddess who grants poets their special gifts. 'Wrath, goddess, sing of Achilles Pēleus's son's / calamitous wrath, which hit the Achaians with countless ills.' We'll come to Achilles and the Achaians in a moment. For now it's enough to note that they are just instruments in the drama – objects caught up in the storms of wrath. What I like about Green's version is that it seems to make wrath itself a goddess, identifying the Holy Muse with the baleful emotion by separating the two terms just by a comma. ('Goddess, sing of Achilles' wrath', would be the more natural way to put it if you were looking to avoid such a reading.) A tale of great complexity unfolds, but every twist and turn can be traced to that one little word and its savage power.

And what was it that caused such terrible rage in the first place? Some slight or loss of face, most likely. A cold shoulder, a mistake in accounting – someone receiving more than his rival did from the spoils of war. Cause and effect are laughably out of kilter. If a woman was involved, then brace yourself, because the anger's going to be stratospheric. Women in this world are little more than chattels to be bargained for, a step or two up from slaves or sheep, and yet they have this uncanny knack of getting under men's skin. To lose a woman is to stand exposed as a fool who can't even keep hold of his closest things. It would be better to lose one's life fighting to avenge the insult than to step back from the fray, dishonoured but alive.

The Iliad is the great foundational European poem, dating to the eighth century BCE. It tells the story of the Trojan War, a conflict waged by Greece after the Trojan nobleman Paris abducted King Menelaus of Sparta's wife, the beautiful Helen. So we know that women have been caught up in all this trouble from the very start. Homer's first stroke of genius, however, is to begin the poem not at the beginning, with the elopement of Paris and Helen, but ten years into the war, in the midst of a whole other argument about a different set of women. The Greeks – aka the Achaians – are camped on the outskirts of Troy, in disarray after the god Apollo has sent a plague to punish them. Their offence can be blamed on Agamemnon, king of Mycenae, who has taken a woman called Chryseis prisoner. Her father, Chryses, petitions for her release, but it does no good: 'Agamemnōn's angry heart remained untouched. / Brusquely he turned [Chryses] away with words of harsh dismissal.'

Here's the first thread of anger in the poem as we read it, though we may remember that Agamemnon's wrath will not be the main event of the drama. That honour belongs to Achilles, who hasn't appeared since the opening fanfare. So what's Achilles' beef? A long story – as every story is, if you stop and think – but to cut it short: Achilles objects to Agamemnon's rashness in dismissing Chryses, who enjoys the favour of Apollo (hence the plague they're all suffering). Achilles thinks Agamemnon should hand over Chryses' daughter and save the Greek armies from disaster. This infuriates Agamemnon, who agrees to return Chryseis but only if Achilles offers compensation by granting him his *own* captive woman, Briseis. And you can imagine how Achilles reacts to that.

These are not admirable quarrels. From a modern point of view they are, at best, extraordinarily petty and, at worst, ugly displays of male entitlement. From these toxic squabbles one could plot a throughline linking up the vast history of misogyny – witch hunts, revenge porn, honour killings. Whether or not they count as admirable from Homer's perspective, however, is a more complicated question. This confrontation between Agamemnon and Achilles is in keeping with ancient Greek honour codes, and Homer's text routinely dignifies their behaviour. Let's look at an interesting example of this phenomenon in action.

At one point in Book 1, a little after the argument between the two men has first erupted, Agamemnon is on the verge of being pacified. Nestor – another king, the eldest and the wisest among the Greeks – has urged for cooler heads to prevail. His intervention seems to have made some headway. Sure, Agamemnon grumbles about Achilles' ruthlessness and ambition, but he accepts that he doesn't have the right to poach his women. A gallant concession, you might think, and one that should surely lead to some kind of truce – though Achilles quickly dispels any mood of compromise.

> Cutting in on [Agamemnon's] words then, noble Achilles
>   responded:
> 'I'd surely be called a coward and a worthless fellow
> if over every matter I yield to you, do as you say!'

It's the first line of this quote that's so revealing. In the first half we have Achilles quite literally 'cutting in' over Agamemnon in a fit of male pique (think of all those braying men who might have interrupted you in meetings over the years). By the end of the line, though, Achilles has been granted the epithet that tracks him throughout *The Iliad* – noble. How can such manifestly *ignoble* behaviour be rewarded with a word that claims the opposite?

To unravel that contradiction, we have to let go of our modern thinking, if only temporarily. What does it mean to be noble? A difficult question at the best of times, and the answer in Homer's case may not be convenient to our values. It isn't that we have to accept that Achilles is right to be so angry. Indeed, Nestor points out why he isn't when he tells Achilles and Agamemnon about the ferocious men he used to know. These former comrades 'fought against the strongest, / the mountain-laired beast-men, and fearsomely they destroyed them'. (Green notes that these exciting-sounding 'beast-men' were centaurs, the race of creatures, half-man, half-horse, who lived on the slopes of Mount Pelion.) Yet what distinguished these mighty warriors from Achilles and Agamemnon is that they were reasonable. 'They listened to my advice,' Nestor admonishes, 'were persuaded by my words. / So do you both be persuaded: persuasion is better.'

Persuasion may be better, but the problem is that it doesn't always prevail. Agamemnon, as we have seen, pays heed to Nestor, but the same words only goad Achilles into new spirals of wrath. This leads us to the crux of our uncertainty about that slippery word, 'noble'. It would be nice if Achilles reacted differently to Agamemnon's offences. It would be great if he showed himself open to persuasion. That would be the wise course. At this point in the poem, the beleaguered Greek armies can't afford to have a rift between two of their leading generals; equally, Agamemnon and Achilles must want to win the war and go home to their lands and families, an objective they can't accomplish while they're at each other's throats. It would be better by far – easier, less wasteful, more productive – if Achilles swallowed his pride, got back to the task at hand, and set about sacking Troy. But would it be more noble?

The modern answer to this, of course, is 'yes'. It's noble to be forgiving, to bury the hatchet and let bygones be bygones. But in Homer's world nobility is a quite different thing. It's about ancestry, prowess and the will to the power. It's a tantalizingly broad word that captures the qualities of a select few. You can be noble and pig-headed, noble and thin-skinned; Achilles certainly is. It isn't a word that precludes flaws, like 'virtuous' or 'holy' would. In fact, being rooted in power, it proves uniquely vulnerable to the flaws that lie on the other side of power – aggression, abuse, obstinacy, anger.

Always, we see, it comes back to anger.

Faced with a poet so alien to modern values, modern readers have dealt with Homer's towering example in a range of ways. We could start with Matthew Arnold, the Victorian poet and critic who delivered a series of lectures in 1860 titled 'On Translating Homer'. This tried to get to grips with Homer's legacy by studying the English-language translations in existence at the time and critiquing everything they got wrong. Arnold measures the translators against four qualities that distinguish Homer in the original Greek, namely:

> that he is eminently rapid; that he is eminently plain and direct, both in the evolution of his thought and in the expression of it, that is, both in his syntax and in his words; that he is eminently plain and direct in the substance of his thought, that is, in his matter and ideas; and, finally that he is eminently noble.

Perhaps unsurprisingly, this turns Homer into a Victorian gentleman ahead of his time. The virtues Arnold latches onto make him seem forthright and industrious – the kind of chap you could imagine going hunting in the morning, then sitting down to decide upon the correct rates of taxation in Eastern India, before dining on a brace of pigeons and washing it all down with a glass of port. Swift, plain, 'noble' thinking, administered with the minimum of fuss. A Homer you could build an empire on.

Homer's nobility, in Arnold's view, is closely tied to him writing in something that he dubs 'the grand style'. This tradition, he says, offers 'something more than touching and stirring; it can form the character, it is edifying'. Homer is being roped in here as an instrument of moral education. Again, this isn't surprising – by the time Arnold was writing, Homer had served this purpose for generations of upper-crust English schoolboys, who would have had to learn his works by heart and imitate them in their own attempts at classical verse. There was a holistic rationale behind teaching the poetry canon like this. By developing the finer aesthetic sensibilities of a child, you would also 'form his character' – two for the price of one.

Arnold, naturally, is all for the canon. His lectures are steeped in reverence for Homer as a Great Mind and font of human knowledge. Nevertheless, they also probe at a difficulty in this long-standing model of learning and imitation – namely, that it is almost impossible to rise to Homer's example. What makes him such an infernally difficult poet to translate, Arnold argues, is the fact that he manages to be noble even while addressing 'prosaic subjects', 'such as dressing, eating, drinking, harnessing, travelling, going to bed'. Poets aren't meant to write about going to bed. Going to bed in order to sleep with a beautiful woman, maybe – but not just the act of retiring for the night. The subject lacks dignity, importance.

Here, though, is Homer, in Green's translation of Book 9 of *The Iliad*, describing just such a sexless bedtime:

Patroklos instructed his companions and the handmaids
to make a thick bed for Phoinix as quickly as might be,
and they obeyed, spread the bed just as he ordered,
with fleeces, a rug, and sheets of the softest linen.
There the old man lay down, and awaited the bright dawn.

A bit of context: Book 9 narrates an unsuccessful mission led by several senior Greek soldiers to persuade Achilles to rejoin their forces. (It probably won't come as much of a spoiler to learn that Achilles has stormed off in a fit of rage, to punish everyone for Agamemnon's insult.) This failed attempt to woo back Achilles isn't a mundane moment. On the contrary, it's filled with dramatic import as Achilles warns his friends not to push their luck by begging him to return. A few stanzas before this, he has said, in effect, that he will sleep on it – 'tomorrow at daybreak / we'll make our decision: whether to go back home or stay' – and has asked Patroklos to make a bed for the elderly Phoinix. Long before this moment, Phoinix had looked after Achilles when he was a child, and this lingering affection shapes an otherwise difficult exchange. In other words, there's human interest and plot galore.

So, the moment itself isn't mundane – but what it does manage to be, in Homer's hands, is plain. The servants make up a bed, 'as quickly as might be'; it is laid with fine bedclothes; and the next thing we know, 'the old man lay down, and awaited the bright dawn'. Just like that: morning turns to night and the story moves on. This is the 'rapid' quality that Arnold identifies in Homer, and I don't think he is wrong to do so. More contentiously – but again, I don't think unjustifiably – one could say that the episode is 'noble'. There is beauty and economy to this scene. It captures more than it overtly states, hinting at reservoirs of feeling at the same time as it describes, with absolute accuracy, an old man going to bed.

Some 60 years after Arnold's lectures, Virginia Woolf expressed a similar sentiment about Homer, albeit with a very different agenda. As a leading member of the vanguard movement in the arts we now know as modernism, Woolf pushed back against the cultural inheritance of the Victorian era. She thought that period had bequeathed a set of repressed, hierarchical values that led directly to the carnage of the First World War. Modernists questioned the dominance of the Grand Style and exploded poetry and prose into new shapes that could capture the topsy-turvy world they found themselves in – a world of trench warfare, radio communication and motorized transport. They had no time for Arnold's view of literature, which seemed to treat Homer like a spoonful of cod liver oil to be taken after breakfast to build up one's immune system.

Nevertheless, like Arnold, Woolf praises Homer's heroic simplicity. In an essay titled 'On Not Knowing Greek', she flips Arnold's argument on its head. Rather than chiding specific translators for their shortcomings, she argues that we are *all* now doomed to ignorance about Homer and his fellow ancients. We just don't know how this stuff was supposed to sound, how it was meant to be performed, or what emotions people would have had while experiencing it. Despite these unbridgeable distances, Woolf follows Arnold in praising how beautifully Homer captures recognizable, worldly actions that should, by rights, be utterly mundane. She illustrates the point with characters drawn from *The Odyssey*, the second great epic attributed to Homer, which details the Greek hero Odysseus' long journey home from Troy. 'Penelope crosses the room,' writes Woolf; 'Telemachus goes to bed; Nausicaa washes her linen; and their actions seem laden with beauty because they do not know that they are beautiful, have been born to their possessions, are no more self-conscious than children, and yet, all those thousands of years ago, in their little islands, know all that is to be known.'

For Woolf, it is one of the joys of reading Homer to visit this Eden of the mind – a place where one can write about the sea, the sky, the bedchamber or the battlefield, without any 'self-conscious' inhibition. The pain, though, is that we can't stay there long. To think like Homer nowadays is impossible, like trying to live inside the ruins of the Acropolis.

On the eve of the Second World War, this Edenic Homer was demolished once and for all. 'The Iliad, or The Poem of Force' is an essay from 1939 written by the French philosopher, mystic and political thinker Simone Weil. It returns us full circle to the dark, furious poem with which we started this chapter, one that is inextricable from human power relations. Weil grew up in Paris between the wars, the daughter of Jewish parents who migrated to the capital after Germany annexed their home territory of Alsace-Lorraine. The Weils would later flee to New York to escape the Nazi occupation of France, though

Simone turned her back on this safe haven and returned to Europe to help with the resistance. As a family they knew hardship, violence, precarity, fear – scourges which Weil saw as the logical outcome of totalitarianism. Four years before she died in 1943, as Europe was breaking apart under fascism, Weil sought out the cultural origins of all this savagery. She found them in *The Iliad*.

'The true hero, the true subject, the centre of the Iliad is force,' she writes. 'Force employed by man, force that enslaves man, force before which man's flesh shrinks away.' Searing words, which she substantiates with a litany of *Iliad* quotations that demonstrate the fallout from this dreadful power. Weil defines her key word – 'force' – as 'that x that turns anybody who is subjected to it into a thing'. 'Exercised to the limit,' she continues, '[force] turns man into a thing in the most literal sense: it makes a corpse out of him. Somebody was here, and the next minute there is nobody here at all.' She quotes the following lines to demonstrate her point:

> . . . the horses
> Rattled the empty chariots through the files of battle,
> Longing for their noble drivers. But they on the ground
>   lay,
> dearer to the vultures than to their wives.

What a terrible, eerie scene Weil picks out here – the horses desperately dragging their 'empty chariots', vessels of warfare that have become mere objects wrenched out of context, weaving in and out of those still more pitiable objects, the corpses strewn across the battlefield.

Reading Weil's essay, one can be swept away by its visionary power, to the point that it seems to foretell the horrors of the Holocaust: that ultimate, genocidal example of a force that turned human beings into things. We need to be careful here. Weil was not a prophet, though she certainly had an acute moral imagination. Nor, it should be stressed, did she condemn *The Iliad* as an instrument of tyranny; rather, she positioned it as the great literary mirror on tyranny. The poem, in her view, reflects the worst of our species: the ugly side that emerges whenever one human, or a tribe of them, sets out to dominate another. And Homer is wise to it all. He shows us these events without sentimentality or judgement. As Weil says, the 'spectacle is offered [to] us absolutely undiluted. No comforting fiction intervenes; no consoling prospect of immortality; and on the hero's head no washed-out halo of patriotism descends.'

This could be why the poem begins where it does. The technique of starting a story in the middle of events is known as writing *in medias res*. (The Roman poet Horace first coined the term, contrasting this mode to stories that are told *ab ovo*, or 'from the egg'.) If Homer wanted to console us, he would have told a neat story *ab ovo*, beginning with the spark that ignited the Trojan War and guiding us through to the end. That way, one could experience these awful events as a one-off cataclysm – a vicious but now safely contained wildfire.

Yet wars are never about just one thing, and no war will ever be the last war. If Paris hadn't stolen Helen from her homelands, then who's to say that another bitter conflict wouldn't have erupted over some lesser quarrel? By starting in the thick of things, with a dispute over prisoners – sex slaves, to be frank – Homer denies us the 'comforting fiction' of a just war pursued with noble motives. That the protagonists are routinely described as 'noble' is an ambiguity we'll just have to learn to live with.

The western poetry canon begins with rage – nasty, arrogant, disfiguring rage. At which point it might be wise to ask: do we want to carry on? Perhaps an answer to this can be found in the opening lines of *The Odyssey*. 'Tell me about a complicated man,' writes Emily Wilson, in a game-changing new translation of this sequel to *The Iliad*. 'Muse, tell me how he wandered and was lost / when he had wrecked the holy town of Troy.' From anger to complication: our next hero, Odysseus, may be thoroughly implicated in the violence of *The Iliad*, but now he's lost and vulnerable. By reading the poem, we follow him on the hazardous journey home, through perils and setbacks, good deeds and ill.

A chronicle could relate the same events as a dispassionate sequence. A fable could mythologize them as a short tale with a learnable moral at the end. Only a poem, though, would filter that same story through the prism of 'a complicated man'. More to the point, it might be the very fact that humans are complicated creatures – wandering, striving, homesick, cruel – that gives rise to the need for poetry in the first place.

2

How to Think Like Sappho

Nobody can say for sure who Homer was, or even vouch that he was a single, unified historical figure. With this chapter, we turn to a poet who almost certainly existed. We also meet our first woman poet, and someone who was mentioned in the same breath as Homer from early on. One of the founders of modern medicine, the Greek physician Galen, claimed, 'You only have to say the Poet and the Poetess, and everyone knows you mean Homer and Sappho.' Sappho shows up in the historical record through varied testimony and archaeological evidence. Nevertheless, many mysteries remain as we haul ourselves out of the primordial soup of Homer's Greece into the murky waters where individual lives can just about be made out against the weeds. Whatever we know of this great poet's work has been salvaged from stray fragments, quotations by other authors, and, in one memorable case, a torn papyrus found in the cartonnage of a 2,600-year-old Egyptian mummy.

Sappho lived on Lesbos, an island off the coast of modern-day Turkey, sometime around the sixth century BCE. She was born to an aristocratic family and seems to have had three brothers, one of whom, the feckless Charaxos, is mentioned in the histories of Herodotus – a key (though not infallible) source of our knowledge about classical civilization. Identifying Charaxos as 'the brother of the poet Sappho', Herodotus relates the tale of how this young man bought the freedom of a beautiful slave woman in Egypt called Rhodopis. After squandering his money on this romantic whim, Charaxos returned empty-handed to Lesbos 'to be much ridiculed in Sappho's poetry'. Though not much of that poetry survives, we can lay a tentative finger on this family squabble in the work now known as Fragment 5. Here are the first two stanzas, in Diane J. Rayor's translation:

> O divine sea-daughters of Nereus, let
> my brother return here unharmed
> and let whatever his heart desires
> be fulfilled.
>
> And may he undo all past mistakes
> and so become a joy to friends,
> a sorrow to enemies – may
> none ever trouble us.

We can't say for certain that this refers to the farrago to do with Charaxos and Rhodopis. However, over the distant historical airwaves, one can clearly make out the sound of a long-suffering sister. She laments her brother's behaviour and prays the gods will give him the strength to 'undo all past mistakes'. Grow up and come home safe, the poem pleads. Stop giving us all a headache. The sentiment could emerge equally from a woman in the East Aegean some two and a half millennia ago or from a big sister today, anxiously checking her phone for a text from the brother who went out clubbing last night and hasn't surfaced yet.

In an important sense, then, it may not matter whether Fragment 5 is an authentic expression of the real-life Sappho's feelings. The point is that it *could* be Sappho, or someone else who happens to share her characteristics (a sister, separated from her brother, wondering when he's coming home). In reading the poem, we follow a disembodied train of thought and understand that it represents a moment of consciousness. This is actually quite a weird and wonderful feat of human imagination. Somehow we intuit that the voice we encounter is making a statement, though that statement isn't necessarily asking us to do anything, like fetch her brother from overseas. Indeed, it's addressed to the gods, though it seems perfectly apt and meaningful for us to overhear. The words may or may not be identical to the feelings of the person who wrote them, yet somebody is certainly speaking – so let's call them 'the speaker', for the sake of argument. The speaker's words have a richness that marks them off from other short snippets of language, like shopping lists or letters. They present as a self-contained work of art.

This mode of poetic thinking is different from the type that we encounter in Homer. Reading *The Iliad*, we're aware of someone telling us the story, but who that person might be is, at best, a secondary question. We know that the speaker isn't telling us about his personal feelings, because everything is subsumed by the heroic exploits of Agamemnon, Odysseus and Achilles. After appealing to the Muse to give him the power of song, the speaker pretty much vanishes from the scene. What follows is storytelling as much as poetry, hence it being assigned to the genre of 'epic' (from the ancient Greek ἔπος, meaning 'word, narrative, song').

In Sappho's poetry, however, we are in the genre not of epic but of lyric. This was one of three poetic modes identified by Aristotle in his *Poetics*, alongside epic and dramatic verse (dramatic, as one would expect, referring to the type of poetry one finds in plays). Aristotle passes brusquely over lyric, barely thinking it worth the trouble of explanation. In the centuries that have passed since then, however, lyric has gradually become the dominant partner in that trifecta. Towards the modern era the term comes to cover any short poem expressing a subjective viewpoint, rising to particular prominence in the Romantic period of the early nineteenth century. 'A poet is a nightingale,' writes Percy Bysshe Shelley in his famous unfinished essay 'A Defence of Poetry', 'who sits in darkness and sings to cheer its own solitude with sweet sounds'. C. Day-Lewis takes a more prosaic approach, defining lyric as 'a poem which expresses a single state of mind, a single mood, or sets two simple moods one against the other'. However one describes it, the lyric poem prizes the interiority of the speaker. It captures a 'mood', a snapshot of personal feeling – an emotional selfie, if you will. That analogy might be less corny than it seems, if one thinks about the fertile crossover between lyric poetry and photographic self-representation on Instagram nowadays.

Whatever lyric is, its origins can be traced to Sappho. In his useful introduction to the genre, Scott Brewster writes that lyric 'derives from the Greek *lurikos* ("for the lyre"), where verses would be sung or recited to the accompaniment of a lyre'. It's not a massive jump from these musical origins to the context in which we most often hear the word 'lyric' nowadays – as the verbal component of popular song. Like Chuck Berry, Bruce Springsteen and any of the other great guitar-slinging modern lyricists, Sappho has been preserved for posterity in a series of iconic images that show her sporting her weapon of choice, in her case, the lyre. We still possess four Athenian vase paintings that depict her either with her instrument or reading from a scroll. These provide a vital counterpoint to Shelley's vision of the poet as a tremulous songbird tweeting into the 'darkness', never sure whether someone will overhear. On these vases the poet is present, but so is her rapt audience. Lyric becomes a matter of performance and projection as much as of personal authenticity.

One of Sappho's most celebrated lines positions the lyre in just this way, as a medium geared towards spectacle and artifice. It's best known in English through Mary Barnard's translation:

I took my lyre and said

Come now, my heavenly
tortoise shell: become
a speaking instrument

Barnard's translations came out in 1958 and did much to popularize Sappho for a new postwar audience, savvy to sexual liberation. Their classical credentials have been debated but their plain-spoken fluency remains a model for translators looking to keep the blood and soul in Sappho's fragments. Here, 'tortoise shell' refers to the material lyres were made out of, and it offers a neat symbol for the alchemical transformations that happen in a poetic performance. An animal furnishes its shell, which is then polished, carved and strung to become a lyre. In turn, that lyre provides a musical accompaniment that elevates mere words from their usual function into something heightened, focused, special. The lyre, but also by extension the poet behind it, becomes 'a speaking instrument'.

One can easily get lost in the labyrinth of lyric theory, wondering what it all means when a poetic 'I' steps up and performs like this – but the essential ingredients are all there in this brief, ecstatic utterance. In fact, we could make the point clearer still by turning to the contemporary poet Anne Carson's translation of the same line: 'yes! radiant lyre speak to me / become a voice'.

Besides her huge contribution to lyric poetry Sappho is best known nowadays for her sexual preferences – or what we imagine them to have been, in any case. There's a salutary lesson to be learned here about the contrasting afterlives of male and female poets. The adjective 'Homeric' tends to mean 'of a type or nature befitting an epic poem; grand, large-scale', gesturing to the lofty status of its (possibly non-existent, but undoubtedly male) progenitor. 'Sapphic', meanwhile, connotes same-sex female desire. It's a word that relates to affairs of the heart rather than to literary achievement.

Same-sex female desire is not nothing, of course – far from it – and we shouldn't shirk from it when reading Sappho's poems. Hers are some of the earliest examples we possess of any sort of love poetry, and they establish sexuality from the start as something bodily, tender, fluid. Fragment 16 provides one of the frankest and most celebrated examples. The queer meanings are resonant even when translated by Rayor, who, wherever possible, opts for sparseness over supposition. The ellipses in the following passage indicate missing material, while Anaktoria is a female name, most likely belonging to one of the women close to Sappho:

> . . . [un]bending . . . mind
>   . . . lightly . . . thinks.
> . . . reminding me now
> of Anaktoria gone.

I would rather see her lovely step
and the radiant sparkle of her face
than all the war chariots in Lydia
and soldiers battling in arms.

Rayor tempers any excitement we might feel when reading this poem by discussing the communal context in which it would have first been performed – as a tune on the lyre, most likely with vocal support from a multi-person chorus. She takes us back into the tangled web of lyric theory, noting that 'when the first-person speaker says that she misses Anaktoria and desires to see her, she acts as a representative of the audience, inspiring the same longing in them. In that case, it does not make much difference for the understanding of the song whether the speaker is Sappho, a chorus, or another woman.' Maybe so, but is it wrong to hold on to the frisson we get from that 'radiant sparkle'? Whether Sappho herself looked longingly on Anaktoria's face is impossible, now, to say – but what we can't doubt is that her words have preserved the sparkle of that face for the ages, and given it lustre.

In any case, perhaps the most radical thing about this poem has little to do with its (quote-unquote) sapphic overtones. The sparkle stanza gains power by contrasting this glinting beauty with 'all the war chariots in Lydia / and soldiers battling in arms'. If ever we were looking for an antidote to Weil's 'poem of force', then here it is, in the 'lovely step' of someone we've never met, undoing all the militarism and clamour of war with a single movement across the room. The fact that this movement is being conjured in Anaktoria's absence is the magic trick of lyric. Pained by separation, the speaker tries to make Anaktoria return through words alone – and in doing so, she invites readers with no knowledge of

Anaktoria to witness this beauty, as if it were fully present before their eyes.

In the millennia since Sappho died, her reputation has gone through numerous ups and downs. Like driftwood on the waves, her work bobs in and out of view, often being buffeted along by the changing moral climate. From its earliest days, Christianity has treated same-sex desire – or any sort of desire, really – with a range of disapproving attitudes, from shame to outright persecution. Sappho has been a regular victim of these moral panics, falling under suspicion during periods of reformist zeal. One early Christian critic, the second-century ascetic Tatian, called her a 'whorish woman, love-crazy, who sang about her own licentiousness'. Though scholars debate the facts, it's likely her manuscripts have been burned by religious authorities on more than one occasion. Perhaps this explains the gaping absences in her work, remarkable even by ancient standards.

Sappho finally found her true readership with the rise of modernism in the early twentieth century. For a school of writers known as the imagists – on whom more in the next chapter – her frank eroticism wasn't a blemish on her verse, but the main event. Boosting their interest was a new selection of her poems, identified from a torn parchment discovered in Egypt. These five poems (which became Fragments 92–97 in her corpus) were published for the first time in Germany in 1902. They included a poem, Fragment 94, that has come to be known as 'Sappho's Confession', since it can be read as an open declaration of queer desire, her most candid on record. A dialogue between Sappho and a woman who is leaving her, possibly to get married, it contains heady references to 'crowns of violets, / roses, and crocuses' and anointments of 'pure, sweet oil', leading to a particularly tantalizing stanza where 'on soft beds / . . . delicate . . . / you quenched your desire' (all quotes from Rayor's translation).

Sappho's greatest modern interlocutor was the poet Hilda Doolittle, better known by her nom de plume H.D. We can trace the line of influence from Sappho in a poem titled 'Pursuit'. Published in H.D.'s first collection, *Sea Garden* (1916), it's a rapturous cat-and-mouse game masquerading as a lover's lament. It begins by misdirecting us with a note of detachment:

> What do I care
> that the stream is trampled,
> the sand on the stream-bank
> still holds the print of your foot:
> the heel is cut deep.

What do I care, in other words, that your feet have left a mark in the sand so entrancing that I've described it in loving detail? The rest of the poem searches for the beloved in a woodland landscape, obsessing over their physical traces. With the 'wild-hyacinth stalk' found 'snapped' along the trail, its buds showing 'deep purple / where your heel pressed', H.D. calls out directly to Sappho's Fragment 105(c), whose three scant lines read, 'Herdsmen crush under their feet / a hyacinth in the mountains; on the ground / purple blooms . . .'

The speaker is clearly pining after a person and their body, so a big part of H.D.'s tribute to Sappho consists in that erotic longing. Bisexual herself, H.D. tunes into Sappho's language of flowers and landscape to give shape to an otherwise genderless desire. But on a deeper level, the poem performs a pursuit of Sappho herself. It chases after the always departing poetic role model, treasuring her elusive form. Absence is fundamental to the attraction, just as it was for modern readers who thrilled over the fragile scraps of papyrus and parchment that preserved Sappho's literary remains.

In an essay titled 'The Wise Sappho', H.D. riffs on the ancient poet Meleager's words that Sappho left behind: 'Little, but all roses.' To this, she retorts: 'Not flowers at all, but an island with innumerable, tiny, irregular bays and fiords and little straits between which the sun lies clear . . .' This, it seems to me, must be an allusion to the dilapidated appearance of the parchment containing Fragments 92–97, officially catalogued as P. Berol. 9722. Dilapidated it may be, but also extraordinary: laid out in an approximation of the document's original structure, with vast tranches missing, it resembles some primordial landmass, frayed at the edges by those 'innumerable, tiny, irregular bays and fiords and little straits' that H.D. visualizes.

This brings us to a final, fascinating paradox in Sappho's story. Where once she was caricatured and dismissed by prudes, she now enjoys an almost legendary status among readers who appreciate the vital essence of her poetry: its passion and sensual energy, its lack of concern for heteronormative strictures. Yet even this love rests on a distortion. The material forms of her surviving work – ragged and worn, with isolated bursts of language surrounded by silence – seem to point to a peculiarly modern mode of thinking. Contemporary literature is comfortable with fragmentation. From T. S. Eliot to Eimear McBride, broken grammar and disconnected logic have been the marks of psychological authenticity in writing – more than nice, fully-formed sentences that tell a story with a beginning, a middle and an end.

The danger, then, is that we turn Sappho into a prophet of modernity: somebody who tells us what we want to hear about the arc of literary history, and the value of contemporary thinking. In 'The Wise Sappho', H.D. lovingly pores over the wreckage of her idol's work, prizing these 'fragments cut from a perfect mirror of iridescent polished silver'. A wonderful image, but a point it leaves unstated is that Sappho thought she was crafting that 'perfect mirror'; she couldn't have foreseen how later it would be smashed into scattered fragments. The truth is that we will never know now exactly how Sappho thought, any more than we can know the sound of her lyre, or the gender of the people she slept with.

3

How to Think Like Li Bai

Daoists don't believe in rules; they believe in ways. 'Way', at least, is the most common English translation of the multilayered term *dao* that lends its name to the philosophy. Originating roughly 500 years before the time of Christ, Daoism has traditionally been pitted against its main ideological rival, Confucianism, in an on–off tussle for supremacy within Chinese politics and culture. Confucianism's concern with order and stability – summed up in the imperative to honour one's ancestors – meets with a tricky twin sibling in Daoism. It isn't that Daoists see honouring one's ancestors as a bad idea, necessarily (quite the opposite); just that doing so offers at most a single way of approaching life, when there will always be many more. As the great Daoist sage Zhuang Zhou once remarked, even thievery has a *dao*. It's a term that lends itself to indefinite articles and endless qualification – your *dao*, my *dao*, the *dao* of the axe as it fells a tree. Poetry and parable are its lingua franca, and no poet speaks the language more beautifully (or mysteriously) than Li Bai.

Li was born in exile in 701 CE, somewhere along the far-western frontiers of the Chinese empire, most likely in modern-day Kyrgyzstan. As an adult, he would be famed for his striking looks and skill in archery and calligraphy, along with his unruly genius as a poet. Measuring nearly six feet in height, he had eyes that were often described as 'piercing', 'bright' and 'flashing'. Such characteristics suggest that the banished Chinese side of his family had married into the local Central Asian community. Despite being of mixed heritage, he traced his name defiantly to the imperial Li family that ruled China from the seventh to the ninth centuries, a period known as the Tang dynasty.

These claims to blue blood may well have had something to them – the Li family was large, after all – yet they never quite brought Bai the influence at court that he craved. (We'll switch here to his given name, to distinguish Bai from others with the Li family name.) Even though his parents made their way back to the motherland, setting up shop and achieving prosperity in Sichuan province, the taint of exile and grubby commerce dogged him for the rest of his life. Being a merchant's son disqualified Bai from the civil service examinations that offered the trustiest pathway to success in Tang China. His one route left was to win patronage from admiring officials who could ease his way up the greasy pole – a cause that wasn't helped by his tendency to write bombastic rhapsodies explaining exactly why they should do so, and to stay up late with fellow poets drinking mammoth amounts of wine.

Lacking a clear destiny, Bai traversed the four corners of the empire looking for a place in the world. He married, twice, but it wasn't enough. He emerges as perhaps the first example we have of that most beloved poetic archetype: the rover. Like Lord Byron many centuries after him, Bai was a handsome rascal with a taste for vice, redeemed by his finer sensibilities. Certainly, there's no doubting his taste for booze, a passion that he articulates with refreshing candour in poems like 'Please Drink' and 'Drinking Alone Beneath the Moon'. His biographer Ha Jin describes Bai composing the former in situ with friends, chanting each syllable in lamplight at the tail end of a heroic binge. 'Boil a sheep and butcher an ox for our feast,' demands the speaker (the translation is Ha's own). 'And let us drink three hundred cups at one go!' A libertine philosophy, to be sure – but a clever one, too. Even as deep in drink as this, Bai offers a compelling logic for opening another flask of wine: 'Since ancient times, saints and sages have been obscure. / Only drinkers have left behind their names.'

In this brash proclamation, Bai puts his finger on an important divide in his character. His ambitions were perennially split between seeking favour in the corridors of power and saying to hell with it and heading for the mountains. He did eventually rise to prominence in the imperial court, but managed to make enough enemies there that he expelled himself back into provincial life. Despite this conscious attempt to avoid conflict, he managed to get mixed up in the An Lushan rebellion that wracked China from 755 to 763. This eventually sent Bai back into exile, where he ended his life, according to a popular myth, by drowning as he tried to grasp the reflection of the moon.

So much for his political career. His spiritual life, on the other hand, could be considered something more like a success. In the countryside he would often end up trying to find one of those same 'obscure' sages he seems to snub in his great drinking song. It's fair to say that this restless oscillation – between company and solitude, abstinence and excess – points to a paradox, but it needn't be a fatal one. Perhaps wisdom can be sought in different places, first at the bottom of a wine goblet and then in a mountain hermitage. The *yin* of intoxication reaches out for the *yang* of silent reflection, the two opposing life forces binding together in a symbiotic embrace.

'Drinking Alone Beneath the Moon' shows Bai brokering this sort of spiritual-drunken pact explicitly. David Hinton, one of Bai's most dedicated translators, casts the encounter as a deep, solitary experience, far removed from the bacchanal of 'Please Drink':

Raising my cup, I toast the bright moon,
and facing my shadow makes friends three,

though moon has never understood wine,
and shadow only trails along behind me.

One's self, one's shadow and the 'bright moon' could be all the companionship a person needs, the poem suggests (provided one also has a glass of wine – so maybe it's four friends, really). A cosmological chain of being is established, ranging from the celestial moon to the immaterial shadow that 'trails along behind' the speaker. In the middle stands a human being with his earthly passions. Though the moon itself has no understanding of wine, the very fact that this is remarked upon implies that it's far more than an inanimate lump of rock. The phrasing invokes a mind, a character, a special lunar consciousness. Perhaps the things it *does* understand will forever remain out of reach for the speaker. Yet while he drinks there, all alone under the Milky Way, these different types of knowledge are brought into tipsy equilibrium.

A more straightforwardly pious Bai poem takes us on another journey into solitude. Though drink is nowhere to be found, the episode unfolds with a sense of absurdist humour that wouldn't be out of place at a tavern fireside. In Arthur Cooper's translation, the poem is called 'On Visiting a Taoist Master in the Tai-T'ien Mountains and Not Finding Him', a splendid riff on the descriptive, tag-like titles that mark many poems of the Tang era ('Seeing Meng Haoran Off at Yellow Crane Tower', for instance, to take one famous Bai example). We call this type of poetry, written to mark a particular event, occasional verse. This, however, seems to be a tremendous *non*-occasion. 'The valley noon: / one can hear no bell'; 'No one here knows / which way you have gone.' Where's that pesky wise man when you need him? He was supposed to be here in his hermitage, like a book of scripture on a dusty shelf. What a bust! The journey, it seems, has been wasted.

Or has it? While the speaker fails in his main goal of meeting the Daoist master, he succeeds in ways he might not have foreseen. He notices other elements of the mountain scene – dogs barking, deer flitting between the trees, bamboo branches cutting across 'bright clouds'. Everything else is at home and its place, which teaches him the only lesson he really needs to know: that the world is an intricate, finely balanced network, which he is lucky to be a part of. The poem is tactful enough not to state this, just as the master was tactful enough not to be at home. The wandering mind finds its own pathway to enlightenment.

This method of 'teaching without words' lies at the heart of Daoism, and is linked to Lao-zi's philosophy of Wu-Wei – roughly translatable, the poet and translator Wong May tells us, as 'self-so', 'as is' or 'let be'. The laissez-faire path to enlightenment, one could say – though that might be harder than it sounds. Cooper hits on a compelling cross-cultural insight in his gloss to 'On Visiting a Taoist Master . . .' The lesson of the poem, he suggests, 'may be compared with that of Ludwig Wittgenstein in *Philosophical Investigations*: "Don't think: look!"'

The art of not thinking could take a lifetime of deepest thought, or it could be gifted suddenly, in the course of an afternoon. This is a paradox that Li Bai brings to life over and over again in his glinting poems. Each one represents a minor epiphany. Its insights flicker in and out of vision, like the deer in the woods by the master's shrine.

In an unexpected subplot, Li Bai would go on to invent modern poetry in English. This is only a modest exaggeration of the impact that Ezra Pound's translations of Bai's work had when Pound published them in 1915, in a volume called *Cathay*. Pound had been turned on to Bai by a series of fortunate events, starting in 1913 when he befriended an employee in the Department of Prints and Drawings at the British Museum called Laurence Binyon. At the time, East Asian and African art forms were all the rage in the European avant-garde. The results could be thrilling – think Picasso's *Demoiselles d'Avignon*, which depicts five naked sex workers turned to confront the viewer, their faces painted to mimic African masks – even if the intentions were often dubious, to say the least. (The style was dubbed 'primitivist', which tells you everything you need to know about this era's esteem for African artistry.)

True to the zeitgeist, Pound was enraptured by Binyon's collection of Japanese prints. They seemed to chime with the spirit of the upstart poetry movement Pound had founded a year or two earlier called imagism – all clean lines and luminous symbols, etched for maximum impact using a minimal number of strokes. The pivotal moment came when Binyon offered to introduce Pound to a woman named Mary Fenollosa. She was the widow of a largely unknown American academic called Ernest Fenollosa, a researcher in East Asian languages who had studied classical Chinese poetry with the help of local colleagues while teaching in Japan. Mary had a chest full of Ernest's papers, which Pound convinced her to let him rummage through. What he found inside thrilled him to the bones.

It's impossible to separate Pound's excitement about Li Bai's poetry from his excitement about the Chinese language more generally. Any understanding he had came filtered through the late Fenollosa, who had himself been only slightly more grounded in Chinese than Pound, and scarcely less impressionable. Pound edited a tranche of Fenollosa's notes for publication under the title 'The Chinese Written Character as a Medium for Poetry'. The following extract gives a flavour of their argument.

> A true noun, an isolated thing, does not exist in nature. Things are only the terminal points, or rather the meeting points of actions, cross-sections cut through actions, snap-shots. Neither can a pure verb, an abstract motion, be possible in nature. The eye sees noun and verb as one: things in motion, motion in things, and so the Chinese conception tends to represent them.

At bottom, this is a praise song for the beauty of the Chinese ideogram. These are the characters that make up the Chinese alphabet, which Pound and Fenollosa thought were uniquely great vessels for carrying poetic meaning. Their reasoning? Ideograms blurred the lines between nouns, verbs and other speech parts, coming closer to how things really happen in the natural world. They allowed one to get rid of all the boring little link words like 'the', 'at' and 'of' that weigh down western languages. Chinese, in their view, had a stripped-down, vigorous, active grammar, illustrated in the following characters representing 'person', 'see' and 'horse'.

人看马

In English you'd have to rehydrate this into a dull sentence like 'The man sees a horse'. Chinese, on the other hand, gets the same message across in only three characters, which seem to interact all at once, with a type of alchemy. The result, wrote Pound, was a language that 'simply HAD TO STAY POETIC; simply couldn't help being and staying poetic in a way that a column of English type might very well not stay poetic'.

The rest, as they say, was history. Pound translated 11 of Bai's poems using Fenollosa's crib notes and gave them pride of place in *Cathay*. Attached to them was the curious inscription, 'By Rihaku'. Rihaku was Li Bai's Japanese name, which points to the cat's cradle of unlikely circumstances that led Pound (an American poet, uprooted to London, working on notes belonging to an American linguist who had studied Chinese literature several decades earlier, in Japan) to him. The poems were written in a new, swaggering English idiom that tried to approximate the vivid economy of Li Bai's Chinese verse. Here, for instance, is Pound's 'Taking Leave of a Friend':

Blue mountains to the north of the walls,
White river winding about them;
Here we must make separation
And go out through a thousand miles of dead grass.

Mind like a floating wide cloud.
Sunset like the parting of old acquaintances
Who bow over their clasped hands at a distance.
Our horses neigh to each other
as we are departing.

Let's start by considering what makes this a poetic triumph in English, regardless of its qualities as a translation. To understand how bracing it is, we could compare it with the poem 'Sea-Fever' written by John Masefield a little over a decade before Pound's translation emerged:

> I must go down to the seas again, for the call of the
>   running tide
> Is a wild call and a clear call that may not be denied;
> And all I ask is a windy day with the white clouds flying,
> And the flung spray and the blown spume, and the
>   sea-gulls crying.

There's lots to enjoy here, from the rollicking, sea-shanty rhythms to chewy phrases like 'flung spray' and 'blown spume' – it feels like a great poem to read aloud with children. For Pound, though, the problem was that *all* poetry of the early 1900s sounded like this: jaunty and slightly infantile, with a baggy syntax that stretched out to fit whatever meter the poet was writing in. (Think about all the padding in the second line of this stanza. It would be so much better to combine 'wild' and 'clear' in a single 'wild, clear call', but the rhythm as it stands won't allow it.)

The antidote, as Pound saw it, lay in Bai's poetry. 'Taking Leave of a Friend' and 'Sea-Fever' are both poems about setting off for the open road (or waves). They both contain images of clouds, symbolizing the restless fate of the wanderer. In almost every other respect, though, Bai's poem and Masefield's couldn't be more different. Masefield's clouds, for example, are bluff and quintessentially English, 'flying' off at a brisk canter across the sky. The clouds in Pound's translation, meanwhile, are – well, they're not actually *clouds*, but a singular entity. What's more, that cloud isn't a cloud so much as a complex metaphor for the speaker's own consciousness ('Mind like a floating wide cloud'). It looms there in the sky as if daring us to hurry it along.

The original Chinese setting of this line illuminates why Pound saw a pathway to modernism in Bai's work:

浮 雲 游 子 意

Reading up on this poem, I came across a helpful transliteration by a native Chinese speaker writing for the website eastasiastudent.net. The five characters in the line can be rendered in English as follows:

[float] [cloud] [roam] [person] [thoughts]

Pound got plenty wrong about Chinese philosophy and Chinese language – to say nothing of the fact that he became a literal fascist in the Second World War, serving Mussolini's Italy as a radio broadcaster – but I don't think he was wrong to see Bai's work as radical or liberatory. The five words in this line interact in ways that seem hard to paraphrase. The cloud is a person is a thought is a cloud. 'Roam' and 'float' are the verbs that shape the utterance, linking human beings to clouds, yet they seem to dissolve the metaphor as much as bind it. Whether or not the poem is unusual by the standards of Chinese verse, it asks a western reader to enter into a wholly new mode of thinking. A mode of thinking which, as we have seen, may in some respects be closer to not thinking – to letting the mind be as a cloud.

The Pound subplot, if we can call it that, has ballooned into something of a distraction across the last hundred years. Commentators weigh in on either side, citing mistakes, appropriations, cancel culture, myths. It's hard to imagine modern poetry evolving in the way it did without Li Bai, which makes Pound's translations of him hard to ignore, at least if you're interested in that narrative. That narrative, admittedly, centres the White cultural inheritance over the original Chinese poetry, valuing Bai for what westerners can extract from him rather than for what he teaches us. It's important to resist such an account. Yet despite all Pound's misunderstandings and linguistic gaffes, his orientalist fantasies and appalling politics, the ghost of *Cathay* still haunts my inner ear. It hogs the stage, so much so that one struggles to hear Bai's original song beneath its fanfare. What to do?

Luckily, in recent years Wong May has given us a new translation of the Tang poets that might just lay these demons to rest. She does so by restoring their linguistic innovation – all the stuff that first enraptured Pound – while grounding them again in lived Chinese experience and a genuine knowledge of the nation's indigenous philosophies. For what it's worth, she rates Pound, too, remarking that his work has 'an ineffable quality: shen-yun', roughly translatable to 'spirit tune/tone', or 'style of the spirit'. Wong's anthology is called *In the Same Light: 200 Tang Poems for Our Century*, and it deserves to be read far and wide, from Shanghai to Shepton Mallet.

Here is the start of Bai's 'Climbing the Phoenix Terrace in Jinling' as rendered by Wong:

The Phoenix Terrace
Once they frolicked

Phoenixes gone
        Terrace defunct

The river flows on.

In some ways the sentiment expressed here couldn't be any simpler: some things change, some things remain the same.

The phoenixes are gone, but the river flows on. On the other hand, the meaning couldn't be more complex. A paraphrase doesn't even begin to touch on the mystery that gathers between the lines, a mystery that Wong draws near to when she talks about 'the beautiful void depicted in Chinese art'. 'Look into this void,' she says, '[and] you are in touch with the one *thing* Chinese landscape painting does so well – *time*. In the ravine, between the cliff-tops, across the waterfall, off the rock-shelves between the lines, the words: time. It is all *about* time.'

It is all about time. Humans know this, deep down, even if we kid ourselves into thinking that time can be manipulated, ignored, brought into line with our designs. After all, what's a story if not an attempt to impose order on time, by saddling it with a beginning, a middle and an end? What's a sentence if not a doomed attempt to cut a slice out of time – to isolate a single action amid the hurly-burly of the universe? Subject, verb, object; the cat sat on the mat.

Bai's poetry has no time for such comforting fictions. It brings us close to the experience of time in its raw state, as a fusion of past, present and future events, filled with strange gaps and overlapping edges. We move through his poems confidently until we stumble, losing our footing on one of those 'rock-shelves between the lines'. Out of nowhere, a ravine opens up. A waterfall crashes down and we wonder how terrible it might be – but also how thrilling; how peaceful, in a sense – to fall and be absorbed into the river. Time would keep moving, with or without us, fulfilling its endless *dao*.

4

How to Think Like Jalal al-Din Rumi

In June 2017, the American singer Beyoncé and her husband, the rapper Jay-Z, named their newborn daughter Rumi, after a thirteenth-century Persian preacher and theologian. When you add the fact that he was a poet, it seems less surprising that a switched-on artistic power couple should be drawn to him as a touchstone. More relevant still, by many estimates Rumi is currently the most popular poet in America. During the last decade, his books have flown off the shelves in their millions, sales figures that would make almost any other poet either pass out or assume an April Fool's prank was being played on them. (This is an industry, after all, where *two* is a more probable annual return than two million.)

Chris Martin is another pop star who has been drawn into Rumi's orbit lately, citing him as a key influence behind Coldplay's seventh album, *A Head Full of Dreams* (2015). Track seven, 'Kaleidoscope', is a short, dreamy piano instrumental with a superimposed voiceover from Coleman Barks, the translator largely responsible for Rumi's recent commercial success. (A hefty proportion of the Rumi units shifted this century will have been Barks-helmed anthologies like *The Book of Love* and *A Year with*

Rumi.) On 'Kaleidoscope', Barks recites lines that sum up Rumi's cross-cultural appeal: 'This being human is a guest house / Every morning a new arrival / A joy, a depression, a meanness, / some momentary awareness comes / as an unexpected visitor.' Across the global north, Rumi has become an avatar of enlightened spiritual virtues – tolerance, compassion, self-acceptance – that can resonate with anyone, regardless of their faith.

It's a phenomenon that has been dubbed Rumimania by Franklin D. Lewis, author of a respected study of the poet. Writing at the turn of the millennium, Lewis spoke to a late-'90s moment summed up in his survey of prominent Rumi fans running the gamut from acoustic supergroups to Donna Karan catwalk models. 'On Lafayette Street in New York City,' Lewis writes, 'a clientele of about four hundred people a day at the Jivamukti Yoga Centre, including such celebrities as Mary Stuart Masterson and Sarah Jessica Parker, do spiritual aerobics to a background beat that sometimes mixes rock music and readings of Rumi.' Truly, if this isn't what the end of history looks like, then what does?

The phenomenon has only gone in one direction since Lewis was writing. Rumi's sheer ubiquity came home to me when I was watching season one, episode five of *The Outlaws*, Stephen Merchant's excellent comedy drama about a gang of misfits who meet on a community service project in Bristol. One of them is Lady Gabby, a vacuous (but deep down very sweet and caring) influencer with anger-management issues and a drug habit. At this point in the show, Lady Gabby is practising a pitch to her rich father. She wants him to invest in a new venture she's been plotting, an exclusive festival that would be held in his garden. She paces back and forth in her living room, intoning a prepared script.

'The great Persian poet Rumi once said, "Only from the heart can we touch the sky."' She takes a deep breath. 'Private Fest comes from the heart – let's touch the sky.'

There follows a perfectly judged half-second of silence – a fleeting moment where Lady Gabby sizes up the enormity and fragility of her dreams, before taking a bump of cocaine.

This scene captures the worst of Rumimania: the narcissistic individualism; the blue-sky business speak masquerading as soulful positivity. Jawid Mojaddedi – a Rumi scholar in the middle of translating the six books of the poet's magnum opus *The Masnavi* – puts the argument more generously. He points to the increasing number of Americans who identify as 'Spiritual But Not Religious' (SBNR), a trend defined by 'disinclination to participate in group worship or to blindly accept theological dogmas, adherence to relativistic ethical values, and liberal political leanings'. Mojaddedi acknowledges that the SBNR crowd are on to something with Rumi. 'The main attraction of being SBNR,' he writes, 'seems to be the preservation of a direct spiritual connection with a higher power and personal development through that connection. There is no doubt that Rumi's poetry supports such attitudes, although his teachings were aimed at those who were already religious in the same way that he used to be.'

And here we come to the nub of the issue. Rumi was religious. Actually, that won't do. Rumi wasn't just 'religious'; he was a Muslim. I've avoided using this term so far to make a point, since all too often 'Muslim' is the word that dare not speak its name in discussions of Rumi. Rozina Ali advances this argument in a perceptive 2017 *New Yorker* article. 'The erasure of Islam from Rumi's poetry started long before Coldplay got involved,' she writes, before going on to trace the roots of the phenomenon to the Victorian period. This was when Rumi first came to prominence in English translation, though, according to Ali, his western champions 'could not reconcile their ideas about a "desert religion," with its unusual moral and legal codes, and the work of poets like Rumi and Hafez'. More recently, colonial condescension has converged with insidious theories that Islam is a uniquely violent religion, a belief that has gone into overdrive post-9/11.

In all this, we should be careful not to break a butterfly on a wheel. None of the critics I've encountered would begrudge Chris Martin drawing on Rumi to help him through a period of post-divorce depression, or a non-Muslim couple using his verses at their wedding. There's a particular couplet that often features in secular ceremonies, translated by Barks as follows: 'Out beyond ideas of wrongdoing and rightdoing, / there is a field. I'll meet you there.' This rather lovely sentiment is typical of Barks's limpid American English interpretations of Rumi's work. It's easy to see why it would recommend itself to a modern, progressive couple as a vision of mutual understanding to take forward into married life.

The only problem is that Rumi never said it. The original verse makes no mention of 'wrongdoing' or 'rightdoing', and its author would likely have been baffled to see such ideas invoked. 'The words Rumi wrote,' Ali points out, 'were *iman* ("religion") and *kufr* ("infidelity").' He was not, in short, talking about universal values, or the many types of good, bad and in-between behaviour that characterize a long and loving marriage. He was addressing the specific context of his Muslim culture, and appealing to fellow believers to see the light. His aim was to prove, in Ali's words, that 'the basis of faith lies not in religious code but in an elevated space of compassion and love'.

This message of 'compassion and love' has certainly proved attractive to Rumi fans across the spiritual spectrum. One can accept and even celebrate this fact with an open mind. What should be clear, though, is that to get close to Rumi himself – let alone attempt to answer the question of how this complicated man thought – one has to reclaim the specifically Islamic content of his worldview.

Rumi would not have been known as Rumi in his lifetime – at least, not by many people, and certainly not as a stand-alone title, as if he were that era's Pele or Cher. According to Lewis, Rumi is a toponym that refers to 'the fact that he lived in Anatolia, what is now Turkey, but was then considered, from the Islamic point of view, Rome'. There would have been other Rumis, in other words – other famous or semi-famous Anatolians who merited the nickname – so to identify the poet among his family and friends, you'd have been better off calling him by his official birthname, Mohammad, or even better, Jalal al-Din, one of several additional monikers given to him by his father. (There are numerous typographic variations on the many names of Rumi, so I've opted for simplified Romanized spellings wherever possible, for the sake of consistency.) In his wider community he was known by an alternative single-word title, 'Molana', an honorific that can be translated as 'Our Master'. This is what he still goes by across the majority of the Muslim world.

Whatever one decides to call him, he was most likely born in 1207. His family came from an area near the border between present-day Tajikistan, Uzbekistan and Afghanistan, but were forced to flee from Genghis Khan's Mongol armies as they descended through Central Asia. Over the next decade the family set upon a westward trajectory, moving from city to city, nation to nation, crossing the linguistic boundaries between the Persian, Arabic and Turkic worlds. In Aleppo, the young Rumi attended a madrasa where he received a rigorous scholastic training in the Qur'an. His father was a respected theologian, preacher and jurist, and by the time Rumi settled in the Anatolian city of Konya, after his father's death, he had entered the family profession.

This early experience of displacement is one of several suggestive parallels between the lives of Rumi and Li Bai, the poet we looked at in the previous chapter. Though separated by some 500 years, these two Central Asian geniuses were both acclaimed in their lifetimes as singular talents with an imposing physical presence. In her introduction to a wonderful new set of Rumi translations titled *Gold*, Haleh Liza Gafori paints a portrait of Rumi's charismatic early ministry: 'Eloquent and magnetic, dressed in a crown turban and silk robe, he evangelized in mosques and theological institutions throughout Konya.' Li Bai and Rumi also shared a love of wine, viewing it as a gateway to higher forms of enlightenment, though in Rumi's case there's an ongoing debate about how literally we should take his writings on the theme. The first poem in *Gold*, for instance, contains the following invocation: 'You who pour the wine, // put the cup of oneness in my hand / and let me drink from it / until I can't imagine separation.' Intoxication is certainly part of the picture here, though traditionalist Islamic commentators point out that it might be of a purely spiritual kind, a metaphor for the intensity of divine love. (Li Bai, on the other hand, unambiguously liked to get sloshed.)

More telling still, both poets had epiphanic encounters with spiritual mentors who set them on a more liberated path. For Li Bai, that path was known as the Dao, a concept that captures the inherent *way* of the universe, and that is often understood in opposition to the rules and moral codes of Confucianism. For Rumi, it was the path of Sufism that opened up to him in midlife. This is a mystical school of thought within Islam that first emerged in the century following the Prophet's death. From its earliest days, Sufism was subject to mistrust and sometimes outright persecution on account of how it challenged the orthodoxies of Islamic law and tradition. As Lewis sets it out in a helpful overview of the movement, 'it involved an individual and personal orientation towards God, often at odds with the communal and legalistic definition of piety expounded by the legal scholars (*foqahâ*) and other men of religious learning'. Mahmood Jamal boils it down further still, defining Sufism as 'the Path of Love'. 'To put it simply,' Jamal writes, 'Sufism in its human essence replaces a fearsome and unforgiving God with a loving, loveable and merciful one.'

The Sufi way stood revealed to Rumi when he met the man who would become his great friend, Shams of Tabriz, 'a scruffy vagabond and rebel in a coarse felt robe, twenty-two years his elder', in Gafori's description. By all accounts this was a meeting of minds, the two men sparking off each other, galvanized by fresh energy and ideas. Shams had travelled to Konya specially to seek Rumi, having heard rumours of his eloquence, though it was the younger man whose mind was most transformed by the encounter. Before their meeting, Rumi's faith had more or less conformed to the Sunni mainstream of Islamic thought. His new friend challenged him to let go of his ingrained piety and concern for public reputation. According to one famous story related by Gafori, 'Shams ordered Rumi to buy a jug of wine, which good Muslims were expected to shun, and carry it home in plain sight' – evidence, perhaps, supporting the liberal side of the great 'did he or didn't he' debate surrounding Rumi's relationship with alcohol.

These experiments in faith had their cost, as Shams discovered when he was driven from Konya barely two years after the two men met, some say by jealous disciples of Rumi. Whatever actually happened, Rumi was distraught, and the loss seems to have been the catalyst to him uncorking as a poet. One of Shams's many challenges to Rumi had been to find his own voice: not to parrot the inherited wisdom of the scholars, but to channel the insights that came from direct communion with God. In Shams's absence, Rumi at last began to assert his artistic liberty, starting with his adoption of the distinctive whirling dance that Shams performed as a *dervish* (an impoverished mystic). 'From that point on,' writes Gafori, 'Rumi would compose poems, while sometimes whirling to drums as friends wrote down his words.'

Shams died soon afterwards in suspicious circumstances, but Rumi continued singing of his love for the great man. The following quatrain, beautifully translated by Gafori, captures the depth and mystery of his feelings:

> How to soar with the moon
> and drown in the sea?
> Listen to Shams of Tabriz.
> Shoreless light lives on his lips.

Rumi operated across several poetic forms, each of which poses unique challenges to his translators. *The Masnavi* is a religious epic with a playful yet didactic purpose, honoured in some quarters as 'the Qur'an in Persian'. It conducts its business in rhyming couplets, a verse structure where the first line rhymes with the second, the third line rhymes with the fourth, and so on. It lends itself to a parallel form in English – the heroic couplet – that also has a history of moral instruction, as we'll see in a future chapter on William Wordsworth. This is handy in one sense but treacherous in another, since it would be tempting to make the poem sound like an English verse tract of the eighteenth century, written by Jonathan Swift, say, or Alexander Pope.

In reality, rhymes have very different nuances across different languages. They can sound loud or quiet, funny or solemn, pompous or subtle. It all depends on how many rhymes are available in the language, how readily they trip off the pen and tongue, how easy it is to combine concrete and abstract vocabulary (like 'coal' and 'soul'), what ritual or social purposes rhyme might serve, and many other largely unquantifiable factors that make translating rhyming verse a minefield. For this reason, *The Masnavi*'s first English translators largely dodged rhyme altogether, opting to render the poem in prose. In his new translations, which do use rhyming couplets, Mojaddedi has succeeded valiantly in playing on the poem's resemblance to English heroic verse, while maintaining the contours of Farsi and Sufi thought – but it's no easy feat.

In any case, many western Rumi fans are unlikely to be enticed by *The Masnavi*, a long and demanding poem that wears its religious faith proudly on its sleeve. Rumi is better known in the West for his ghazals, another couplet-powered verse form with closely patterned end-words, though in most other respects providing an entirely different experience from *The Masnavi*. A ghazal gives an espresso-strength shot of poetic thought. It consists of somewhere between five and fifteen couplets with consistent but not exact line lengths. A refrain (a repeated word or phrase) appears at the end of both lines of the first couplet and at the end of the second line in each succeeding couplet. This creates a wonderful tension between flexibility and formal pattern, predictability and surprise, as the refrain word absorbs layer upon layer of fresh meaning with each return. The effect is perhaps easiest to demonstrate using a contemporary English-language ghazal, such as Kazim Ali's 'Rain'. Here's the opening of that poem:

> With thick strokes of ink the sky fills with rain.
> Pretending to run for cover but secretly praying for more
>   rain.

Over the echo of the water, I hear a voice saying my name.
No one in the city moves under the quick sightless rain.

Each couplet of a ghazal should work as a self-contained unit.
This enables strange leaps of logic to take place, in a form that
circulates rather than travelling along a linear path.

These fluid formal rules mean that the ghazal presents
a radical challenge to rational thought. This quality is
underscored in Rumi's work because his poems often pose the
challenge explicitly, an element that is drawn to the fore in
Gafori's translation. 'Don't think!' begins one poem, startling
us awake with a command that it's almost impossible to carry
out. Already the mind is on the back foot, trying to think its
way around the problem of being told not to think. Helpfully,
Rumi suggests an alternative way of operating:

Be a fool! Drunk on Love, soaked in awe
till dry reeds are sweet as sugarcane.

A lion leaps out of its cage.
A man leaps out of his mind.
Bravery is delicious madness,

not some circumspect, cagey thought,
sly and ungiving.

Again, we can see how easily such sentiments might collapse
into New Age platitudes. ('Get drunk on love! Be brave and
mad! Eat, pray, love!') Worse, the injunction not to think
could be interpreted as a free pass, encouraging the western
reader to ignore all the tricky Islamic stuff and enjoy Rumi on
whatever terms they please.

The distinction between utter carelessness and the
intellectual abandon Rumi has in mind might seem wafer-thin.

He is, indeed, telling people not to think. He wants us to let go of our inhibitions and leap out of our minds. Yet despite this superficial likeness, the distinction matters. Rumi isn't telling us to leap anywhere we please. He's asking us to leap onto the path of Love – a Love so strong that it can make you drunk, precisely because it emanates from the Almighty. If one takes the message of Sufism to heart, then this Almighty being proves infinitely less scary than we supposed Him to be – more 'loving, loveable and merciful', to use Jamal's formulation – but He can't be absolutely anything that we choose. Gafori's Rumi puts it nicely: 'The heart is a door, / the soul, an alley, / and the wine flows from God's jug.'

Not *your* jug: God's. Now lift up your cup, Rumi urges us, and drink your fill.

5

How to Think Like Dante Alighieri

The Basilica of Santa Croce in Florence boasts a higher density of geniuses per square metre than anywhere else in Europe. The geniuses may all be dead, but their names still conjure up the supernova brilliance of the Italian Renaissance. Niccolò Machiavelli, Galileo Galilei, Michelangelo: all Florentines, all buried in Santa Croce, and all in their different ways revolutionaries. Each agitated against the status quo in his respective field – politics, science, visual art – stripping back thick layers of convention to stare at a deeper truth. Each enjoyed a close, fraught relationship with authority in his lifetime, landing in hot water on more than one occasion. Yet at the end of their lives, these three geniuses were each able to assume their final resting place in a church that would become known as *Tempio dell'Itale Glorie* – the Temple of Italian Greats.

A fourth, no less illustrious name could be added to that list from the world of poetry. Dante Alighieri's cenotaph is also in Santa Croce, as one might expect of a Florentine who served the city as a prior (a senior local politician) and ambassador at various points around the turn of the fourteenth century. What makes him the odd one out is the fact that his bones lie 80 miles to the east, in Ravenna. I visited them one day, almost by chance, before I'd even read a page of Dante's work. I was on holiday with my sister at the time, a mainly food-related jolly to nearby Bologna that had descended into a very pleasant stupor fuelled by mortadella and wine. One morning Hannah and I decided to blow out the cobwebs and catch a train to Ravenna. Nestled on the northern Adriatic coast, the city was briefly the capital of the Western Roman Empire until it fell to the Ostrogoths in 476. Shortly afterwards it was conquered by the Byzantines – the eastern offshoot of the Roman Empire, which outlasted its western cousin – and governed from Constantinople, initially by the Emperor Justinian I.

The main reason we'd travelled to Ravenna was to see its religious monuments. Like any Italian city worth its salt, it has some handsome churches, mausoleums and baptistries. Unlike most Italian cities, however, several of these buildings have glittering mosaic interiors, a legacy of Ravenna's eastward-facing history. For anyone bred on frescoes and gloomy chapels, nothing can prepare you for the sheer luminosity of Ravenna's Galla Placidia mausoleum. Its ceilings are adorned with blue, green and gold tiles, tessellating in geometric patterns around biblical tableaux and a gorgeous cross at the centre. That golden cross, winking from the highest vault, seems to carve out an alternative history for Christianity. It cancels out any thoughts of hellfire, shame and guilt to hint at a gospel of pure light.

I like to think Dante visited the Galla Placidia towards the end of his life, when he needed an image of heaven. As for Hannah and myself, we got there eventually, but only after we'd stopped for lunch. And so it was, on the other side of a huge platter of *polpette e piselli* – meatballs and peas – that we came to waddle past Dante's tomb. It hadn't been on the agenda.

'Huh,' I said. 'Dante. I thought he was from Florence?'

'Yeah,' said Hannah. 'But he was exiled, wasn't he?'

She's more up on this stuff than I am, the product of an English degree where they ground you in global classics as well as the anglophone canon. Until then, I'd only really had a vague, pub-quiz idea of Dante as the author of *The Divine Comedy*. This I knew as a long Italian poem about a journey through the afterlife, which nobody got to the end of any more. A poem in three parts, Hell, Purgatory and Paradise, all kicking off in the nine circles of the *Inferno*. Big influence on T. S. Eliot. *Abandon all hope, ye who enter . . .*

'Ah right,' I said. 'Yeah. That rings a bell.'

We decided we'd better go inside.

I've taken this rather frivolous approach to a serious poet for a couple of reasons. One is to show my hand and dispel any lingering pretence to mastery in a book like this. We all have different depths and densities of knowledge, and we all start our journeys with individual poets somewhere.

The other is to emphasize just how important Ravenna was to Dante's life. He only spent three years there before his death in 1321, but in that time he completed *Paradiso*, the third and final canticle of *The Divine Comedy*, which follows his poetic alter-ego into the celestial spheres. Paradise is a place so beautiful, so beyond mortal comprehension, that it can scarcely be described, though Dante gives it a go. Up until this point in the poem, Dante's visual recall has been sharp-edged and specific. The higher he ascends through Paradise, however, the more his language surrenders to paradox and allusion. In the final reckoning with God, he can only hint at what he saw in terms of shape, colour and light. Here is that moment, in Mark Musa's translation:

Within Its depthless clarity of substance
>I saw the Great Light shine into three circles
>in three clear colors bound in one same space;

the first seemed to reflect the next like rainbow
on rainbow, and the third was like a flame
equally breathed forth by the other two.

Dante's divine vision chimes suggestively with the experience of staring at the ceilings of the Galla Placidia. All those iridescent shifts in tone and scale; the floating, abstract circles; the way one thing seems to reflect another, 'rainbow / on rainbow'. It's impossible to prove a theory of direct influence, alas, but it's easy to imagine Ravenna as a place where Dante could finally achieve spiritual and aesthetic release.

The city would also have been a place of exquisite sadness. This much, perhaps, is less a matter of speculation. By the time he arrived there, some 16 years after his original exile, Dante must have known that he was unlikely to make it back to Florence. Giuseppe Mazzotta summons a wonderful portrait of the poet in Ravenna, a place that had become in Dante's day 'an after-thought of the Roman empire', enduring in 'the after-glow of its Byzantine art'. Here's the rest of what Mazzotta has to say:

> For a man like Dante, who more than ever roamed in a world of internal phantasms and broken dreams, and who needed the most concentrated effort to finish the *Divina Commedia*, the dreamy immobility of Ravenna, the quality of posthumousness it conveyed, was the right place for his imagination. The dense woods of pine trees near the city; the tombs and reliquaries of the Caesars; the memory of Boethius and of the Emperor Justinian [. . .]; the riddle of shadows and the prodigy of the golden light in the mosaics of San Vitale and Sant' Apollinare in Classe (replicas of which Dante saw in Venice and Torcello) – these are the images of Ravenna that Dante evokes and crystallizes in the conclusive part of *Purgatorio* and in those parts of *Paradiso* he wrote or revised while in Ravenna.

These days it's the spiritual joy of Ravenna that rings out to me – not the 'riddle' of its shadows so much as its parade of 'golden light' – but Mazzotta hits on something vital by emphasizing its melancholy, end-of-an-era ambience. Paradoxically, the city might have seemed older to Dante than it does to us now, since he was that much closer to the reality of its imperial decline. It would have been a bittersweet place in which to live out one's years – a sunset kind of city, pointedly removed from the political pulse.

There's a glorious moment in Canto 17 of *Paradiso* that captures these complex feelings of loss. Dante is talking to his ancestor Cacciaguida in the sphere of Mars, the planet representing the virtue of courage. The Dante we encounter in the poem – often referred to by commentators as Dante the Pilgrim, to differentiate him from the real-life Dante doing the writing – has no knowledge of his impending exile, though by the time he encounters Cacciaguida he's picked up on dark hints that something bad is coming down the line. (A quick explanatory note: even though the poem was written entirely in exile, Dante the Pilgrim's journey in *The Divine Comedy* takes place in Easter Week 1300, at a time when he would have been approaching the peak of his political influence in Florence.)

Finally, Dante's curiosity gets the better of him and he begs Cacciaguida to spill the beans about his future. Cacciaguida's response is an object lesson in how to break bad news – tactful and empathetic, without trying to sugarcoat the truth. It could speak for anyone uprooted from their home:

> You shall be forced to leave behind those things
> you love most dearly, and this is the first
> arrow the bow of your exile will shoot.

And you will know how salty is the taste
>   of others' bread, how hard the road that takes
>   you down and up the stairs of others' homes.

I'd eaten a similar salty bread in the restaurant that lunchtime. It tasted normal to me, the way bread ought to taste, though Florentines such as Dante would almost certainly disagree. Even today Tuscan bread remains defiantly unsalted, a culinary quirk unchanged since Dante's time. Elsewhere in *The Divine Comedy*, Dante addresses his feelings of exile in elemental terms, as a cosmic injustice befitting his cosmic pilgrimage. But it's this small, telling detail – an emblem of common homesickness, rather than monstrous betrayal – that keeps Dante's hurt fresh into the present day.

How had it come to this? To untangle the dense political context of Dante's exile is no easy feat. The first thing to note is that medieval Italy was not the united country we know today, but rather a loose conglomeration of kingdoms and city-states that were often at each other's throats. To thicken the plot, thirteenth- and fourteenth-century Florence was riven with factional infighting, of a fierceness and complexity that make the five-season arc of *The Wire* seem like *Spot the Dog*. The essential split was between two parties, the Guelfs and the Ghibellines, who backed different sides of the major geopolitical conflict of the time, a power struggle between the Pope and the Holy Roman Emperor that turned the Italian peninsula into a theatre of war. As a Guelf, Dante belonged to the papal faction that controlled Florence throughout the first three decades of his life, hence his being able to serve the city as prior in 1300, and to join the influential Council of the Hundred the year after.

Unfortunately for Dante, around this time the Guelfs split into two sub-factions, the Whites and the Blacks, and this time he ended up on the wrong side. Dante was a White Guelf. For a short time this was the ascendant faction, until Pope Boniface VIII lined up behind the Black Guelfs and enlisted Charles of Valois, brother of the French king, to invade Florence on his behalf. (Like I say – it's complicated.) In October 1301, Dante was dispatched to Rome on a diplomatic mission whose aim was to dissuade Boniface from sending in his French allies. Unfortunately, while Dante was there Charles invaded Florence anyway, leading to a Black Guelf coup d'état. The price put on Dante's safe return was a whopping 5,000-florin fine and a two-year ban from public office. Dante spurned these terms and fled from Rome to seek refuge elsewhere. In 1303, he settled for a time in Verona under the protection of the ruling della Scala family. He never returned to Florence.

It would be nice if one could urge the modern reader to dive into *The Divine Comedy* and ignore the arcane Guelf and Ghibelline psychodrama. That might make for an easier sell, but it wouldn't really be accurate, or fair, and it might inadvertently end up selling short some of the most compelling features of the poem. For a start, it includes some terrific, highly specific score-settling, particularly in the *Inferno* and *Purgatorio* canticles, where Dante's enemies (and frenemies) are condemned to lurid punishments intimately linked to their crimes in life. Pope Boniface, for instance, gets it in the neck. Indeed, Dante shows great ingenuity in placing Boniface among the damned in the first place, since at the time the poem was set – 1300 – Boniface was still in rude, warmongering health. Dante gets around this by taking us to the eighth circle of hell, reserved for those guilty of fraud, which is itself divided into ten *bolgias*, or ditches, each devoted to a different category of fraud. (Each realm of Dante's afterlife, it should be said, is about as intricate and sub-divided as Florentine politics at the time.)

In the third *bolgia* we find the simonists, the worst fraudsters of the lot. Simony is the sin of selling ecclesiastical offices for financial gain, named after Simon Magus, a nefarious magician from the biblical book of Acts. In other words, to be a simonist, one first has to be a powerful person in the Church – somebody capable of profiting from the sale of holy office. Lo and behold, the third *bolgia* is full of popes. (Never let it be said that Dante pulls his punches or picks easy targets.) The bespoke punishment dreamed up for the simonists is as slapstick as it is terrifying: they are thrust headfirst into a rocky landscape filled with holes. Musa's translation captures the scene with a nice, pulpy colloquialism:

> From the mouth of every hole were sticking out
>> a single sinner's feet, and then the legs
>> up to the calf – the rest was stuffed inside.

> The soles of every sinner's feet were flaming;
>> their naked legs were twitching frenziedly—
>> they would have broken any chain or rope.

Dante the Pilgrim sees that one pair of legs is twitching more frenziedly than the others, so he asks his guide, the Roman poet Virgil, to be taken to meet him. When the man these legs belong to hears Dante and Virgil speaking, he asks, 'Is that *you*, here already, upright? / Is that you here already upright, Boniface?' Dante is taken aback – no, of course he isn't Pope Boniface VIII! Whatever could Mr Legs mean by that? Once Dante disabuses him of this notion, it becomes clear that Mr Legs is none other than Boniface's last but one predecessor as pope, Nicholas III. This particular hole has been carved out for bad, greedy popes, and each time one of them dies he is spirited there and jammed on top of the last, compacting all the others further down into the rock, like rubbish in a chute. Boniface's place there has already been foretold, a fact we infer from Pope Nicholas's double take. It's a sizzling burn.

These could be petty pleasures: scenes of torture and comeuppance whose superficial details may be exciting, but whose deeper relevance has to be painstakingly reconstructed. There's certainly something curious about the fact that Dante has the whole of the afterlife in which to wander, and yet ends up bumping into a lot of people born in Tuscany during the century leading up to the poem's composition. Perhaps this is to be expected: one could imagine a modern-day *Divine Comedy* that gravitated towards Margaret Thatcher, Nelson Mandela and Silvio Berlusconi. (I'll leave it to the reader's imagination to decide which realm each of these various figures belongs to.)

This in itself touches on a useful lesson, reminding us that politics is ephemeral and culturally relative. Whatever priorities, squabbles and personalities seem dominant today will eventually be dust in the wind of history. This might not be quite Dante's point; I suspect he fully believed in the enduring relevance of Boniface and Cacciaguida, and wanted the reader to be stunned or inspired by their respective fates. In any case, his ultimate concern is not human history but divine justice. Whether or not Boniface and Cacciaguida will be remembered by anyone except readers of the poem, their crimes and virtues are of eternal relevance to God. Nevertheless, as modern readers, we can set these theological issues aside, to some extent, to swoon at the poem's hyper-detailed alternative reality, most of whose inhabitants might as well be characters in a fantasy novel (Dante would have been a master of the genre, one suspects). And we are free, whatever our faith, or lack of it, to use the poem as a springboard to meditation – to ponder what will endure from our own chaotic life and times, and what will perish.

One thing that can't be doubted is that Dante has endured. In his homeland alone, *The Divine Comedy* proved so influential that the Tuscan dialect it was written in became the blueprint for the language we now know as Italian. Prior to Dante, nobody had dared to execute such a bold and ambitious literary project in the vernacular language. His success proved what might be possible, and encouraged writers across Europe, gradually, to cast off Latin as their lingua franca and experiment in their native tongues. (Geoffrey Chaucer was certainly inspired, as we'll see in the next chapter.) None of this would have been possible if the poem hadn't touched on matters of lasting importance amid its local skirmishes. For medieval readers, the higher truth of the poem would have been obvious: it spoke directly to the deepest mysteries of the one true faith, and opened a thrilling window onto the world beyond this mortal coil.

In a secular age one has to drill a little deeper to find significance. It's there, though, abundantly, in every canto. For a start, the poem offers a stinging rebuke to factionalism that resonates today, reflecting our own bitterly divided culture. 'O wretched Italy,' the Pilgrim opines in *Purgatorio*, Canto 6, 'search all your coasts, / probe to your very center: can you find / within you any part that is at peace?' Moreover, Dante begins to model how trust in civil society might be repaired. Time and again in the *Comedy*, divine providence – and by extension the poet's sympathy – breaks along surprising lines. Sienese people, bitter rivals of the Florentines, turn up in Purgatory among the saved, while mentors and personal acquaintances of Dante languish in Hell. Families lie separated across different realms, underscoring how conduct and faith trump blood or tribal allegiance.

Most importantly of all, Dante insists on his own fallibility. The first canto of the poem presents the Pilgrim at a moment of crisis, wandering lost in a shadowy landscape:

Midway along the journey of our life
    I woke to find myself in a dark wood,
        for I had wandered off from the straight path.
[. . .]

How I entered there I cannot truly say,
    I had become so sleepy at the moment
        when first I strayed, leaving the path of truth [. . .]

This is what I first responded to in Dante – this sense of disillusion and moral urgency; his willingness to take readers far into the 'dark wood' of error, in the hope that they'll emerge somewhere different, somewhere better. This is gnarly, grown-up poetry, for the moments when one's purpose in life seems to have gone astray. It makes a special type of sense to read it in your late thirties, if you can, the age Dante would have been when he first embarked on the project.

I was getting to such an age in Ravenna that afternoon, feeling sleepy and full of meatballs as we strayed from the straight path leading to the Galla Placidia. Dante's mausoleum is relatively modest, a small, dignified space next to the Basilica of San Francesco, wonderfully cool and welcoming on a hot day. A marble bas-relief portrait of Dante overlooks his sarcophagus, which is adorned with a Latin inscription that hints at his bitterly contested earthly afterlife. 'Here in this corner lies Dante,' reads the official translation, 'exiled from his native land, born to Florence, an unloving mother.' Ouch.

Remarkably soon after Dante's death, the unloving mother started to regret how she had treated her famous son.

According to Guy P. Raffa, who has written the authoritative account of this story, 'Dante's bones, cherished no less than the remains of a saint, acquired the aura of holy relics' for Florentine admirers. Leading the calls for repatriation was the great poet Giovanni Boccaccio, and his appeal was swiftly taken up as municipal policy. By the middle of the fifteenth century, the ruler of Florence, Lorenzo de' Medici, had turned Dante's bones into a key demand in negotiations with the Venetian empire, which now ruled Ravenna. Yet it was all to no avail. When Florence made another attempt to retrieve its great poet in the next century, a group of canny monks decided to take matters into their own hands, and hid his bones. Eventually, in 1829, Florence settled for the Santa Croce cenotaph as the next best option. It still lies empty, and the city still sends olive oil to Ravenna every year, to fuel the lamp burning in Dante's tomb.

6

How to Think Like Geoffrey Chaucer

You are going on a journey. It's springtime and the weather is set fair. You are one among a motley crew, most of them unfamiliar, so to make sure you don't end up hating each other, you'll have to find some common ground. Break the ice. Share a drink. Tell someone to watch his step when he's had a few too many and seems like he's about to fall over.

One of the gang's a chippy tradesman. He's doing all right for himself, thank you very much. He's a grafter with a grudge against lawyers, scholars, busybodies or anyone for that matter who's never known the sweat of an honest day's toil. Bringing up the rear is some middle-management type, a thin fellow who suspects he's the butt of the joke. Soon, rivalries emerge. Too many different personalities are jostling together for it to be any other way. As ever, the loudmouths hog the conversation while wiser heads keep their counsel, but by and large the kind-hearted, upbeat types soften the edges of the selfish, sarcastic or pious. The crucial thing holding it all together is the shared project. You've all started off somewhere, you're all travelling under the same sun, and you'll all end up in the same place, too, unless you lose someone along the way. So for now just rub along, learn how to take a joke, and enjoy the fresh air. You'll miss this part when it's over.

Is all this a metaphor for life? Possibly – and presumably that's Geoffrey Chaucer's point. This rough overview of *The Canterbury Tales* goes some way to outlining the range of a text so ambitious in design that Chaucer never finished it. The travellers are pilgrims bound for St Thomas à Becket's shrine at Canterbury Cathedral: 29 of them in total, including Chaucer himself and the landlord of the Tabard in Southwark, the inn where they've lodged the night before setting off on their pilgrimage. It's a text that ebbs and meanders in the way of all good journeys, and dissolves at the final hurdle into a farewell address that has the flavour of a deathbed confession, perhaps even a retraction. We never make it to Canterbury.

But don't worry about that for now. Above all, *The Canterbury Tales* is great fun to read, a medieval smorgasbord filled with comedy, pathos and wisdom. The scene is set in April, and no poet is better equipped than Chaucer to evoke the pleasures of an English spring. Here are the opening lines of the 'General Prologue', the poem before the poem that sets the work in motion:

Whan that Aprille with his shoures soote,
The droghte of March hath perced to the roote,
And bathed every veyne in swich licour
Of which vertú engendred is the flour . . .

Wait. No doubt this prompts a fair question in the new reader's mind: namely, how on earth am I supposed to *have fun* reading a poem that seems to be written in a different language? Let's try flipping the record, then, to read the same opening passage in David Wright's excellent modern translation, proceeding a little further this time:

> When the sweet showers of April have pierced
> The drought of March, and pierced it to the root,
> And every vein is bathed in that moisture
> Whose quickening force will engender the flower;
> And when the west wind too with its sweet breath
> Has given life in every wood and field
> To tender shoots, and when the stripling sun
> Has run his half-course in Aries, the Ram,
> And when small birds are making melodies,
> That sleep all the night long with open eyes,
> (Nature so prompts them, and encourages);
> Then people long to go on pilgrimages . . .

Reading Chaucer 'in translation' is of course not the same thing as reading, say, Dante in translation. The bridge being crossed passes not from nation to nation but from century to century within a single linguistic tradition. All the same, Wright's translation can help many of us to access this 600-year-old text in ways that might otherwise not be possible.

Chaucer starts his epic about pilgrimage not with God, or even humankind, but with the natural world. Before we even get to thoughts of heaven or the Church, Chaucer suggests we look at the soil instead. Consider how rain arrives in April, just at the moment when the flowers most need it. These opening lines create a symphony of mutual exchange: April's showers 'pierce' the hard earth, releasing vital, life-giving 'moisture' (one can't help but prefer Chaucer's 'licour' here). The west wind lends its 'sweet breath' to 'wood and field', helping them to bud with 'tender shoots'. The sun is revolving through the zodiac and the birds respond with song.

A key line that could go unnoticed is: 'Nature so prompts them, and encourages'. Primarily, this is an afterthought explaining the folk belief that spring makes songbirds 'sleep all the night long with open eyes'. The genius, however, lies in how it touches the next line, delivering our first sign of those other creatures who are quickened by the springtime: humans. 'Then people long to go on pilgrimages' frames this activity not as a religious duty so much as a natural instinct, akin to a bird's migration. If the poem didn't open out into a tapestry of Christian experience, one might be tempted to call its religious sensibility pantheistic (corresponding to a pagan belief that God is no more or less than the forces of the universe).

Or maybe those two worldviews – Christianity and paganism – aren't as far apart as we've been led to believe. The rhythm of the seasons and the pattern of divine providence might all be part of the same great mystery. The key is to find your place among these overarching structures, and to live richly and variously within them.

Chaucer was a career civil servant. A high-ranking one at that: he served in several different senior offices for two kings, Edward III and Richard II, living long enough (just) to draw a pension under Henry IV as well. The list of his job titles has a poetry of its own: Esquire of the King's Household; Controller of Customs and Subsidy of Wools, Skins and Hides; Clerk of the King's Works; Deputy Keeper of the Royal Forest of North Petherton. One imagines a stolid administrator, good at handling money and cosying up to the most powerful person in the room. Granted, he'd have needed a sharp eye for figures to be trusted with gathering taxes from all those lucrative wools, skins and hides unloading in the London docks. But he also saw plentiful action abroad, from serving in the Hundred Years War between England and France to thrashing out trade deals with Italian dukes. It was in Italy that most historians assume he must have encountered the work of the Italian poets Petrarch and Boccaccio, from which he adapted several of his most famous works (*Troilus and Criseyde*, for instance, and 'The Knight's Tale'). For a long time scholars cherished the belief that Chaucer, Petrarch and Boccaccio must all have been in the same room at one point, perhaps at a society wedding. Alas, this theory has fallen out of favour in recent years, but Chaucer nevertheless seems to have been a mover and shaker – a cosmopolitan with a wide-ranging government portfolio.

He came from the upwardly mobile middle classes, his father working as a London wine merchant. As well as being successful commercially, John Chaucer boasted social connections good enough to establish the young Geoffrey as a page in the household of Elizabeth, Countess of Ulster. Chaucer rose swiftly through the ranks from page to squire, securing an advantageous marriage to Philippa de Roet, a lady-in-waiting to the Queen. From here, he progressed serenely into the realms of sinecured public service.

Clearly, he was an able and likeable man with a knack for landing on his feet. Yet there's more to his life than luck and social climbing. *The Canterbury Tales* depicts a world poised precariously on the verge of a huge paradigm shift. On one side stands the old feudal order, a rigid hierarchy with the King at the top, the aristocracy and the Church beneath him, and below that everyone else – the vast majority of whom were peasants, owing their entire living (and regularly collected taxes) to the local lord. On the other side is the prospect of a more liberal and mobile society, the type of country where a wine merchant's son could rise to be on good terms with the King. And Chaucer never takes that for granted. His poetry is fully alive to the tensions involved in making the journey from the old world to the new.

Nowhere do these complexities show up more clearly than in his use of a particular word: 'gentil'. This roughly translates to 'noble' in contemporary usage, and wouldn't have meant 'gentle' in the modern sense of 'tender and kind'. Reading the *Tales*, however, it's possible to hear that new sense slowly taking shape, as Chaucer and his pilgrims tease out what it means to be not just a 'gentil' person – an aristocrat born to power and accustomed to its privileges – but someone worthy of the title.

In the first story, 'The Knight's Tale', we see this ambiguity flicker into life. The tale concerns two rather hapless knights called Palamon and Arcita, who have been taken prisoner by Theseus, Duke of Athens. Languishing in their cell, both men fall desperately in love with the beautiful Emily, a woman they can see wafting through the palace grounds beneath their window. By several fantastical twists, both men escape captivity, only to find themselves drawn back to Emily and Athens, where they bump into each other in the forest. As two men obsessed with the same woman are wont to do, they engage in bloody combat, until Theseus and his retinue stumble on them fighting. This is a bit awkward because, by rights, Theseus should probably chop off their heads to make an example of them. Yet, as Chaucer writes, 'pitee renneth soone in gentil herte' – and, encouraged by the women in his hunting party who plead with him to show mercy, Theseus spares their lives.

These days, to say that 'pity soon reigns in gentle hearts' is to come close to saying nothing at all. Gentle people take pity, almost by definition. However, Chaucer is saying something more substantial, which comes out in Wright's translation: 'For pity soon repairs to noble hearts.' In other words, noblemen such as Theseus are naturally disposed to show mercy, almost as if it were a natural law. We might well disagree with the sentiment, and in 'The Knight's Tale' there's no sense that 'pity' and nobility might be one and the same thing; just that they tend to go together, like bacon and eggs.

At this point it's worth asking the question: who's speaking? For it isn't Chaucer, exactly, but his Knight – someone who would have been invested wholesale in the same feudal order that Chaucer was starting to probe. Consider the source, as the saying goes. In a knight's world, we inevitably end up stuck with this dull, deferential version of gentleness, a concept that seems closer to what nowadays we'd call *noblesse oblige.*

For an example of Chaucer interrogating the concept directly, with wicked comedy and moral courage, we have to turn to another voice on the pilgrimage. It belongs to a woman with a salty tongue and a zest for life. She's been with five husbands in her time, and isn't about to apologize to any monk or prioress for enjoying what the marriage bed has to offer. In the centuries since the *Tales* first circulated, she's become Chaucer's best-loved and most enduring creation. Her name is Alison, but we'll address her using the title she's usually known by, the Wife of Bath.

If a historical novelist invented the Wife of Bath today, seeking a sex-positive medieval feminist to appeal to contemporary audiences, people would think they were laying it on a bit thick. She's just too brazen, they'd say, too modern – too much like Megan Thee Stallion in a smock and garters to be credible. She likes receiving oral sex. She reckons that all men owe a debt to women and that the only way for them to pay it is by using their 'sely' – or 'little' – 'instrument'. She rails against controlling husbands who won't let her go out and about with friends. Some of those friends, scandalously, are male. Indeed, there's a dubious overlap between husbands four and five, and she admits to finally pouncing on the fifth at the fourth husband's funeral. Husband number five, the nefarious Jankin, is half her age, and though he starts by giving her the pleasure she expects, he quickly becomes controlling and abusive in his turn, beating her about the ribs and conning her out of her inheritance – that is, until she turns the tables and conquers him, fair and square.

Above all, time and again she refuses to be shamed for her body, her desires, or the fact that she has a past. There's a beautiful moment in the prologue to her tale when she looks back on the high jinks of her youth. Wright captures the mood of fond reminiscence with the modern cliché 'It warms the very cockles of my heart', but the original is better: 'It tikleth me aboute myn herte roote.' This image of tickling is her all over. It summons thoughts of laughter, touch, flirtation – all the things that make life pleasurable and good. A host of podcasts dispensing guidance to anxious millennials could be set aside if more people channelled the Wife of Bath. 'Unto this day it dooth myn herte boote,' she continues ('boote' meaning roughly 'good' in this context), 'That I have had my world as in my tyme.' No regrets, in other words. I love how this last line brings together two huge abstracts – the world and time – and links them with a single pronoun (*my* world, *my* time) that insists on the integrity of her own experience. It's a line that lends weight to the view of the Scottish bishop and poet Gavin Douglas that Chaucer 'was evir (God wait) all womanis frend' (i.e. all women's friend).

Like much else in the Wife of Bath's account, her meditation on gentleness begins in the prologue, with a witty deconstruction of the Bible's take on sex and marriage. Doesn't the Good Book tell us to be fruitful and multiply? In her view, this command from Genesis is (in Wright's translation) 'A noble text, and one I understand!' There's that weird historical parallax again – the blur between our modern-day 'noble' and her Middle English 'gentil'. When in the original she proclaims, 'That gentil text kan I wel understonde,' it's hard not to hear the word reaching for its modern meaning, like a flower leaning towards the sun. For the Wife, it goes without saying that God is gentle in the formal sense (literally, by being the Lord). Yet on top of this, she must be saying that God is gentle in another way – that He embodies lordliness by being good and generous, and having a sensible attitude towards sex. The term sucks us forward in time, because Chaucer is teaching us how to think about it in new ways.

In the story that follows, the same tension plays out with an added class dimension. It's a funny little squib, really – not a patch on her prologue, which occupies roughly double the space. 'The Wife of Bath's Tale' begins when a knight in the court of King Arthur rapes a young maiden in the woods. Rather than paying with his life, he is banished for a year and told to use his time profitably finding the answer to a riddle. What is it that women most desire? With the year almost up, and despairing of his chances, he happens across an ugly old hag who offers to tell him the answer, providing he grants her whatever she requests. What women want, she says, is simple – they would have sovereignty over their husbands. The grateful knight rushes off to tell the court, thereby earning his reprieve from Queen Guinevere and her astonished ladies-in-waiting. But relief soon turns to a new type of despair, when afterwards the hag returns to claim her quid pro quo of marriage to the knight. Being chivalrous, he's beholden to grant her wish – but he does so with an almighty sulk, as he struggles to pay his debt in bed. She's just too ugly, too low-born.

From a modern perspective, much about this story could strike us as distasteful. Chaucer adapts it from the so-called loathly lady genre – a category that, in itself, tells a story about medieval misogyny – and we may not think it much of a consolation that the hag succeeds in teaching this awful young knight a lesson, when as a reward she magically transforms into a beautiful young woman, clearing the way for them both to live happily ever after. Nevertheless, it's worth listening in while she schools him. Rather than rebuking him for his slight against her ugliness, she bridles at his class snobbery. Look for the person who does the right thing in private as well as public, she says – that person is the *real* gentleman. What's more, to lord it over others because of inherited privilege isn't just crass; it's close to being ungodly as well. 'Crist wole we clayme of hym oure gentilesse,' she says. 'Nat of oure eldres for hire old richesse.' (Roughly: 'We claim our gentleness from Christ – not the wealth of our ancestors.') To clinch the point she goes on to say, 'Thanne comth oure verray gentillesse of grace,' a formulation that explicitly coaxes gentleness out of the clutches of 'nobility', into the open, democratic arms of 'grace'.

Chaucer was no revolutionary. We know as much because he lived in a time of actual social tumult and chose the side of power. It's worth reflecting on just how unlikely it was for him to have survived the fourteenth century unscathed. Thomas Usk, a fellow writer and public servant, called it a period of 'confederacie, congregacion, & couyne', three archaic words that, in a nutshell, mean 'conniving and plotting'. Usk chose the path of political agitation and ended up being beheaded. Below the higher ranks of society, too, there were huge upheavals, from the Black Death of 1348 to the Peasants' Revolt of 1381. Although 30 years apart, these two seismic events might well be linked. The Black Death decimated somewhere between a third and a half of England's total population, radically reshaping the national economy. For a while, pay and conditions improved for the surviving population, until the aristocracy hit back with legislation designed to curb wage inflation – but the feudal link between land and labour had been irrevocably damaged.

In the world of *The Canterbury Tales*, these social tremors are at most a distant vibration. Outside 'The Nun's Priest's Tale' – where we catch a quizzical, sideways reference to Jack Straw, the fabled leader of the uprising – the Peasants' Revolt might have never happened. Chaucer was nothing if not a diplomat, meaning there's little in his work that could scare the patrons. Yet the wheel of social fortune is turning regardless, and more often than not it's Chaucer who's giving it a nudge. He does so not by riling up the masses or decrying injustice – though there are some choice words against religious fat cats and charlatans – but by taking a more radical step. He actually seems to *like* the people he's writing about. He respects them as individuals with talents, resentments, aspirations and histories, rather than slotting them in as interchangeable cogs in the cosmic machine. And what's more, through the fog of centuries we recognize them. Despite any number of changes to the way we live, think and interact, this imagined journey continues to hold up a mirror to the human condition. This was what William Blake was getting at when he declared (in the eighteenth century), 'Every age is a Canterbury pilgrimage; we all pass on, each sustaining one or other of these characters.'

So will you be a greedy, ingratiating friar, 'versed in small talk and in flattery'? Or will you own your life with the conviction of the Wife of Bath? Given the choice, I know which of these I'd aspire to. And if it's neither, well then, just turn to your left – there's another woman riding at your shoulder, and she's not much like anyone you've met so far. What's her story?

7

How to Think Like William Shakespeare

Shakespeare is one of the few poets who may genuinely need no introduction. When I write 'To be or not to be', I expect a majority of readers can fill in the blanks with what comes next. Shakespeare's words are both common property and big business. *Hamlet*, the play that first gave us 'To be or not to be', has been performed in 75 different languages since 1960, including Klingon and Esperanto. On the silver screen, his plays have inspired everything from American teen comedies (see *10 Things I Hate About You*, a post-feminist spin on *The Taming of the Shrew*) to chilling samurai noir (see *Throne of Blood*, Akira Kurosawa's transplantation of *Macbeth* to feudal Japan). Every year, from every corner of the globe, some six million visitors troop to Shakespeare's birthplace of Stratford-upon-Avon. Although the regional tourist board has reported a sluggish recovery from the coronavirus pandemic, there's every reason to believe that the numbers will bounce back. The Bard has seen off worse during his 400 years of immortality, and will likely be around for many multiples of that to come. The smart money would be on him sticking around forever – or at least for as long as humanity still has the means to perform plays, read books and talk about itself.

An aura of greatness has clung to Shakespeare from the very beginning. In 1623, seven years after his death, two actors named John Heminge and Henry Condell clubbed together to publish *The Workes of William Shakespeare, containing all his Comedies, Histories, and Tragedies: Truely Set Forth, according to their first originall*. Heminge and Condell could make this claim about textual authority because they were actors in Shakespeare's company, the King's Men, and therefore would have received his scripts hot off the writing desk. In their dedication, Heminge and Condell boast that Shakespeare's 'mind and hand went together; and what he thought, he uttered with that easiness, that we have scarce received from him a blot in his papers'.

Shakespeare's poetry and plays were popular during his lifetime, but this 1623 publication is probably the first instance we can find of an extra, Shakespeare-specific layer of acclaim attaching to his work. More than just a very good playwright, Shakespeare is presented here as someone who had an almost supernatural fluency. His 'mind and hand went together', we are told, as if there was scarcely any barrier between his powers of imagination and his powers of expression. What he thought, he wrote, without even needing to 'blot' the paper with a scratched-out word or scrawl in the margin.

This is mythmaking, of course, though from a fairly trustworthy source. It's corroborated in the same edition – now known universally as the First Folio – by a set of dedicatory poems written by Shakespeare's peer and sometime rival, Ben Jonson. In the longer of the two poems, Jonson calls Shakespeare 'Soul of the age!', 'The applause, delight, the wonder of our stage!' and 'Sweet Swan of Avon!' Over the centuries, these epithets have done much to promote a view of Shakespeare as some sort of universal ambassador. The 'soul' apparent in his work comes to stand not just for a single author with a peculiar sensibility, but for an entire 'age', just as the Beatles would later be claimed as avatars of the Swinging Sixties. By the time Jonson's near-namesake Samuel Johnson was preparing his eight-volume edition of Shakespeare's plays over a century later, Shakespeare's ability to speak for others had spread from his immediate audience to all mankind. 'Shakespeare is above all writers,' writes Dr Johnson, 'at least above all modern writers, the poet of nature; the poet that holds up to his readers a faithful mirror of manners and of life.'

It's possible at this point to feel a little claustrophobic. Who's to say that when a reader looks into the mirror of Shakespeare's works, they'll see their own image reflected back? Not for the first time in this journey through the canon, one has to make the awkward point that, well, it depends very much on the reader. But even if Dr Johnson's mirror could latch on to some ideal, homogeneous beholder, the metaphor would still leave a lot to be desired. It reinforces the view, first put forward by Heminge and Condell, that Shakespeare's mind and work were somehow perfectly harmonious and transparent: that his brain delivered thoughts which transfigured into lines, and that these lines passed serenely into public circulation on account of their obvious truthfulness. And brains are rarely as simple as that; nor is the public, for that matter.

Against this squeaky clean and frictionless Shakespeare, the earlier, h-less Jonson had already provided a bulwark of sorts. Where Samuel Johnson sees nature as something static and unchanging – a self-evident reality that a great writer should simply try to represent – Ben Jonson casts it in more complex terms. Midway through his longer dedication poem, Jonson elevates Shakespeare above a host of celebrated classical poets like Aristophanes, Terence and Plautus, remarking that 'they were not of Nature's family'. So far, this is a similar claim to

Dr Johnson's, granting Shakespeare privileged access to that capital-letter abstract, 'Nature'. But what comes next throws Nature for a loop.

'Yet must I not give Nature all,' warns Jonson: 'thy art, / My gentle Shakespeare, must enjoy a part.' Art is an extra element in the mix, which Jonson triangulates with those other key factors – the poet himself and Nature – using an image drawn from the blacksmith's forge:

> For though the poet's matter nature be,
> His art doth give the fashion; and, that he
> Who casts to write a living line, must sweat,
> (Such as thine are) and strike the second heat
> Upon the Muses' anvil; turn the same
> (And himself with it) that he thinks to frame,
> Or, for the laurel, he may gain a scorn;
> For a good poet's made, as well as born;
> And such wert thou.

Jonson, a bricklayer's stepson, would have known the meaning of hard work, so it's telling that his tribute restores the 'sweat' and 'heat' to Shakespeare's work. With a craftsman's pride, he insists that 'a good poet's made, as well as born' – a simple fact that should always be kept in mind when considering a seemingly immutable literary god like Shakespeare.

Ironically, given these images of bodily toil, Jonson's poem has also contributed to a tenacious myth that Shakespeare may not have been born at all – or else, if he was born, that he couldn't possibly have written all those sublime works that were credited to him in his lifetime. Earlier in the poem, Jonson lands a glancing blow with a remark that Shakespeare had 'small Latin and less Greek'. This slight against Shakespeare's schooling feeds into a more dubious modern belief that he came from too lowly a background to wield a pen with such grace.

The two most common names put forward as rival claimants to his work are the English polymath Francis Bacon and the 17th Earl of Oxford, Edward de Vere. The reasons for their eligibility needn't detain us here, so much as the strange phenomenon of the conspiracy itself. 'Over time, and for all sorts of reasons,' writes James Shapiro, in his examination of the authorship controversy, *Contested Will*, 'leading artists and intellectuals from all walks of life joined the ranks of sceptics. I can think of little else that unites Henry James and Malcolm X, Sigmund Freud and Charlie Chaplin, Hellen Keller and Orson Welles, or Mark Twain and Sir Derek Jacobi.'

Of all the names in Shapiro's roll call, Twain is the Shakespeare truther whose reasons for doubting are funniest and most illuminating. In 1909, Twain published his views on the matter in a short book called *Is Shakespeare Dead?*, chapter three of which lays out the bald biographical facts of his life. Though the modern reader would be advised not to take all of these 'facts' as gospel, Twain fastens on one in particular that can be corroborated – the existence of a will in Shakespeare's name that, notoriously, bequeathed his 'second-best bed' to his wife, Anne Hathaway. 'And not another thing,' Twain adds, in disbelief; 'not even a penny to bless her lucky widowhood with.' At this point there's a paragraph break. Resuming his case, Twain hammers a nail into Shakespeare's coffin: 'It was eminently and conspicuously a business man's will, not a poet's.'

Another break. Another nail.

'It mentioned NOT A SINGLE BOOK.'

Funny as this is, we should be very sceptical of Twain's hard dichotomy between 'business man' and 'poet'. Must the two be mutually exclusive? Partly to address this supposition, Shapiro tells the story of how Bard-fanciers from the mid-1700s onwards set upon a quest to find Shakespeare's papers. Alas, those documents that could be safely linked to Shakespeare tended to the 'business man' side of the ledger, with precious few pointing towards the vocation of 'poet'. Besides the will, there was a mortgage deed to a London townhouse in the Blackfriars district (so, Shakespeare wasn't poor) and an undelivered letter from a Stratford neighbour named Richard Quiney asking for a loan (definitely not poor, then: he was lending money). By the mid-1800s, evidence had even emerged that he kept up a family interest in malt production. Malt, for goodness' sake! How stubbornly unromantic.

The problem with such reasoning – that Shakespeare cared more about his valuable assets than his literary legacy, ergo he can't have written *Hamlet* – is that it puts the chronological cart before the horse. It judges Shakespeare by a modern ideal of authorship founded on the glamour of the personal archive. Nowadays, when studying an author, literary experts expect to be able to rummage through a trove of notes, drafts and personal correspondence. Yet Shakespeare would have had a very different relationship with paper than we have today. It would have been an essential tool of his trade, but also a valuable commodity, priced at '4 pence a quire, or roughly a penny for six sheets' according to Dr Heather Wolfe, a librarian and curator at the Folger Shakespeare Library.

Suppose that in a good day's work Shakespeare would have got through a whole quire (or 25 sheets). Using Wolfe's price index, that would be a daily expense equating to almost half the average daily wage of most labourers in early modern London. As such, paper would have been something you'd reuse for memos, notes, shopping lists, kindling – or, indeed, for distributing among the players in your company, to make sure that they learned their lines. The paper you preserved, on the other hand, would have been the stuff that made a material difference to your wealth or status: wills, deeds, depositions, debts.

The fact that William Shakespeare emerges from the historical record as a man of business shouldn't cast aspersions on his achievements as an artist. On the contrary, it makes those achievements all the more poignant, and believable – that a man who had to work hard to keep the lights on at his theatre and provide for his family back in Warwickshire was also able to articulate, as no one had before, what it means to be human.

These considerations give another slant to one of the most oft-quoted speeches in Shakespeare's plays. In Act 1 of *Hamlet*, the nobleman Polonius sees off his son, Laertes, on an overseas voyage. He delivers a catalogue of fatherly advice, winding up for the final thought as follows:

> Neither a borrower nor a lender be;
> For loan oft loses both itself and friend,
> And borrowing dulls the edge of husbandry.
> This above all – to thine own self be true
> And it must follow, as the night the day,
> Thou canst not then be false to any man.

First, Polonius gives Laertes an affectionate, worldly cuff about the shoulders, warning him off lending money to friends or oiling the wheels of his own business (his 'husbandry') with loans. In the next breath, however, he pivots to a moral affirmation that captures the very essence of Renaissance humanism: 'to thine own self be true'.

It takes a great poet to condense all this proverbial wisdom with a sense of clarity and freshness. But it also takes someone who knows the sting of a loan gone bad. Business and higher matters of the soul go side by side. Polonius doesn't make hard distinctions, and neither should we.

In the search for Shakespeare, there's an ever-present risk of losing sight of why we're trying to find him in the first place – that is, for the brilliance of his work. His plays are one place to be reminded of this, though their plots and language have so seeped into the public imagination that it can be hard to filter them out from the wider myth. The words rebound around our collective consciousness with the nagging, time-worn quality of a proverb. Friends, Romans, countrymen, all the world's a stage: the course of true love never did run smooth. The last sentence is a mash-up of famous lines from *Julius Caesar*, *As You Like It* and *A Midsummer Night's Dream*, but I flatter myself to think it could hoodwink the unsuspecting reader into thinking it was the real McCoy.

From time to time, then, it's worth blanking out the noise. Try flipping open one of Shakespeare's plays and tuning into just the verbal frequencies. They're filled with glorious poetry written in diverse forms, from blank verse (where each unrhymed line consists of ten syllables following a regular iambic stress pattern) to the delicate, interlinked sonnet that Romeo and Juliet craft with one another when they first meet.

ROMEO
[To JULIET] If I profane with my unworthiest hand
This holy shrine, the gentle fine is this:
My lips, two blushing pilgrims, ready stand
To smooth that rough touch with a tender kiss.

JULIET
Good pilgrim, you do wrong your hand too much,
Which mannerly devotion shows in this;

For saints have hands that pilgrims' hands do touch,
And palm to palm is holy palmers' kiss.

What lends this moment dramatic credibility is the fact that
sonnets are a shared resource. Fourteen lines long, with a
closely patterned rhyme scheme, the form can be thought of
as a poetic argument. The opening eight lines (the octet) set
up a proposition, which leads towards a leap in logic known
as the volta, before the final six lines (the sestet) resolve the
matter in a satisfying or surprising way.

Here, Romeo and Juliet collaborate on the octet, teasing out
a complex line of thought about holiness and pilgrimage, lips
and hands. It works because of the intrinsic way that sonnets
set possibilities in motion. An idea is floated ('Let's say this
beautiful hand is a shrine . . .') and then tested; one thought
leads to another, with a familiar choreography of rhythms,
rhymes, entrances and exits. It's an inherently reciprocal form.
That this budding couple can so effortlessly co-author a sonnet
bodes well for their erotic and spiritual chemistry. (Anyone in
doubt should watch Baz Luhrmann's filmed interpretation of
the scene, in which Leonardo DiCaprio and Claire Danes frisk
one another around the edge of a party while intoning these
lines, before snogging in a lift once the sonnet concludes.)
Yet it's a chemistry based on rules and expectations – a set of
fizzing reactions that take place inside a solid flask.

Sonnets ran deep through Shakespeare's soul. Aside from
their occasional appearance in his plays – there are good
examples in *Henry V* and *Love's Labour's Lost* as well as in
Romeo and Juliet – he wrote at least 154 stand-alone works
in the form, which were collected for the first time in a
volume published in 1609. What strikes one reading these
today is exactly how modern and mysterious they are. They
offer perhaps the biggest, most direct hit of Shakespeare's

mind at work, while revealing that mind to be something many-angled and genuinely weird. Love is their theme, and their shifting modes of address have kept scholars guessing about Shakespeare's love life for centuries. The first 126 are addressed to an unnamed 'fair youth', a man for whom the speaker has complex but clearly homoerotic feelings, before the focus shifts to a woman widely known as the 'dark lady' on account of her 'dun' skin and wiry hair.

It would be a mistake to overplay the obscurity of Shakespeare's sonnets. Several are almost as well known as the blockbuster plays, chief among them Sonnet 18, 'Shall I compare thee to a summer's day?' This tends to be remembered as an untrammelled praise song for the beloved, and there are certainly some beautiful lines of celebration, culminating in the claim that 'thy eternal summer shall not fade'. Less remarked upon, however, is the poem's self-reflexive quality – the fact that Shakespeare is constructing a hymn not just to a lover, but to the art of poetry itself.

The final couplet projects a glorious, symbiotic afterlife: 'So long as men can breathe or eyes can see, / So long lives this, and this gives life to thee.' In other words: yeah, you might be a hottie now, but my poem is the elixir that will give you life eternal. It's a wonderfully arrogant, domineering rhetorical move, as if Shakespeare has already got one eye on his posthumous celebrity. It has also turned out to be something of a half-truth, since nobody really cares about the person the poem's addressed to any more (not outside the geeky halls of Shakespeare studies, anyway). Sonnet 18, on the other hand – now *that* lives on, in wedding ceremonies, Valentine's cards and earnest recitals by national treasures, with the addressee shifting eternally to fit the occasion. Shakespeare 2, Fair Youth 1.

Elsewhere, the sonnets are anything but swaggering and self-possessed. More often they reverse the roles of submission and domination, so that it is the poor poet who comes to the relationship pining, jealous, in need of affirmation. Time and again, thinking itself is at the heart of the drama: what the beloved thinks of the speaker; what the wider world would think if they were to be together; what the speaker himself is thinking in the depths of his soul. Thinking takes on a riddling, knotted quality, full of rebounds and repetitions:

> Yet in these thoughts myself almost despising,
> Haply I think on thee, and then my state . . .
>
> (Sonnet 29, 'When, in disgrace with
fortune and men's eyes')

> No matter then although my foot did stand
> Upon the farthest earth removed from thee;
> For nimble thought can jump both sea and land
> As soon as think the place where he would be.
> But ah! thought kills me that I am not thought . . .
>
> (Sonnet 44, 'If the dull substance
of my flesh were thought')

> Nay, if you read this line, remember not
> The hand that writ it; for I love you so
> That I in your sweet thoughts would be forgot
> If thinking on me then should make you woe.
>
> (Sonnet 71, 'No longer mourn for
me when I am dead')

This is some high-level, painful mental gymnastics. 'But ah! thought kills me that I am not thought' is a line that agonizes over another person's indifferent mind. It embodies thought as a ghostly double presence, possessing an active element and a negative shadow. The active element covers whatever might actually be in this beautiful, maddening person's mind, from idle musings about what to have for dinner to lovelorn yearnings for someone else. Then there's the shadow-thought that causes the speaker so much pain – the fact that this person *isn't* thinking about them. Behind it all lurks the anxious spirit of the speaker himself, conjuring this psychodrama in his overheated brain. The thought that kills him could originate in the mind of the beloved, or it could be his own feverish realization that 'I am not thought.'

If we consider the challenge of 'how to think like William Shakespeare', chances are that most people will gravitate to the plays. They'll fasten on to those breathtaking passages where the modern self seems to be taking shape before our eyes – a form of personhood that is private, unique and intelligible to itself, with motives that extend far beyond the claims of family, faith and nation. Few might look to these wild frontiers of the sonnets, where the self is many things, but rarely intelligible. This, though, is an equal part of the story, and perhaps even more revealing of how language, poetry and human thought would evolve together in the centuries to come.

8

How to Think Like John Donne

The sixteenth and seventeenth centuries were an extraordinary time in English poetry. The Anglocentric canon has a lot to answer for, but this much, at least, should be admitted. Something was in the water. Call it confidence; call it novelty; call it crisis; call it wealth: whatever was sloshing around England at the time, it fed a kind of protracted growth spurt among the nation's poets. New words became possible, new forms of speech. At the same time, London fattened on the profits of England's ascendant global empire – a bloodstained enterprise that enabled new forms of exploitation and disease. Poets were right there in the thick of it, helping themselves to the banquet. There wasn't, and there never has been, any ivory tower.

John Donne is the poet who more than any other sums up the excitement and voracity of this era. Born in 1572, eight years after Shakespeare, he's the first English poet who takes the New World in his stride, rather in the way that digital natives today live and breathe the internet. 'O my America! my new-found-land,' he exclaims in one poem.

My kingdom, safeliest when with one man mann'd,
My Mine of precious stones, My Empirie,
How blest am I in this discovering thee!

This might sound like the exultation of a man setting food on a 'new-found-land' for the very first time. But Donne isn't talking about the real America, the continent plundered by Sir Walter Raleigh in a series of voyages starting in 1584. He's talking about a woman, as readers will be aware of from the opening line ('Come, Madam, come'), or before that, even, if they're reading the poem under its common title, 'To His Mistress Going to Bed'. (Donne wasn't much of a titler, so those that we have are mostly the work of later anthologists and editors.) In other words, it's a poem that has thoroughly digested the shock of the new and regurgitated it as a metaphor. America is well enough understood, by this point, that it can serve as a symbol for an older but continually enigmatic subject (for male poets): women.

Sex tantalized and enraptured Donne, provoking his brain as well as his body. By this, I don't mean that he thought with his genitals – to put a polite gloss on a crude contemporary cliché – so much as that sex is cerebral in his poems, and thinking erotic. Katherine Rundell writes wonderfully about this side of him in a recent biography, *Super-Infinite*, arguing that Donne 'wrote sex as the great insistence on life, the salute, the bodily semaphore for the human, living infinite'. 'Insistence' is an especially apt word to use in connection with Donne's poetry, which is forever reaching out to persuade, bargain or seduce, often exhaustingly so. Some nights the mistress will simply want to go to bed, without being pestered for sex – not least because, as Rundell points out, extramarital sex carried a severe social and religious sanction at the time Donne was writing.

In merry disregard for these niceties, 'To His Mistress Going to Bed' cajoles the potential lover to offer up her virtue and disrobe. 'As liberally, as to a Midwife, shew / Thy self,' runs the counterintuitive invitation at the end of the poem. There's intellectual as well as moral risk to this analogy. Lovers shouldn't be like midwives – especially not lovers who are men. For one thing, the simile renders the swaggering male seducer disarmingly feminine and homely. For another, it comes at sex from entirely the wrong end of the spectrum, at least for someone whose main priority is to have a hassle-free orgasm. At the precise moment when Donne's speaker might prevail and get his lady into bed, he puts an inconvenient thought in her mind, by reminding her that sex can sometimes lead to babies.

That's the edgy and perverse side of Donne's imagination at play. It's this side that provoked Samuel Johnson to coin the term 'metaphysical' to describe Donne's work, alongside that of other seventeenth-century poets drawn to the new domains of scientific and geographical knowledge. Johnson argued that the Metaphysicals valued 'wit' – the dazzling, unexpected display of intelligence – above other more important artistic virtues, like elegance or truth. As a result, their work abounds in far-fetched metaphors. 'The most heterogeneous ideas are yoked by violence together,' harrumphs Johnson; 'nature and art are ransacked for illustrations, comparisons, and allusions.' In a famous example of such 'heterogeneous' yoking, Donne compares two lovers separated by distance to a set of mathematical compasses. 'Thy soul, the fixed foot, makes no show / To move, but doth, if the other do,' he posits.

> And though it in the centre sit,
> 　　Yet when the other far doth roam,
> It leans and hearkens after it,
> 　　And grows erect, as that comes home.
> 　　　　　　　　　　('A Valediction: Forbidding Mourning')

For Johnson, these conceits made for bad wooing as well as roughshod verse. They were distracting and self-important, shining the spotlight on the poet's ingenuity rather than on the proper object of attention.

There's a grain of truth to this. Donne's best poems are nothing if not self-important. They vaunt and preen. Yet there's another nuance that Johnson misses altogether – their vital element of sincerity and tenderness. The compass simile appeals first to the intellect, but after that it settles into something deeply felt and tactile: an image of two lovers spiritually conjoined yet bodily apart, tracing the shape of a circle with their devotion. To make it work, you have to shut down the rational part of your brain and trust to subconscious instincts – in the same way, perhaps, that someone using a set of compasses might measure a precise interval between the points before handing over to their motor skills to finish the job. The comparison is a stretch because long-distance love is a stretch. Donne understands that we need a complex, unromantic image to make sense of an essential complexity in love itself.

In similar fashion, 'To His Mistress Going to Bed' plays serious metaphorical games. At the last gasp, the midwife image swaps the poem's penetrative male stance for one of gender-fluid partnership. The speaker encourages his mistress to set out on this intimate adventure as if they were both collaborating towards some higher end. In this light, it makes sense that the speaker seems to be excited not so much by the physical prospect of sex as by the intellectual sport leading up to it. Perhaps at some level this makes sex feel safe and fun, an activity where foreplay is as essential as the main event. Perhaps it even creates a space where sex can exist solely, and satisfyingly, in the flirtatious exchange of words. Or perhaps all these verbal pyrotechnics suggest, in time-honoured fashion, that a man will simply say anything to get a woman into bed. The signals are mixed. What's clear, though, is that Donne is getting his kicks out of the process of thinking itself, and out of inviting a woman to enjoy sex – and thinking – on the same level as him.

T. S. Eliot likewise latched on to the sensuality of Donne's mind. In an influential essay from 1921, Eliot turned the tables on Dr Johnson's sniffy appraisal, which had set the agenda in discussions of the Metaphysical poets for well over a hundred years. Where Johnson saw the Metaphysicals as a blind alleyway for English verse, Eliot saw them as the great example of a road not taken. In trying to define that road, he hit on a broader narrative of cultural decline, a gulf in outlook that divided the Victorian era from the anthology of seventeenth-century poetry he was reviewing:

> It is something which had happened to the mind of England between the time of Donne . . . and the time of [Alfred, Lord Tennyson] and [Robert] Browning; it is the difference between the intellectual poet and the reflective poet. Tennyson and Browning are poets, and they think; but they do not feel their thought as immediately as the odour of a rose. A thought to Donne was an experience; it modified his sensibility.

For Eliot, then, to think like Donne meant far more than just thinking. It meant sensing thought, inhaling thought, letting it percolate through every fibre of one's 'experience'. 'When a poet's mind is perfectly equipped for its work,' he continues, 'it is constantly amalgamating disparate experience; the ordinary man's experience is chaotic, irregular, fragmentary. The latter falls in love, or reads Spinoza, and these two experiences have nothing to do with each other, or with the noise of the typewriter or the smell of cooking; in the mind of the poet these experiences are always forming new wholes.'

Eliot, as we'll see in a later chapter, had a vested interest in making 'the noise of the typewriter' a legitimate subject for poetry. For now, it's enough to note that, in his view, Donne was the supreme poet of 'amalgamating disparate experience' – a man who would almost certainly have compared the sensation of falling in love to the noise of a typewriter, if he had only known that one day typewriters would exist.

Donne's life was as eventful and multifarious as his poetry. Rundell teases out the full story in a series of glinting pen portraits, or 'transformations', that follow Donne from his risqué youth to a well-heeled and respectable old age. In later years he served as Dean of St Paul's Cathedral, an ultra-establishment position that would have astonished many of his long-standing friends and enemies. He came from a trenchantly Catholic family that counted among its recent dead Sir Thomas More, a senior Tudor politician who was executed in 1535 for defying Henry VIII in his first attempts at a Protestant reformation. (Donne's mother, Elizabeth, was long rumoured to carry More's skull among her personal effects.)

Out of a dicey, recusant childhood he emerged as a gifted scholar at Lincoln's Inn, the breeding ground for many illustrious young lawyers and men of court. It was here that Donne started to write the erotic and satirical verse that made his name. Granted, salacious poetry was no way to make a living, though for whatever reason Donne never quite knuckled down to a career in law either. After finishing his studies, he embarked on a brief cameo as a soldier, joining the Earl of Essex's successful voyage to sack the Spanish city of Cádiz in 1596. While this didn't lead to any further military adventures, it did furnish him with an alternative career path courtesy of his friend and fellow soldier, Sir Thomas Egerton the younger. For the next four years Donne served Egerton's father (also Sir Thomas) as his private secretary.

Egerton senior was Lord Keeper of the Great Seal, one of the most prominent roles in Elizabeth I's court, with a significant legal brief. More than your average private secretary, Donne seems to have enjoyed Egerton's trust, even being gifted the parliamentary seat of Brackley, Northampton in 1601. Yet no sooner had Donne started to build his political career than he unceremoniously blew it up. His downfall, predictably, was love.

In a clandestine ceremony held three weeks before Christmas, 1601, Donne married a young woman named Anne More. More was Egerton's niece and ward – in other words, someone wholly and inappropriately out of Donne's league – and the star-crossed lovers must have begun the courtship under Sir Thomas's roof, while Anne was only 16 to Donne's 28. When Egerton and Anne's father, Sir George More, found out about the wedding, they, to put it mildly, hit the roof. More had his surprise son-in-law locked up in the Fleet prison, where Donne had to write grovelling letters begging for his release. These pleas eventually succeeded, and the marriage was grudgingly acknowledged as valid, but Donne never again regained favour in Egerton's household.

The coming decade was gruelling and precarious, with the taint of an illicit marriage dogging the young couple's footsteps while their family grew larger by the year. Donne's first biographer, Izaak Walton, called his marriage to Anne 'the remarkable error of his life'. We can't know what Anne would have made of that, but I imagine marriage must have often felt like a mistake to her, too. The union with Donne seems to have been founded in genuine love and commitment, but it brought with it hardship, endless maternal labour and exile from her family. She died in August 1617, five days after giving birth to her stillborn 12th child. Donne preached the funeral sermon himself.

Altogether, it's a sad story, albeit with a surprising upswing towards the end when Donne found his calling as a clergyman. Donne's trajectory has none of the inevitability that we expect from Great Men narratives. An awkward and brainy boy, tainted by an illegal faith; a young rake circulating manuscripts of saucy poems; a headstrong eloper: none of these identities is an obvious preparation for high office in the Anglican Church. Accordingly, there has long been a tendency to accentuate the gap between Donne's rollicking young-courtier and elder-statesman phases. At the root of the myth is a short line Donne wrote himself to enclose with a copy of a book he'd written in 1608 titled *Biathanatos*.

This prose treatise would have caused serious scandal had it ever been published in his lifetime. It justified the individual right to suicide, and more than that advanced the sizzling hot take – borderline insane, really, given the fractious religious climate of the time – that Christ's death on the cross was itself a kind of glorious suicide. Donne wavered, it seems, over whether or not to destroy *Biathanatos*, but eventually sent the manuscript to his friend Sir Robert Ker with a note of warning: 'It is a book written by Jack Donne, and not by Doctor Donne.' This playful act of self-fashioning offers 'an irresistible formulation', writes Catherine Nicholson, 'with the snap and symmetry of an epigram, and it has become a shorthand for the puzzle of Donne's mercurial being.'

To explore these binaries more fully – worldly Jack versus the pious Doctor of Divinity – we can turn to one of Donne's great poems. 'Good Friday, 1613. Riding Westward' was written two years before he took holy orders, long after his Jack Donne period should have drawn to a close. By that point he had fathered nine (legitimate) children and started to claw back respectability at court. You wouldn't know it, though, to read the poem, which cringes with a sense of personal sin. It all turns on the coincidental but piquant detail that Donne is travelling 'westward' on this holiest of days, away from Christ's crucifixion in the East. His daily business quite literally averts his gaze from the only sights that should matter – that is, the holes pierced in 'those hands which span the Poles', and Mary, Christ's grieving mother, 'Who was Gods partner here, and furnish'd thus / Halfe of that Sacrifice, which ransom'd us.'

Donne starts to resolve this predicament by triangulating between his own gaze and God's.

Though these things, as I ride, be from mine eye,
They'are present yet unto my memory,
For that looks towards them; and thou look'st towards
    mee,
O Saviour, as thou hang'st upon the tree . . .

The subject matter may be worlds apart from his erotic verse, yet we might recognize something in the manner of his argument – the restless bargaining, the attempt to win God over by force of logic, making Him swallow some questionable rapid-fire premises along the way. The final couplet even casts salvation as a kind of come-hither game, putting the onus on God to make the first move: 'Restore thine Image, so much, by thy grace, / That thou may'st know mee, and I'll turne my face.'

It's a fiendishly intricate argument which depends fundamentally on the splitting of selves. To unpack its multiple planes of vision, one almost needs a whiteboard scrawled with diagrams and arrows: here is the speaker's body, facing in one direction; here is the personification of his memory, which faces in the other; and here, meanwhile, is God, who is simultaneously looking at the back of the speaker's head and meeting the chastened gaze of his memory, eye to eye, as it were. No wonder Dr Johnson puffed his cheeks in exasperation.

That's the uncharitable view, in any case. But there's a different way of reading this strange scattering of thought and image. A. S. Byatt is best known nowadays as the Booker Prize-winning author of *Possession*, though in a previous life she was an English professor, and in critical mode she has written one of the finest essays there is on Donne's fascinating brain. 'Feeling thought: Donne and the embodied mind' returns to Eliot's famous pronouncement about the thinking poet and the reflective poet. It agrees with Eliot's thesis, up to a point, but insists even more strongly on the supercharged role of thinking in Donne's poetry. 'The pleasure Donne offers our bodies is the pleasure of extreme activity of the brain,' writes Byatt.

> He is characteristically concerned with the schemas we have constructed to map our mental activities – geometry, complex grammatical constructions, physiology, definitions. He is thinking about thinking. (And about smelling roses, but he is not immediately inducing us to smell any in our imaginations.)

In Byatt's view, what matters for Donne is the process of connection itself – the thrill we get when we correlate objects and ideas that are normally stored in different compartments of the brain. To flesh out this hypothesis, she dips a toe into contemporary neuroscience and cognitive literary studies, borrowing the concept of 'radiant ignition' from the writer Elaine Scarry. Byatt paraphrases radiant ignition as 'the verbal calling up of sharp bright lights in the mind', positing that

Donne's poems are constantly involved in summoning such a cerebral lightshow. They delight in forging neural pathways that we didn't know we had, less concerned with the real-world phenomena their lines describe than with the act of mapping these new mental territories in the first place.

In practice, these radiant effects often consist in lists, adverbs, metaphors of position and space. Byatt's main example is a couplet from 'To His Mistress Going to Bed': 'Licence my roving hands and let them go, / Before, behind, between, above, below.' Something comparable takes place, I would argue, at the climax of 'Good Friday, 1613. Riding Westward'. This time imagining the Passion of Christ rather than the nooks and crannies of his lover's body, Donne nevertheless constructs a similarly multidimensional map. I am here, another part of me is there, and God is somewhere else again, calling out across the gap. Whether or not we have faith in the theology behind this vision, our minds light up with the effort to make it real.

9

How to Think Like John Milton

As we saw in the last chapter, English poetry's early-modern growth spurt would have been unthinkable without the religious strife unleashed by the Reformation. This is a shorthand term for the gruelling, centuries-long process by which England wrenched itself away from Catholic Christendom and established a Protestant national Church. British propagandists have tended to glorify this era as a long march towards freedom, a Brexit of the soul. In reality, this is unlikely to be how it felt or looked at the time. As Clare Jackson puts it in an eye-opening new history, 'To contemporaries and foreigners alike, seventeenth-century England was a failed state: a discomfiting byword for seditious rebellion, religious extremism and regime change.'

The Reformation is never far from the surface in the work of Shakespeare and Donne, two outwardly conforming Protestants who we can say with varying degrees of certainty carried a torch for the old Catholic faith. Shakespeare's Sonnet 73, for instance, imagines autumnal trees as 'bare ruin'd choirs', which some critics have claimed stand for the stripped and whitewashed walls of post-Reformation churches. Donne dealt with doctrinal arguments more directly in his sermons and prose treatises, bashing the Jesuits, for instance, in an unlovely tract called *Ignatius His Conclave*. His poems, meanwhile, inhabit a thousand shades of spiritual grey. We only see the full blood and thunder of this period come into focus, therefore, with the next poet in our survey. John Milton had no such lingering affinity for the rituals of the Catholic Church. If anything, he saw them as the work of the Devil.

Which is not to say that he lacked an interest – in either Catholicism or the Devil. Milton imagined Hell in sensuous, lurid detail. For this Christian visionary, Hell was not a vague word for eternal punishment, leveraged by priests to guarantee good behaviour on earth. It was a realm with specific dimensions, lighting and interior decoration. In his masterwork, *Paradise Lost*, Milton even coined a new word to capture Hell's physical presence: Pandemonium. This is an ingenious portmanteau, mashing together the Greek word 'pantheon' (an assembly of the gods) with the demons who populate this space in Hell.

What he finds in Pandemonium is at first blush rather glorious:

Anon out of the earth a fabric huge
Rose like an exhalation, with the sound
Of dulcet symphonies and voices sweet—
Built like a temple, where pilasters round
Were set, and Doric pillars overlaid
With golden architrave; nor did there want
Cornice or frieze, with bossy sculptures graven;
The roof was fretted gold.

Music, pillars, artworks; gold upon 'fretted gold'. Who wouldn't want to spend time in a Hell like this? Twenty lines earlier, Milton has already tried to forestall this reaction by warning the reader, 'Let none admire / That riches grow in Hell'. Yet one could be forgiven for thinking that the subsequent description rather undermines the point. It's a bit like introducing a sex-education lesson with a stern lecture on abstinence before proceeding to show an erotic film.

Above all, Pandemonium is a suggestively Catholic space. All those cornices, friezes and sweetly mingled voices mirror the trappings of worship that Europeans would have imbibed for centuries as part of the Roman Church. Granted, this is a particularly grand version of that tradition; not so much a country parish in a rural backwater as one of the great cathedrals of Christendom. 'It is likely that Pandemonium is represented as a parody of a gorgeous Counter-Reformation building,' ventures Andrew Hadfield, 'possibly St Peter's in Rome, which Milton saw in 1638.' The Counter-Reformation followed hot on the heels of the Reformation itself, as Catholic Europe sought to repel the Protestant barbarian at its gates by doubling down on priestly ritual and sacred beauty – not to mention violence.

However, Milton's youthful travels to Rome offer our first hint that his religious allegiances might not be as simple as they seem. To put it bluntly, why would such an avowed critic of Catholicism stray into the enemy's lair? In a new biography, Joe Moshenska explores the moral and intellectual hinterland of Milton's journey to the continent. Moshenska is keen to stress the complex networks that would have enabled Milton's travels – alliances that by no means kept to a straight and narrow Protestant path. Here is Milton wowing the Florence Accademia; here he is in the Vatican Library, relishing its collection of esoteric manuscripts; here, now, in the audience at a recital by the great singer Leonora Baroni, a maestra of the new musical style that would come to be known as opera.

All these rich Italian experiences fed the soil that gave rise to *Paradise Lost* some 25 years later back in chilly England. Nevertheless, Milton concluded his grand European tour in Geneva, the home of a more severe strain of Protestantism, named after its progenitor, John Calvin. In Geneva, Milton signed the friendship album of a new acquaintance with a line from the *Epistles* of Horace, best translated as 'I change the skies, but not my mind, when I cross the seas.' To anyone who might have disapproved of his adventures in Italy, Milton was issuing a firm rejoinder: in effect, 'I may have seen some things in Rome, but rest assured I know what I'm about – no foreign, popish muck for me.' The irony is that it took a Roman poet to help him find the right words for this complex sentiment.

Let's lay our cards on the table: Milton was a Puritan. Nowadays, to assign somebody this label – most likely with a lowercase 'p' – has the flavour of a character assassination. You would be calling that person intolerant, mean-spirited and rigidly orthodox: holier than thou. The word gets bandied about in modern culture wars, often to smear the left in their efforts (so the argument goes) to police free speech. In recent years there has even been a polemical book called *The New Puritans: How the Religion of Social Justice Captured the Western World*. Its author, Andrew Doyle, argues, 'One of the key aspects of this ideological movement is that its adherents treat all challenges as a form of heresy that must be quashed.' According to this jaundiced vision of twenty-first-century life, the cry of injustice trumps rational evidence; victimhood confers sainthood; sensitivity readers desecrate literature, and statues are toppled, all while well-meaning artists and cultural commentators are cancelled in their droves by an amorphous woke mob. You know the drill.

John Milton was a Puritan, but not like that. For a start, the term, spelled with a capital 'P', had a more precise descriptive function in the seventeenth century. It summed up a loose coalition of radical Protestant groups – Calvinists, Anabaptists, Congregationalists, Millenarians, Quakers – whose common denominator was divergence from the Anglican Church. In various ways, these sects felt that the Church of England hadn't gone far enough in cleansing Christianity of its Catholic past. There were still too many ornaments and baubles; too many liturgical extras that distracted from the literal word of God. Above all, Puritans resented the secular power of the Church. What was the point in leaving Rome if bishops still had the right, enshrined in law, to dictate how someone should worship? That, in their view, was a matter concerning nobody except the individual and their maker.

From the 1630s this broader critique coalesced into revulsion for a particular cleric, William Laud, the Archbishop of Canterbury under King Charles I. We catch the reverberations of this antagonism in Milton's great elegy 'Lycidas'. Primarily, the poem mourns the death of Edward King, a companion of Milton's at Cambridge University who drowned while travelling from Wales to Ireland. However, 'Lycidas' also provides a platform from which Milton can survey the contemporary political moment. Written in 1637, it seems to gesture to a grisly incident in the summer of that year, when three prominent Puritans – a doctor, John Bastwick; a clergyman, Henry Burton; and a lawyer, William Prynne – had their ears cut off at the behest of Archbishop Laud, on the charge of seditious libel.

Reflecting on the fact that King had plans to take holy orders, Milton laments the loss his friend's death has brought to the ministry, a profession riddled with cruelty and corruption. Milton riffs on the conventional image of the bishop with his

flock, a pastor following in the footsteps of the original Good
Shepherd, Christ – only now the bishops are more like wolves
sneaking into the fold. In an extraordinary outburst, he gives
it to the English bishops full blast:

> Blind mouths! that scarce themselves know how to hold
> A sheep-hook, or have learn'd aught else the least
> That to the faithful herdman's art belongs!
> [. . .]
> The hungry sheep look up, and are not fed,
> But, swoll'n with wind and the rank mist they draw,
> Rot inwardly, and foul contagion spread [. . .]

The people of England, 'hungry' for spiritual guidance, are
compared here to sheep whose empty stomachs bloat with
wind for want of sustenance. It's an appropriately gross and
flatulent image, telescoping Milton's contempt for religious
hierarchy. Even more striking is the expostulation 'Blind
mouths!', a blurt of apparently nonsensical frustration that
contains another tremor of anxiety about sense organs. This
is a land, after all, where ears are mutilated when people speak
the truth, so it stands to reason that those responsible for the
violence – the people who ironically most need to use their
ears and listen – are just bloviating 'mouths'. The fact that they
are also *blind* mouths is par for the course. Everything here is
malfunctioning, topsy-turvy, inside out.

'Lycidas', then, indicates one way in which we can reclaim
Milton's Puritanism from the modern meanings of the slur –
that is, by attending to the many ways in which it has nothing
to do with us. Laud is not J. K. Rowling, and Bastwick, Burton
and Prynne are not social justice warriors on a mission to
cancel him. The power dynamics and moral nuances are
completely different, and most likely alien to our present-day

understandings of what morality should be. At the same time, we should remember that the original Puritans were serious, intelligent people fighting for their conscience in the teeth of specific challenges. Their crusade often had less to do with scolding or policing others than with vehemently protecting their own rights of worship and assembly – values which place them more on the side of today's free-speech absolutists than with the loudly feared snowflakes who cramp their style.

Which brings us to the second way in which Puritanism has to be re-evaluated in light of Milton. Rather than believing that opposition viewpoints 'must be quashed' (a belief which Doyle attributes to the modern variant of the species), Milton believed passionately in letting debate circulate. *Areopagitica*, Milton's prose tract from 1644, offers one of the most robust defences for freedom of speech that has ever been published. 'I cannot praise a fugitive and cloistered virtue,' he declaims, 'unexercised and unbreathed, that never sallies out and sees her adversary'. Anyone who seriously believes in their cause should stand their ground, he argues. Seek out dissent; meet it head on. Tellingly, he reaches for the concept of purity itself to prove his point. 'Assuredly we bring not innocence into the world, we bring impurity much rather: that which purifies us is trial, and trial is by what is contrary'. Milton has no time for those who feel safe in their personal virtue. He reminds us that humans 'bring not innocence into the world', but endless fallibility and error – or 'impurity', we might say, if we can stomach a word that has been so dragged through the mud in the centuries since Milton.

I don't want to overcorrect, by suggesting that Milton was some nice, misunderstood liberal before his time. *Areopagitica* places certain ideas beyond the pale of free speech, in particular Catholicism, which for Milton was nothing more than a vexatious blot on true religion, the spiritual equivalent of yelling 'Fire!' in a crowded theatre. This, after all, was a man who held political office in the famously illiberal government of Oliver Cromwell. A Puritan himself, Cromwell ruled England through the 1650s, after leading the parliamentary forces to victory against King Charles I in the brutal English Civil War that gripped the nation from 1642 until 1651. Cromwell's Britain is maligned these days as a joyless place – the Land that Banned Christmas – and Milton continued dutifully to serve it, even addressing Cromwell as 'our chief of men' in a sonnet of 1652. However, as Blair Worden demonstrates, Milton's enthusiasm for the regime waned palpably across its final years. In 1653 the republic became a protectorate, organized under the increasingly despotic personal rule of Cromwell. 'Milton's pen offers no tribute to the military and naval exploits of the protectorate,' observes Worden, 'no lament on Cromwell's death. His silence is loud.'

Milton's final public address to Cromwell can be dated to 1654, in a Latin prose work called *Defensio Secunda*. This sought to justify the regicide of King Charles – a cause Milton passionately believed in – while defending the new regime, with increasing wariness, as it grappled with the burdens of power. Following the fall of the regime, in 1659, Milton condemned the years of the protectorate as 'a short but scandalous night of interruption'. Whether Milton felt personally sorry for the part he'd played in this 'short but scandalous night' is another matter – but given how every sinew of his written work strains to protect the dignity of individual conscience, I find it hard to imagine that he didn't.

All in all, then, Milton remains a tough sell. On the charitable side of the ledger, one could follow Moshenska in saying that he is 'a national monument rather than a national treasure'. We know that *Paradise Lost* is one of the most outstanding literary achievements of all time, though we'd rather do almost anything else than sit down and read it. Even Milton's fans have a tendency to talk about his brilliance as a problem to be wrestled with. William Blake first set this train in motion when he proposed that '[t]he reason Milton wrote in fetters when he wrote of Angels & God, and at liberty when he wrote of Devils & Hell, is because he was a true Poet and of the Devil's party without knowing it'. The underlying assumption here is that an orthodox Christian couldn't possibly be a 'true Poet', and that – ergo – Milton reveals his heretical impulses by being a great poet. Anyone who has felt their blood rise reading Satan's soaring hymn to liberty from Book I of *Paradise Lost* ('Better to reign in Hell, then serve in Heav'n') might be inclined to agree. But it remains a curious form of admiration.

Then there are the sceptics. Running parallel to the narrative of greatness (grudging or otherwise) is a rich history of Milton-bashing. The spectrum encompasses everything from backhanded compliments to outright vituperation. Dr Johnson has been a faithful companion to our excursions through the English Renaissance, so we might as well start with him. Despite penning a biography of Milton, Johnson wrote elsewhere that his poetry is composed of 'a "Babylonish dialect," in itself harsh and barbarous; but made by exalted genius, and extensive learning, the vehicle of so much instruction and so much pleasure, that, like other lovers, we find grace in its deformity'. 'Babylonish dialect' alludes to Milton's famously Latinate diction, which led him to coin a host of new words like 'omnific' and 'convolved'. Some might see this as a mark of the man's genius rather than a 'deformity' to be excused – those coinages also include such modern-day essentials as 'lovelorn' and 'terrific' – but many readers have followed Johnson in finding Milton too weird, too foreign, to sit neatly in the English canon.

Doubts about Milton's style sometimes shade into personal misgivings. T. S. Eliot – who, as we saw in the last chapter, proved to be a generous and penetrating critic of Donne – becomes a pearl-clutching snob when it comes to Milton. 'As a man, he is antipathetic,' Eliot sniffs. 'Either from the moralist's point of view, or from the theologian's point of view, or from the psychologist's point of view, or from that of the political philosopher, or judging by the ordinary standards of likeableness in human beings, Milton is unsatisfactory.' To this (quite funny) slander one might add A. D. Nuttall's judgement, harder to shrug off, that Milton was 'dead from the waist down' – that is, frigid and overbearingly cerebral, with a lack of ease among the opposite sex that bordered on misogyny. At one point in *Paradise Lost*, Milton appears to confirm Nuttall's hypothesis via a moment of wincing body horror in which Sin is depicted as a monster. Like a wretched earth-dwelling mermaid, the creature is 'woman to the waist, and fair' but below that blemished with 'many a scaly fold / Voluminous and vast', 'a serpent arm'd / With mortal sting'. This is only the cherry on the cake of a long Christian tradition of fearing women as sensual, snaky *femmes fatales* – though it is quite a juicy one.

Why, then, for all these faults, is Milton worth fighting for? Moshenska's book, *Making Darkness Light*, presents an eloquent case for the defence, never excusing the unpalatable aspects of Milton's life or works, but setting them firmly in place beside his virtues. As a schoolmaster, Milton zealously beat his students, and by all accounts he was impossible to live with. Yet for every snub or justified rebuke, we should venture a countervailing tribute. Milton was a radical thinker who adopted courageous, often lonely positions. He bristled righteously at the abuse of power. More than that, he was someone who knew his own mind and made painstaking efforts to enrich it. I would not want to be Milton – or even be like him, in any meaningful sense of the idea – but perhaps more than any other poet he reveals the poverty of that line of thinking. On an ethical level, what I get from spending time in his company is not a warm glow of recognition but a bracing ice bath of difference. His Puritanism is a goad to think harder, think deeper, and hold oneself to account.

Finally, there is the side of Milton that needs no apology or special pleading, at least not in my house – and that is the wonder of his poetry as poetry. This is where it becomes most important to push back on the image of Milton as a dusty monument. I first read and admired *Paradise Lost* as an undergraduate English student, but I didn't fully appreciate it until I encountered it as a creative writer during my master's degree. This is where it flared into life as a rhythmic animal full of swing and syncopation. Our teacher, Timothy Donnelly, got us to read passages from *Paradise Lost* aloud, so that we could feel the cadences build and resolve across epic intervals. Forget about meaning for a moment, Tim said. Just listen to the music.

I recall us reading the invocation to light at the start of Book III, where Milton finally turns to beauty and goodness after two books spent sweating with Satan's fallen angels in Hell. The poignant twist is that Milton can't see the light himself. By this point in his life he was blind, a condition that he writes about with exquisite, tactile understanding:

> Thus with the year
> Seasons return; but not to me returns
> Day, or the sweet approach of even or morn,
> Or sight of vernal bloom, or summer's rose,
> Or flocks, or herds, or human face divine;
> But cloud instead, and ever-during dark

Surrounds me, from the cheerful ways of men
Cut off, and for the book of knowledge fair
Presented with a universal blank
Of nature's works to me expung'd and ras'd,
And wisdom at one entrance quite shut out.
So much the rather thou, celestial Light,
Shine inward, and the mind through all her powers
Irradiate; there plant eyes, all mist from thence
Purge and disperse, that I may see and tell
Of things invisible to mortal sight.

One can appreciate these lines with or without any prior knowledge of Milton's life – but it does enrich the experience to situate this passage at the likely time of its composition, sometime in the 1660s.

Following the restoration of the monarchy at the turn of that decade, Milton could very easily have joined the ranks of the senior officials in Cromwell's government who were executed as traitors to the nation. Had he played an active part in the regicide – as opposed to cheerleading it from the sidelines – he'd have been a goner. Thanks to some canny intercessions by influential friends, he survived. But it's doubtful that Milton would have felt in any way 'lucky' to be granted this reprieve. The dominant note in these lines, at least to begin with, is regret. With their talk of 'a universal blank' and a world of 'works' that have been 'expung'd and ras'd', I hear not just a man coming to terms with his disability in old age, but an avid republican acknowledging that the project he believed in was dead.

Does it add to the lustre of the poem that Milton would have had to dictate these lines aloud to an amanuensis? Not as such, though this has long been a cornerstone of his legend, and it must certainly have been a technical feat – to put it mildly – to manage the iambic rhythms of the verse without being able to see the shape of the poem emerge on paper. There is an ableist tinge to this narrative, however, that marvels at the practical 'how' of blindness while ignoring more important questions of form, content and meaning. A better question might be: how does Milton ask us to experience blindness? How does the warp and weft of his language embody his new reality? The beginnings of the lines in this passage seem almost designed to trip us up: 'but not to me returns / Day'; 'ever-during dark / Surrounds me'; 'from the cheerful ways of men / Cut off'. We become like the speaker himself as he tries to navigate the world, constantly being startled into new sensitivities. By a similar token, when the mood of the passage shifts from minor to major key and the speaker enjoins the light to 'Shine inward, and the mind through all her powers / Irradiate', we experience each new line as a dawning of hope and resolve.

Further wonders await in every book of *Paradise Lost*. So next time you're feeling blocked, 'cut off' or uninspired, try to break through that inner wall of resistance pretty much everyone feels when faced with a massive canonical tome. Sit down with it as a poem of breath and spirit, flesh and blood. Break it into manageable chunks. Let it irradiate your mind.

10

How to Think Like Matsuo Bashō

Sometime between 1680 and 1686 – experts are divided on the exact date – Matsuo Bashō saw a frog jump into a pond. The amphibian may have been real or imaginary, a single frog or a generalization from many frogs, and the pond in question may or may not have belonged to the fish merchant Sugiyama Sanpo, who bequeathed Bashō a hut in which to meditate and write his poetry. These all remain matters for scholarly disagreement. For now, then, it's best to stick with what we can say for certain, which is that some combination of a frog, a jump and a body of water seared itself into Bashō's mind. The experience moved him to write a haiku, a 17-syllable poem written in the courtly form that he had mastered as a young man in the castles and temples of Kyoto. In the centuries since it was written, that haiku has gone on to become one of the most widely known and reproduced poems of all time.

Here it is, in the original Kanji:

古池や
蛙飛こむ
水のおと

And again, in Romaji, the westernized form of Japanese that captures the phonetic sound of the original:

Furuike ya,
kawazu tobikomu,
mizu no oto.

Beyond that, any reader who lacks Japanese will be beholden to a translator. As we've seen in previous chapters, transposing a poem from one language to another is far from a simple matter, even on such a restricted canvas as this. In English alone, there are over 100 versions of Bashō's frog poem, each emphasizing a slightly different element of action or phrasing. These translations run the gamut from the reverent and serene:

The old pond;
a frog jumps in—
the sound of the water.
(Robert Aitken)

to the anarchic:

pond
frog
plop!
(James Kirkup)

But between the kaleidoscopic variations, three elements are non-negotiable: the pond, the leaping frog and the sound of the water as it swallows the creature. Each occupies one of three interwoven lines, forming a delicate but sturdy knot.

Prise apart one of the threads, and you end up with a different poem altogether. This is the elusive magic of the haiku form, and Bashō remains its most gifted – and influential – exponent.

Born under the name Matsuo Kinsaku in 1644, Bashō lived through a pivotal era in Japanese history. Having won power in 1603, the Tokugawa shogunate moved the nation's capital to Edo, modern-day Tokyo. The seventeenth century was a time of paradoxical expansion and retraction in Japan. The expansion was economic, driven by urbanization and an emergent merchant class growing wealthy off the trade in silk, cotton, porcelain and sake. Simultaneously, the nation turned inward, forbidding foreign travel and only allowing overseas trade through the southern port of Nagasaki. Despite – or perhaps because of – this authoritarian streak, the Tokugawa shoguns presided over a period of remarkable social harmony. They wouldn't be usurped until the second half of the nineteenth century, when Emperor Meiji's government aggressively modernized the country and started to build Japan's colonial sphere of influence.

Bashō came from the older Japan. The son of a minor samurai, he grew up in the relative backwater of Iga Ueno, a city in the wider orbit of Kyoto. From provincial origins, he managed to set Japanese literary culture on its modern path with his witty, urbane renovations of the haiku. As a poetic form, haiku had for centuries been bound up with the tradition of courtly verse called *renga*, where multiple poets collaborated in writing interlinking stanzas of 5-7-5 and 7-7 syllabic patterns.

Haiku takes its name from the *hokku*, or originating piece, that would set in motion this collaborative artwork. The hokku could only be written by a master poet, and over time the form evolved further conventions, beyond the syllabic. It had to contain a seasonal reference, indicating the time of year, and also a *kireji*, 'a short emotionally charged word', in Nobuyuki Yuasa's definition, 'which, by arresting the flow of poetic statement for a moment, gives extra strength and dignity'. These constraints would be carried forward into the freestanding haiku of Tokugawa Japan, not to mention the thousand limpid imitations in western languages, detailing autumn leaves and migrating swallows.

Throughout his life Bashō stayed tight-lipped on the subject of politics. He preferred to observe surface tensions of human society, converting them into images drawn from the natural environment. At times in his work, humankind and nature are set quizzically at odds, as in the following haiku from his masterpiece *The Narrow Road to the Deep North*, as translated by Yuasa:

The chestnut by the eaves
In magnificent bloom
Passes unnoticed
By men of this world.

Throughout Bashō's work, we catch this note of admiration for the imperturbability of trees. Indeed, it might be worth reflecting on the fact that he adopted his own writing name from a variety of tree – not a chestnut, but the banana tree that he received as a gift when he retired to his hut in 1680. Admiring his arboreal namesake, Bashō wrote:

The big trunk of the tree is untouched by the axe, for it is utterly useless as building wood. I love the tree, however, for its very uselessness . . . I sit underneath it, and enjoy the wind and rain that blow against it.

Whether they are beautiful chestnuts or 'useless' bashōs, most trees end up being neglected by the 'men of this world', Bashō suggests – the implication being that he is not such a business-like and worldly chap himself. He treasures the bashō tree on its own terms, inviting us to scoff, very gently, at those who would only value it as an inanimate lump of construction material. By sitting under the tree and embracing the same rough weather it endures, he establishes a crucial act of solidarity. If you want to call it useless, he implies – well, then you'll have to call me useless, too.

Nevertheless, it's possible to view this most quiet and meditative of lives in subtly political terms. Reading between the lines of Bashō's work, one finds a response to the challenge of surviving, and finding meaning, in a rigid but rapidly evolving society. Not for nothing did he write his greatest, most innovative work in the genre of the travelogue. As if to test the restrictions imposed by his shogun, Bashō journeys to the far limits of his island nation, seeking out the bracing beauty of the Deep North. Along the way he meets people, mooches on them for hospitality, rubs shoulders with peasants and priests alike.

To encompass this variety, he invents a hybrid, self-consciously cosmopolitan form called the *haibun*, which switches between prose and haiku. Late in his journey, he shelters from a storm in a 'suspicious' gatekeeper's cottage near Dewa Province. The treatment he receives there is not what you would call five-star:

Bitten by fleas and lice,
I slept in a bed,
A horse urinating all the time
Close to my pillow.

It takes a particular mind to see a pissing horse as a subject worthy of poetry, on a par with the cherry tree. Bashō never shies away from earthy realities: the necessities of the shivering body or the full bladder. These, like the blossom of the tree, are phenomena of the world, and deserve to be noticed.

That incontinent horse might also change the way we think about Bashō's more famous frog. There are two broad schools of thought about how to read this great – and some would say overbearing – heirloom of Japanese culture. The common interpretation is to see the frog poem as a moment of beauty and enlightenment, in keeping with the training in Zen Buddhism that Bashō undertook around the time of the poem's composition in the 1680s. The frog jumps, the water makes its deeply satisfying froggy sound, and Bashō's mind and soul are realigned as a result. This is the interpretation favoured by Bashō's western readers, many of whom have come to his work through an interest in eastern philosophy more generally.

The alternative perspective comes from Susumu Takiguchi, a Japanese poet, artist and haiku expert. Putting forward a 'contrarian viewpoint', Takiguchi points out that in Japanese culture frogs aren't usually considered to be symbols of Zen perfection. Rather, they represent 'the merriment, colour, noises, life (sex) and bustling movements of spring', serving as 'a celebration of life on earth'. Not so much a stepping stone on the path to enlightenment, then, as a reflection of what is already palpable, here and now. Takiguchi points to an account of Bashō developing the poem with his disciple Kikaku, who suggested that 'yamabuki ya' – or 'the mountain roses' – would have been a nice opening to the two-line fragment about a frog that Bashō had shared with him. Bashō disagreed, finding it too conventional, and settled on the less picturesque 'old pond' as the poem's instigating image.

I'm not a Buddhist, so far be it from me to hold forth on what the true path of Zen might be. As a reader of poetry, however, who believes that the art form can have transformative powers, I'm drawn more to Takiguchi's reading. It emphasizes the role that chance, imperfection and labour have to play in the making of this poem – or any poem, for that matter. Yes, there's the key detail of Kikaku offering up his image of mountain roses, inspiring his master to reach for the better image – at once more humdrum and more profound – of an old pond. But just as important is Takiguchi's claim that Bashō had the poem knocking about for years, in multiple drafts, until he settled on the version that we know and love. According to Takiguchi, the final eureka moment came at a hokku competition held in 1686 at Bashō's writing hut, where 41 participants shared their poems and decided upon the winner by a process of collective deliberation. By this account, Bashō might have been inspired just as much by one of his peers as by the scene outside his window.

In other words, I don't want to put my finger on the frog. I don't want it to have plopped into the water at just the right moment to produce a decisive moment of awakening in its author's mind. I want the frog to be an idea, hopping about in a playful dance with other ideas, until the moment that it plunges onto the page.

Though it might sound like a lot to place on the shoulders of a single creature, at stake is a whole dilemma about the way that poets think and write. Does a poem act as a pure record of experience, almost in the manner of a recording? Or does it constitute the experience itself – an event in language first and foremost, that activates disparate ideas in the minds of individual readers? To put it another way, your frog won't be my frog, and it certainly won't be Bashō's frog – and even at the moment that Bashō wrote about it, all those years ago, the animal in the poem had already hopped onto a different lily pad, far away from the frog that inspired it in the first place.

None of which should detract from the view that something authentically spiritual is going on in this poem. We take a leap into the unknown and end up somewhere different. If spirituality means anything, then it is surely connected to this powerful fusion of the senses – air and water; sound, movement and vision – that we meet in the poem. No doubt it's a strange thing that mere words on a page can produce such effects, lighting up parts of the brain – dare we say the soul? – that we hardly knew existed. But spirituality itself might be a strange and troubled thing, and we might do more harm than good by looking to it for a pathway to inner bliss. In any case, this is not what Bashō seems to promise in his poetry of restless wandering and silence.

In Japanese there is an expression, *shizen ichimi*: 'Poetry and Zen are one.' To most western minds, the word 'Zen' conjures up thoughts of pagodas, koi ponds and herons, trees of cherry blossom framing the tableau. These beautiful images may well be part of the picture, and they're motifs that recur throughout Bashō's work. However, Bashō describes poetry in rather less soothing terms in his early travelogue *Nozarashi Kikō* ('The Records of a Weather-exposed Skeleton'). At one point, passing through Nagoya, he thinks affectionately about one of the region's famous sons, a person called 'crazy Chikusai', a fictional character who 'is said to have practised quackery and poetry'. Bashō inserts the following poem as a counterpoint:

With a bit of madness in me,
Which is poetry,
I plod along like Chikusai
Among the wails of the wind.

Sleeping on a grass pillow
I hear now and then
The nocturnal bark of a dog
In the passing rain.

Poetry as Zen; poetry as madness: according to the western connotations of Zen, we've just walked slap bang into a contradiction. Yet Bashō coaxes us to think outside of these narrow parameters. It is *mad* to devote one's life to poetry, just as it is mad to take the grass for a pillow, to listen for dogs barking in the night, or to let yourself be driven to distraction by lice and urinating horses in a stranger's cottage, far away from home. The reason one does it is that the rewards are astonishing. Beyond the gatekeeper's cottage lies the narrow road to Kisagata, the most northerly point on Bashō's journey, and the joint most beautiful along with Matsushima.

And yet, even here we aren't free from distress. However beautiful Kisagata and Matsushima may be, there is a key difference between the two. 'Matsushima is a cheerful laughing beauty,' Bashō writes, 'while the charm of Kisagata is in the beauty of its weeping countenance.' So far, so good – we're used to poets finding loveliness in nature and comparing it to a woman. But Bashō goes a step further in his description of Kisagata – a step closer to madness, perhaps. 'It is not only lonely,' he suggests, 'but also penitent, as it were, for some unknown evil. Indeed is has a striking resemblance to the expression of a troubled mind.' This, remember, is the great spiritual terminus of Bashō's journey: a moment of beauty and achievement that is nevertheless identical to 'the expression of a troubled mind'.

The sound a frog makes when it enters the water could also be cast as a type of madness: an interruption in the normal order of things that most people breeze past without a care in the world. Pity the poets, then, who not only notice it, but feel compelled to turn that innocent frog into a phantom creature made out of syllables, lines and human breath.

Pity them, but also honour them, because they've seen something mysterious and real – something, indeed, which it might be worth devoting one's life to, as Bashō did. Plop!

11

How to Think Like William Wordsworth

Imagine, at this point, a short intermission. Between Bashō's frog and the first poems by William Wordsworth, a hundred years elapse during which the writing, publication and circulation of verse dramatically increase across the western world. So why no poet to represent this fertile period? One, slightly flippant, way of accounting for the gap is to say that it took this long for European poets to catch up with Bashō. With his intense focus on nature and the senses, Bashō anticipates Romanticism, a cultural and poetic revolution that flowered towards the end of the eighteenth century.

Born in the Lake District in 1770, Wordsworth was at the forefront of the movement in Britain. 'Come forth into the light of things,' he writes in 'The Tables Turned', with a rapture worthy of Bashō at his pond. 'Let Nature be your teacher.' First published in *Lyrical Ballads* (1798), a hugely influential volume Wordsworth co-authored with his friend and collaborator Samuel Taylor Coleridge, these lines could serve as an all-purpose bumper sticker advertising the main tenets of Romanticism – close attention to the world, direct contact with nature, the self-conscious embrace of freedom.

There is, however, a key distinction to be made between Bashō and the Romantics. Where Bashō's immersion in nature ultimately serves to dissolve the bonds of self – a project in keeping with his Zen Buddhist philosophy – Wordsworth and his fellow travellers saw nature as the supreme way to access the self, even to glorify it. Their work exemplifies what Charles Taylor has called 'the massive subjective turn of modern culture, a new form of inwardness, in which we come to think of ourselves as beings with inner depths'. In the West these days, we don't just look at a burst of 'sun above the mountain's head' (to lift another line from 'The Tables Turned') and take it as a sign of nature's magnificence. We take it as a sign of our *own* magnificence. Just think of anyone today photographing themselves on a mountaintop or swimming near a coral reef – we love nature, but more than that, we love how nature makes us feel. This impulse can be traced back directly to the Romantics.

Wordsworth's greatest hit embodies this Romantic fusion between the self and nature. Originally left untitled, the poem is officially known by its opening line, 'I wandered lonely as a Cloud', but millions of people prefer its colloquial title, 'The Daffodils'. There's a decent chance that, like me, you first encountered it at school.

> I wandered lonely as a Cloud
>   That floats on high o'er Vales and Hills,
> When all at once I saw a crowd,
>   A host of golden Daffodils;
> Beside the Lake, beneath the trees,
> Fluttering and dancing in the breeze.

In this first stanza, the speaker makes only a couple of entrances. He's there in the first line, wandering 'lonely as a Cloud', and he pops up again in the third line as a witness to the main event, this glorious 'crowd' of daffodils. We might think that this is entirely appropriate. How else is he, as the poet, supposed to register his presence in the poem? In its long history from Sappho to the present day, lyric poetry has always been defined by the relationship between the speaker, their thoughts and emotions, and the world they inhabit. To this extent, Wordsworth is just slotting in and using the tools at his disposal – a tiny but momentous pronoun, 'I', that orchestrates the whole affair.

It's worth pausing here, however, to state the obvious: the 'I' doesn't have to be there. Very often in haiku it isn't. Here, too, it could butt out. How much more meaningful might the poem be as a tribute to daffodils if Wordsworth removed himself from the picture? This is a version of the complaint that many contemporary poets make, not just of Wordsworth, but of all poetry in this vein. The lyric form has been much criticized for its self-centred approach, and you can start to appreciate why if we skip ahead to Wordsworth's final stanza:

> For oft when on my couch I lie
>   In vacant or in pensive mood,
> They flash upon that inward eye
>   Which is the bliss of solitude,
> And then my heart with pleasure fills,
> And dances with the Daffodils.

These lines switch the scene from nature, where the speaker first encountered the flowers, to the parlour or study where he remembers them. With his image of the speaker swooning on his couch, 'In vacant or in pensive mood', Wordsworth does a lot to shape the modern cliché of the poet as a kind of sensitive malingerer. I love the sudden 'flash' that transmits the daffodils from their home in the wild to the poet's 'inward eye' – a stranger, more unsettling image than it seems at first glance. But I'd probably agree that it's a self-important move, relegating nature to second place. Although rhetorically the poem ends on the word 'Daffodils', in spirit, by this point, it's become a celebration of the lyric moment itself. The poet's own dancing heart elbows out the original 'sprightly dance' of the flowers, as Wordsworth describes it in the second stanza.

Poor old Wordsworth. I've started a chapter on how to think like him with a case for the prosecution, detailing why his thinking might be problematic. I've done so not to be awkward or mean, but to point to an important fissure in the history of poetry. Romanticism has come to dominate how we think about the role of the poet in society, so it's only natural for that supremacy to generate mixed feelings. Nevertheless, history could always have taken a different path, so I hope this chapter will shed light, also, on the literature that was eclipsed in Romanticism's rise to power. To do that, we'll take a quick detour into Alexander Pope, an English poet from the early eighteenth century who is often thought of as the opposite of everything Wordsworth stands for – the Darth Vader to his Luke Skywalker, the chalk to his cheese. Apart from anything else, the comparison with Pope helps to illustrate why Wordsworth's thinking remains startling and vital, in ways that can get muffled beneath his status as a hoary old classroom staple and national treasure.

Pope was a product of the European Enlightenment: a time of encyclopaedias, scientific breakthroughs and political advancement. It was an era when poets contributed to a wider project of manufacturing and gatekeeping intelligent thought. Pope's 'An Essay on Criticism' (1711) is an especially revealing – and paradoxical – example of this phenomenon, since it betrays an anxiety about whether there's *any* worthwhile role for poetry in a rational and progressive world. Pope sneers at the pretentions of his fellow poets, comparing them to painters who 'hide with ornaments their want of art'. He goes on to crystallize an alternative vision of what literature could do:

> True wit is nature to advantage dress'd,
> What oft was thought, but ne'er so well express'd,
> Something, whose truth convinc'd at sight we find,
> That gives us back the image of our mind.

'Wit' is meant here not in the modern sense of 'witty' (that is, amusing) but as a synonym for intellectual ability itself. The eighteenth century cared deeply about wit: who had it, who didn't, and how it could be cultivated or squandered.

'True wit', in Pope's view, is a quality found only in the best writing. It stands revealed in those rare moments when we come across something so perceptive, so in tune with how things really are, that it 'gives us back the image of our mind'. This is generous, up to a point. It suggests that thinking can be a hard task that leads us astray from ourselves – something that requires reparation, a process of 'giving back'. But it is also a fundamentally conservative way of looking at the world. (Pope was an avowed Tory, back when that word was starting to mean something we might recognize today.) It suggests that the best we can hope for, in art as in life, is to elevate something that already exists. There is little room here for the radical, the visionary, the disruptive: for poetry as an engine for exploration and dynamic change.

Such a political worldview is implicit in the formal character of Enlightenment verse. Along with his contemporaries, Pope's weapon of choice was the heroic couplet, an iambic pentameter verse form divided into rhyming pairs. It's a brilliant mode for delivering comparisons and pithy insights, since the rhymes knit together to map a complex but ultimately stable worldview. Pope often deploys heroic couplets to articulate his conservative ethics, as in the resounding finale to 'An Essay on Man':

> All Nature is but Art, unknown to thee;
> All Chance, Direction, which thou canst not see;
> All Discord, Harmony not understood;
> All partial Evil, universal Good:
> And, spite of Pride, in erring Reason's spite,
> One truth is clear, Whatever Is, Is Right.

'Whatever is, is right.' Heroic couplets are both a symptom and perhaps a cause of such a belief. The mind that sees a direct convergence between reality (what 'is') and justice (what 'is right') naturally reaches for a poetic form where A mirrors A and B mirrors B. Wordsworth vented his dislike of heroic couplets in a letter to the poet Hans Busk, confessing, 'Reading such verse produces in me a sensation like that of toiling in a dream, under the night-mair.'

From today's vantage point, we don't need to feel as terrorized by heroic couplets as Wordsworth did. Pope is mightily unfashionable these days – more so than Wordsworth, and that's saying something – but there's a lot to enjoy in his work. The contemporary critic Helen Vendler captures his talent brilliantly. Pope's poetry presents thinking as a knotty phenomenon, she argues, 'something that can be parodied, jested with, coarsened, inhumanly speeded-up; something mobile in its flickering, ever tumbling over into nonsense, smooth at times, rough at times, serious and funny by turns, giddy and solemn, wittily resourceful in its self-expression in language; something that can always bring an edge to the mind and a smile to the lips.'

A noble defence, for sure, and one that I tend to go along with – yet it doesn't altogether dispel Wordsworth's misgivings. With his jesting, rough, 'giddy and solemn' verse, Pope can come across as the dinner-party guest from hell: an argumentative chatterbox straining to get the last word, hitting you over the head with his intelligence. These days we're free to read him for as long as we find him entertaining or insightful and then change seats, so to speak, to spend time with a less sweaty and exhausting poet. Yet for Wordsworth and his peers, the eighteenth century must have seemed like one big drawing room from which there was no escape. You could mount a pretty solid case that the Romantic period was a prolonged attempt to break poetry out of that stuffy atmosphere and breathe some oxygen again.

All this puts a more positive spin on 'The Daffodils'. Read as an antidote to Pope's worldly sophistication, Wordsworth's paean to nature sprouts a backbone that it didn't previously seem to have. A tone of quiet resistance creeps into the speaker's claim that 'A Poet could not but be gay, / In such a jocund company.' (How would Pope react to a bank full of lovely flowers? He'd probably sneer and turn it into a metaphor for a gaggle of vain young airheads swanning about town.) I'm not quite prepared to let Wordsworth off the hook, though. 'The Daffodils' remains a whimsical, corny, fleetingly brilliant earworm, like many greatest hits. If Wordsworth's genius only rests on its heartfelt simplicity, then we're setting him up for a fall.

For the full expression of that genius, we can turn to *The Prelude*. Addressed to Coleridge, this multi-book autobiographical epic carries the reader from Wordsworth's childhood in the Lakes, through his unhappy days at Cambridge University and even more miserable postgrad life in London, to his triumphant embrace of a new, self-styled Romantic philosophy. More than any sequence of biographical events, then, its real subject is the 'Growth of a Poet's Mind', as the subtitle puts it – a self-regarding mission that makes the homely lyric 'I' of 'The Daffodils' seem positively humble in comparison. What 'The Daffodils' lacks, however, is the sense of awestruck complexity that we meet in *The Prelude*. It's an epic where the human hero, the poet himself, is constantly rediscovering his place in a world that exceeds the limits of his knowledge.

Book I begins with a praise song to the wind, almost as if tuning in at the very moment that the speaker busts out of the Enlightenment drawing room and runs for open air.

> Oh, there is blessing in this gentle breeze,
> That blows from the green fields and from the clouds
> And from the sky; it beats against my cheek,
> And seems half conscious of the joy it gives.
> O welcome messenger! O welcome friend!
> A captive greets thee, coming from a house
> Of bondage, from yon city's walls set free,
> A prison where he hath been long immured.
> Now I am free, enfranchised and at large,
> May fix my habitation where I will.

In the fourth line, Wordsworth ennobles the breeze by saying that it 'seems half conscious of the joy it gives'. This is a revealing moment, since it implies that the breeze is so wonderful it's almost conscious – that's to say, almost human. Indeed, it's the explicit subjective turn of the ninth line ('Now I am free, enfranchised and at large') that really gets the juices flowing through the poem. The all-conquering 'I' receives its blessing from the wind and runs with it.

Let's linger a moment on the word that follows directly after 'free'. 'Enfranchised' vibrates with possible meanings, coming at the start of a work whose first iteration was completed in 1805, at a time of huge debate about the proper scope of political liberty in Britain and beyond. Book XI even takes us to the site of a recent revolution in France, which Wordsworth visited between 1790 and 1791. 'Bliss was it in that dawn to be alive,' goes his famous adage about those years, 'But to be young was very heaven!' Book I's opening fanfare builds to an echo of that other great literary republican, Milton.

> The earth is all before me – with a heart
> Joyous, nor scared at its own liberty,
> I look about, and should the guide I choose
> Be nothing better than a wandering cloud
> I cannot miss my way.

Paradise Lost concludes with a mournful glance at Adam and Eve in their newly fallen state, as Milton notes, 'The World was all before them.' Wordsworth loved Milton, though he didn't share his theology. When the speaker of *The Prelude* describes the earth as being 'all before' him, the elegiac tone of Milton's original thought is flipped on its head, transformed into a boast of the speaker's own revolutionary potential.

From here, *The Prelude* only grows in stature. Later in Book I, the speaker recalls his childhood memories of skating on the icy lakes during winter, 'Proud and exulting, like an untired horse, / That cares not for its home.' At first he is part of the throng of children, but before long he peels away. In one particularly gorgeous image his skates 'cut across the image of a star / That gleam'd upon the ice'. It's as if he is learning to trace the connectedness of things, scrawling his own contribution on top of the natural world.

Soon afterwards, however, the natural world reasserts itself. When the skating child comes to a sudden stop, the landscape keeps spinning. A bank of 'solitary Cliffs / Wheeled by me,' he recalls, 'even as if the earth had roll'd / With visible motion her diurnal round'. This leads to a breathless expostulation from the adult speaker, reflecting on the meaning of this formative experience:

Ye Presences of Nature, in the sky
And on the earth! Ye Visions of the hills!
And Souls of lonely places! can I think
A vulgar hope was yours when Ye employ'd
Such ministry, when Ye through many a year
Haunting me thus among my boyish sports,
On caves and trees, upon the woods and hills,
Impress'd upon all forms the characters
Of danger or desire, and thus did make
The surface of the universal earth
With triumph, and delight, and hope, and fear,
Work like a sea?

Contrast this with Pope's 'An Essay on Criticism', which assumes that the writer's project is to capture 'naked nature'. On this view, Nature is presented as something quite simple and intelligible – a passive surface that the skilled intellectual craftsman can hope to 'trace' if he only concentrates his thinking. For Wordsworth, here at least, Nature is nothing so biddable or pliant. The natural world trembles with 'triumph, and delight, and hope, and fear', an inventory of emotions that could serve as a handy summary of the 'Sublime'. Theorized in 1757 by the philosopher Edmund Burke, this was a concept that proved increasingly potent through the Romantic era. 'The passion caused by the great and sublime in nature . . . is

Astonishment,' Burke wrote, 'and astonishment is that state of the soul, in which all its motions are suspended, with some degree of horror. In this case the mind is so entirely filled with its object, that it cannot entertain any other.' The Sublime was routinely contrasted with Enlightenment rationality, as a slightly terrifying force that suspends our higher faculties.

Another telling contrast with Pope can be found in the formal patterns of *The Prelude*. Adapting the blank verse of Milton, Wordsworth rejects end rhymes in favour of enjambment. This is the technical word for lines that break in the middle of a sentence, so that the reader has to continue to the next line to find out how a phrase resolves. Christopher Ricks mounts a brilliant analysis of Wordsworth's enjambment in *The Force of Poetry*, starting with the ice-skating episode from *The Prelude*. It all hinges on the moment when the young Wordsworth 'Stopp'd short, yet still all the solitary Cliffs / Wheel'd by me'. After quoting this passage, Ricks pauses for emphasis: '"Stopp'd short": yet these lines are about – and supremely evoke – the impossibility of stopping short.'

This seems exactly right, though the insight carries me slightly further down the passage, to the long question Wordsworth poses to 'Ye Presences of Nature' quoted in full above. That sentence snakes down the page for a full 12 lines, coming to a point with the claim that Nature has

> Impress'd upon all forms the characters
> Of danger or desire, and thus did make
> The surface of the universal earth
> With triumph, and delight, and hope, and fear,
> Work like a sea [. . .]

The verse here is itself being made to 'Work like a sea'. The rhythm imitates how the oceans pulse and divide the land

– liquid, mobile, windblown, surging from crest to crest. No matter how many times I read this passage, I struggle to get to the bottom of it. Even as Wordsworth steers me from line to line, like a mountain guide who knows every crag of his terrain, the full meaning eludes me. How could one begin to frame an answer to his question? The poem is, properly speaking, sublime.

Today, the Lake District is home to a flourishing Wordsworth tourist industry, rivalled only by Stratford-upon-Avon in the pecking order of literary pilgrimages. Wordsworth Country trumps Shakespeare's hometown, however, in its undeniable claim to *terroir* – a French word for the unique combination of soil, climate and culture that gives local specialities like wine and cheese their character. Shakespeare was born and raised in Stratford and made investments there; beyond that, one needs the visual cues of timbered shop fronts, theatres and gift shops to be reminded of the town's literary pedigree. Wordsworth's imagination, on the other hand, was demonstrably shaped by the landscape he called home. A holiday to Grasmere therefore promises more than just a stroll in a genius's postcode. It grants access to the very sights that inspired Wordsworth's budding mind.

By the time of Wordsworth's death in 1850, he'd moved very far from the idealistic young man who set out at the turn of the century to start a poetic revolution. The first half of the nineteenth century saw technological innovations that left the steady progress of the Enlightenment era in the dust, none of them more seismic than the birth of the railways. Suddenly the countryside was a place of transit, not a hallowed and self-enclosed ecosystem. Wordsworth looked on aghast and adopted a series of increasingly conservative political positions through later life. He campaigned for the Tory interest in the 1818 general election, opposed the 1832 Great Reform Bill (which extended the vote to any man whose home had a lease of £10 or more a year), and wrote doggerel to shore up the reputation of his patron, the Earl of Lonsdale, who manoeuvred tirelessly against the Bill in northwest England – all of which could make *The Prelude*'s celebration of the free and sovereign soul, 'enfranchised and at large', ring a little hollow. Who gets to be enfranchised, then? Not everyone, clearly – and certainly not those whose homes were worth less than a tenner per year.

True enough, the elderly Wordsworth understood perfectly well what he'd written back in 1805. He suppressed the first draft of *The Prelude* during his lifetime and produced a bowdlerized update to be published after his death. This 1850 *Prelude* performs reverse surgery on his earlier hymn to liberty and the wind, reducing it to cliché:

Whate'er its mission, the soft breeze can come
To none more grateful than to me; escaped
From the vast city, where I long had pined
A discontented sojourner: now free,
Free as a bird to settle where I will.

'Free as a bird'? Come on, William, you're better than that. The revision does one useful thing, however. It reminds us that poetry is always a deliberate activity, even – or especially – where it purports to be most natural and authentic. Poets make a thousand good or bad decisions at every juncture of their career; their works aren't gifts from the heavens. Luckily, in Wordsworth's case we're free to disregard the reactionary he became, and remember him as the thrilling poet that he used to be, back when the earth was all before him.

12

How to Think Like Walt Whitman

Walt Whitman was born on 31 May 1819, shortly before the United States of America turned 43. The relative youth of his nation would haunt Whitman's work until his death in 1892. By that point he was widely feted as the 'Good Gray Poet', a venerable institution who had almost single-handedly invented modern American poetry. Throughout the final decade of his life he held court with passing dignitaries such as Mark Twain and Oscar Wilde, alongside a host of lesser acolytes who made the pilgrimage to Whitman's cottage in Camden, New Jersey, eager to parlay with a latter-day prophet. The long white ragged beard he wore in later years confirmed the Methuselah-like impression. As for his beloved United States, by that point it was ageing too. In Whitman's lifetime, the country had undergone a horrendous civil war, abolished slavery, and more than doubled in size from 21 to 44 states, widening its reach across the full mass of the American continent. Yet to many it still felt like a fresh experiment – an upstart democracy, forever in thrall to the European nations out of which it grew.

Whitman was sensitive to these historical pressures, and not shy of boasting that he was the man to address them. In one of

'Inscriptions' that he placed at the start of his life's work, *Leaves of Grass*, he made the following address 'To Foreign Lands':

> I heard that you ask'd for something to prove this puzzle
>   the New World,
> And to define America, her athletic Democracy,
> Therefore I send you my poems that you behold in them
>   what you wanted.

If nothing else, one has to admire the chutzpah. Whitman knows that America remains a 'puzzle' to the rest of the world, an 'athletic Democracy' that stands in marked contrast to the sclerotic Old World monarchies across the pond. Each of America's citizens is free 'to define' the country in a way that could never be said for Europeans. But how could you make such a cacophonous free-for-all actually work?

One approach might be to turn the clashing voices of democracy into harmony, as Whitman does in another of the *Leaves of Grass* inscription poems, 'I Hear America Singing':

> I hear America singing, the varied carols I hear,
> Those of mechanics, each one singing his as it should be
>   blithe and strong,
> The carpenter singing his as he measures his plank or
>   beam,
> The mason singing his as he makes ready for work, or
>   leaves off work,
> The boatman singing what belongs to him in his boat, the
>   deckhand singing on the steamboat deck,
> The shoemaker singing as he sits on his bench, the hatter
>   singing as he stands,
> The wood-cutter's song, the ploughboy's on his way in the
>   morning, or at noon intermission or at sundown,

The delicious singing of the mother, or of the young wife
    at work, or of the girl sewing or washing,
Each singing what belongs to him or her and to none else,
The day what belongs to the day – at night the party of
    young fellows, robust, friendly,
Singing with open mouths their strong melodious songs.

Working-class voices had been heard before in English-language poetry. For instance, Wordsworth's preface to the second edition of *Lyrical Ballads* claimed that its poems captured 'the real language of men in a state of vivid sensation', a category that included shepherds and other humble rural folk. Whitman, however, is doing something more radical: not ventriloquizing individual speakers, but orchestrating the many trades of America as a social mass. By reading his verses, he assures the sceptical or foreign reader, they might start to understand why this raw and vibrant nation held the key to the future.

The first half of Whitman's life showed few signs that he was destined for such a role. Born in the hamlet of West Hills on Long Island, he came from a family that could trace its American roots back to the 1660s. His English-American ancestors had risen to prosperity, amassing a modest fortune in land and slaves, but by the time it passed down to Whitman's father the legacy had shrunk. Walter Sr set up shop as a carpenter and moved the family to Brooklyn to take advantage of a budding construction boom in this small town overlooking the metropolis of Manhattan. The Whitmans were comfortable but far from rich, and Walter Jr slipped through the school system without distinction. Many years later his teacher B. B. Hallock dredged up an unflattering memory of the young Whitman, calling him 'a big, good-natured lad, clumsy and slovenly in appearance'. On finding out that this klutz had somehow become America's foremost poet, Mr Hallock remarked, 'We need never be discouraged over anyone.'

Whitman's early career was almost equally undistinguished. He flitted from job to job, in the way of many budding writers before and since. Between the ages of 11 and 15, he was apprenticed as a printer, a trade that took him briefly into the big city of New York, before he moved back to Long Island to teach school. His twenties were a hotchpotch of unsatisfying teaching positions and journalism, taking in stints as an editor for local rags like the *Long-Islander*, the *Aurora*, the *Evening Tatler* and the *Brooklyn Daily Eagle*. David Reynolds paints a vivid picture of Whitman's year at the helm of the *Long-Islander*. 'Not only did he serve as the paper's editor, compositor, and pressman,' Reynolds writes, 'but also each week he did home delivery by riding his horse, Nina, on a thirty-mile circuit in the Huntington area.'

These may seem like wasted years to the Whitman scholar, but they paved the way for his poetic flowering in the 1850s. It's impossible to disentangle *Leaves of Grass* from its origins as an object crafted by someone with first-hand knowledge of the printing trade. First published privately in 1855, the book went through at least eight major reissues, right up to the so-called Deathbed edition of 1892, and Whitman maintained a firm hand on the tiller to the end. It expanded from a relatively trim, self-made volume of some hundred pages to a commercially printed behemoth containing numerous other 'clusters' of poems that Whitman wrote across his later years. These included *Drum-Taps*, a sequence bearing witness to the Civil War, and *Good-Bye My Fancy*, a valedictory collection appended to the Deathbed edition. As Whitman wrote to a friend when preparing the Deathbed edition, the book was 'at last complete – after 33 y'rs of hackling at it, all times & moods of my life, fair weather & foul, all parts of the land, and peace & war, young & old'.

The business of printing shows up at several key points in Whitman's poetry, fusing with his perennial themes of democracy, America, and the valour of the human spirit. Section 13 of 'Starting from Paumanok', for instance, sets up the parallels between printing and humanity as a complex two-stanza simile:

> Of your real body and any man's or woman's real body,
>   Item for item, it will elude the hands of the corpse-cleaners, and pass to fitting spheres,
>   Carrying what has accrued to it from the moment of birth to the moment of death.
>
> Not the types set up by the printer return their impression, the meaning, the main concern,
>   Any more than a man's substance and life, or a woman's substance and life, return in the body and the soul,
>   Indifferently before death and after death.

The metaphysics of this passage could be rather airy if it weren't for the printing metaphor nailing them to the ground. Roughly, Whitman is saying that the individual's body and soul will stamp their 'impression' on the cosmos, in the same way that the printer sets up his types (or fonts) to make solid marks upon the page. In Section 18 printing machinery makes another appearance, as a fleeting entry in one of Whitman's epic catalogues of America:

> See, pastures and forests in my poems – see, animals wild and tame – see, beyond the Kaw, countless herds of buffalo feeding on short curly grass,

See, in my poems, cities, solid, vast, inland, with paved
    streets, with iron and stone edifices, ceaseless vehicles,
    and commerce,
See, the many-cylinder'd steam printing-press – see, the
    electric telegraph stretching across the continent,
See, through Atlantica's depths pulses American Europe
    reaching, pulses of Europe duly return'd [. . .]

Printing, then, is not to be demeaned as grub-work. It is a
thrilling, technological, quintessentially American trade, firing
(almost literally) on all cylinders. This is one way in which
Whitman sought to distinguish himself from his Old World
ancestors. By embracing his origins as a common artisan, he
hoped to clear space for a new literature that would likewise
be useful, open-hearted and frank, unfettered by prejudice
or deference. He imagines the Atlantic Ocean as a medium
of commerce between Europe and America, transmitting
'pulses' of industry and imagination like the electric telegraph
network 'stretching across' his home continent. Telegraphy was
a European invention, but it took the geography and enterprise
of America to turn it into a truly modern technology operating
at scale. Something similar could be said for the poetic tradition
Whitman was bringing to fruition in *Leaves of Grass*.

To get to this point, Whitman had to overcome a nation-sized
inferiority complex. By the mid-nineteenth century, many in
America had grown restless about its lack of a truly original
literary tradition. American colonists had long ago asserted
their political self-confidence by winning a revolution and
establishing a republic. But where were the comparatively
new forms of expression, fit to tell the story of this innovative
nation? Where were its authentic bards, singing off a hymn
sheet that hadn't been prepared centuries ago in England?

Chief among these critics was the transcendentalist philosopher, essayist and poet Ralph Waldo Emerson. Transcendentalism is a school of thought that can be compared to European Romanticism, beefed up with a distinctly American brand of self-reliance. Regina Schober provides a useful introduction to its influence on Whitman, pointing out that 'transcendentalists believed in the liberating potential of the individual in opposition to the constraints of systems and institutions'. Prominent fellow travellers included Bronson Alcott, Margaret Fuller and Henry David Thoreau, though the movement centred on Emerson and his home in Concord, Massachusetts. One of Emerson's cornerstone essays was 'The Poet', where he set out in bombastic detail what he was looking for in the great American poet.

The problem, though, was finding somebody who had the skill and sense of mission to answer the call. In the following passage, he throws down the gauntlet:

I look in vain for the poet whom I describe. We do not with sufficient plainness or sufficient profoundness address ourselves to life, nor dare we chaunt our own times and social circumstance. If we filled the day with bravery, we should not shrink from celebrating it. Time and nature yield us many gifts, but not yet the timely man, the new religion, the reconciler, whom all things await.

Enter Whitman. We know that in 1842 Whitman attended a lecture delivered by Emerson which served as a trial run for 'The Poet', and reviewed it favourably in the press. Later, Whitman would confide that 'I was simmering, simmering, simmering; Emerson brought me to a boil.' Upon publishing the first edition of *Leaves of Grass*, Whitman duly sent a copy to Concord and received a reply that must have exceeded even his wildest expectations. 'DEAR SIR –' began Emerson's letter, dated 21 July 1855, 'I am not blind to the worth of the wonderful gift of "LEAVES OF GRASS." I find it the most extraordinary piece of wit and wisdom that America has yet contributed.'

Alert to an opportunity for self-promotion, Whitman rushed out a new edition of his book with Emerson's letter tacked on at the end, alongside a much longer open missive of his own. In it, Whitman presented himself in no uncertain terms as the poet Emerson had been searching for. Americans need wait no longer:

> Swiftly, on limitless foundations, the United States too are founding a literature. It is all as well done, in my opinion, as could be practicable. Each element here is in condition. Every day I go among the people of Manhattan Island, Brooklyn, and other cities, and among the young men, to discover the spirit of them, and to refresh myself.

What Emerson couldn't intuit yet, on reading the 1855 *Leaves of Grass*, is that there was a sexual undercurrent to these boasts about consorting 'among the young men'. Whitman was, in the modern parlance, queer, and as he grew in confidence his poems spoke with increasing boldness about his love of sex, with men and women alike. The 1860 edition of *Leaves of Grass* contained a new set of poems grouped under the title *Enfans d'Adam* ('Children of Adam'), depicting the poet admiring 'Potent mates, daughters, sons, preluding, / The love, the life of their bodies'.

The second section of *Enfans* ups the ante. The speaker goes from admiring the human form with some degree of plausible deniability – as, say, a classical sculptor might – to proudly 'singing the phallus, / Singing the song of procreation'. It builds to a rhapsody of 'From' phrases that don't quite seem to check out grammatically – but why would someone in such ecstatic raptures have any need for grammar?

> From sex – From the warp and from the woof [. . .]
> From privacy – From frequent repinings alone,
> From plenty of persons near, and yet the right person
>   not near,
> From the soft sliding of hands over me, and thrusting of
>   fingers through my hair and beard,
> From the long-sustained kiss upon the mouth or bosom,
> From the close pressure that makes me or any man drunk,
>   fainting with excess [. . .]

Even in today's more liberated culture, these lines remain pretty spicy. For Emerson they were erotic dynamite, and entirely beyond the pale. He met with Whitman in Boston in 1860 and pleaded with him not to include the poem in *Leaves of Grass* – but Whitman was not to be cowed. 'In a true act of self-reliance,' writes Schober, 'Whitman did not concede to this suggestion, noting that "I felt down in my soul the clear and unmistakable conviction to disobey all, and pursue my own way."' The irony here is that transcendentalism had given Whitman the tools he needed to reject one of its core principles: that is, the primacy of the soul over the material body. For Whitman, body and soul were thoroughly inseparable, and he owed it to himself to celebrate this fact.

The self is the dominant subject of Whitman's poetry – more so even than America. Without self, indeed, there can be no nation: this is one of the many lessons Whitman gives us, and the reason his work transcends its grand civic mission. The original 1855 *Leaves of Grass* underlines this order of priority by kicking off with a poem he would later title 'Song of Myself'.

Here is the ravishing start of that poem, set as it was in 1855 with ellipses punctuating the lines.

> I celebrate myself,
> And what I assume you shall assume,
> For every atom belonging to me as good belongs to you.

> I loafe and invite my soul,
> I lean and loafe at my ease . . . . observing a spear of
>   summer grass.

> Houses and rooms are full of perfumes . . . . the shelves are
>   crowded with perfumes,
> I breathe the fragrance myself, and know it and like it,
> The distillation would intoxicate me also, but I shall not
>   let it.

Again, it's instructive to compare Whitman's ideas with those of Wordsworth and the European Romantics. Wordsworth boldly placed himself at the heart of *The Prelude*, and insisted that a single man's life and thoughts were a fitting subject for epic poetry, but only after taking pains to assure the reader he was aware of the pitfalls of such a project. He never comes close to the swagger of Whitman's opening line, whose three short words jab the air with unapologetic bravado. Likewise, Whitman pushes into uncharted territory with his boast, 'I breathe the fragrance of myself, and know it and like it'. With one hearty gesture, this sweeps aside centuries of Christian body horror and moral shame, attitudes that are still lurking in the background for the reliably demure Wordsworth.

Whitman's anti-moralism reaches its peak in perhaps the best-known lines from 'Song of Myself'. The quote below has become an all-purpose motto for mavericks and flakes, often paraphrased, misquoted, or called upon ironically as the mother of humble brags:

> Do I contradict myself?
> Very well then . . . . I contradict myself;
> I am large . . . . I contain multitudes.

This is one instance where – with apologies to the elder Whitman – I must insist on the 1855 version of the poem. Those ellipses add more than just typographic flavour; they breathe life and movement into a passage that has somehow been hijacked as a catchphrase. To be fair, Whitman led the way in this fossilizing process. Compare and contrast the lines above with the Deathbed setting of this passage:

> Do I contradict myself?
> Very well then I contradict myself,
> (I am large, I contain multitudes.)

Same words, in the same order, distributed across the same number of lines – but somehow all the air's been beaten out of them. In particular, the third line now stands as a full stop, a closed-off proof, rather than a moment of discovery. These lines are all about fickleness and chance, so to hear them properly we have to tune in to how they were first composed, long before Whitman had started to flirt with his status as a national monument.

From the start, Whitman's posturing and contradictions had a tendency to grate on people. Even his admirers could be sniffy, emphasizing his rougher edges. Charles Eliot Norton called Whitman 'a compound of New England transcendentalist and New York rowdy'. With a similar gist, Emerson once remarked that *Leaves of Grass* was 'a combination of the *Bhagavad-Gita* and the *New York Herald*. Both these quotes put their finger on something important – Whitman's oracular, renegade spirituality – while sneering at the poet's less containable energies, the parts of his work that seem to have been swept up like litter from the Manhattan streets. Taking the snideness even further, Thoreau wrote to H. G. O. Blake that, with Whitman, 'It is as if the beasts spoke.' As Helen Vendler pithily responds, 'Whitman has never been granted much intellectual capacity.'

There is plenty to object to in Whitman's work. Apart from the obvious complaints about long-windedness or arrogance, his views on race will sound paternalistic and clumsy to modern ears, and likely always did to many of his African American and Native American readers. A staunch opponent of slavery and a cheerleader for Abraham Lincoln, Whitman landed on the right side of enough key issues for him to retain his status as America's Shakespeare – a unifying presence whose humanist values and artistic virtuosity have helped the country to tell a positive, adaptable story about itself. Vendler guards against this tendency, however, issuing a firm warning against feelgood narratives:

> [Whitman] is too subtle to be comprehended by such wide-grained leading ideas as nationalism, democracy, the body, and gender. He is too intellectual to be seen solely as a poet of enthusiastic sociological transcription of American scene and event, too mournful to be summed up as a celebrant of nineteenth-century expansion, too idiosyncratic to be subsumed into the history of American oratory.

Like Shakespeare, then, it might be best to appreciate Whitman these days for his peculiarity rather than his universality. Like Shakespeare, he can be awkward, weird and demanding.

We see this side of him vividly in 'By Blue Ontario's Shore', a long poem written in the aftermath of the Civil War addressing the strange, nervous atmosphere of Reconstruction. In the first section, a 'gigantic' Emersonian phantom accosts Whitman and throws down yet another challenge for him to rise to:

Chant me the poem, it said, that comes from the soul of
  America, chant me the carol of victory,
And strike up the marches of Libertad, marches more
  powerful yet,
And sing me before you go the song of the throes of
  Democracy.

So far, so familiar. Whitman is rallying the troops and tuning up for the victory march – except that short word 'throes' pulls the celebration short. This means 'intense or violent pain and struggle, especially accompanying birth, death, or great change', and it alludes here to the terrible, protracted growing pains the nation had undergone during wartime.

In this disillusioned, conflict-torn landscape, Whitman takes on a thornier role than that of national bard, something closer to that of a national gadfly or doomsaying prophet. He wanders the States 'with a barb'd tongue, questioning everyone I meet'. The message he bears the nation amounts to a new, spiritual call to arms:

Piety and conformity to them that like,
Peace, obesity, allegiance, to them that like,
I am he who tauntingly compels men, women, nations,
Crying, Leap from your seats and contend for your lives!

So, the poet 'tauntingly' asks us, are you content to sleepwalk along the path of 'Piety and conformity', or will you dare to march to a different drum? Reading Whitman, we are exhorted to leap from our seats and contend for life, in all its desperate glory.

13

How to Think Like Emily Dickinson

In 1850, Emily Dickinson wrote a letter to an old school friend, Abiah Root, complaining about her lot.

> Mother is still an invalid tho' a partially restored one – Father and Austin still clamor for food, and I, like a martyr am feeding them. Would'nt [*sic*] you love to see me in these bonds of great despair, looking around my kitchen, and praying for kind deliverance, and declaring by 'Omar's beard' I never was in such plight. *My* kitchen I think I called it, God forbid that it was, or shall be my own – God keep me from what they call *households*, except that bright one of 'faith'!

This cryptic excerpt from an intimate letter, sent from one young woman to another in nineteenth-century America, naturally requires a bit of context. Dickinson was 19 at the time she wrote it and adjusting to her new life as a deputy housewife. Her mother had occupied the main role through her childhood, but now that Dickinson had finished school she was expected to pitch in with the chores – the more so at times like these, when Mother was suffering from one of her periodic neuralgia attacks. With their insatiable 'clamor for food', her father and brother Austin are presented almost as greedy chicks, and Dickinson understands that the buck now stops with her when it comes to keeping them fed.

In hindsight, we can appreciate this as a *Sliding Doors* moment in Dickinson's life. If she'd got on the wrong train (so to speak) then it's highly unlikely that she'd be remembered today as one of the geniuses of American poetry. An unusually intellectually fulfilling childhood lay behind her, centred around Amherst Academy, the school where she met Root. The Academy had close links to its sister establishment, Amherst College, and pupils were encouraged to attend undergraduate lectures from a young age. On the other side of youth stood this boring, laborious Sunday afternoon at home. It's as if she's been visited by a ghost from her future, who shows her what things will be like if she capitulates to her family's expectations and allows the room where she prepares their meals to turn into '*My* kitchen'.

An eternity of drudgework looms in that one little pronoun, *my*, a fate Dickinson tries to keep at bay with her lightly sacrilegious prayer, 'God keep me from what they call *households*.' It's only by pivoting quickly to "'faith'", and implying that this is the (metaphorical) household she longs for, that Dickinson can keep her remarks on the right side of social acceptability. Yet it's a 'faith' safely cordoned off by quotation marks, and I have a hunch that by this point in the letter Root would have twigged the mischief in her friend's voice, and figured out that her real desire was to be saved from the tedium of '*households*', full stop.

In a roundabout way, Dickinson got her wish. She never married. By staying at home and preserving her status as a daughter and sister, she enjoyed a more ambiguous status. A daughter or sister could avoid taking responsibility for the household, even if she could not quite avoid doing her share of the work. These burdens lightened, however, as the family fortunes improved. In 1856, the Dickinsons returned to the comfortable house in Amherst where Emily was born, affectionately dubbed the 'Homestead', and Austin moved across the street into the Evergreens with his new wife, Susan Gilbert. Back in the Homestead, the Dickinsons hired help and Emily was able to enjoy a life of reasonable leisure alongside her modest rota of garden and kitchen tasks. (She was a dab hand at jellies and gingerbread.) One of the family's maids, an Irishwoman named Maggie Maher, kept a special eye out for the lively but peculiar woman with whom she shared a kitchen and a roof. She shooed away callers and kept Mistress Emily topped up with oil for her lamp so that she could retreat to her bedroom and write.

From this perspective, Dickinson's later life might be considered a success. She dreaded becoming a housewife, and largely got her way. To a remarkable degree she was spared the Stepford-ish routines of church and social visiting. She did what her heroes did, and wrote, sharing her work with an engaged circle of confidants, usually via letter. Yet viewed from another angle, we might consider these years a failure. Her work often seemed to baffle people, and with some minor exceptions was never published in her lifetime (her family discovered the great majority of the 1,800-plus poems she wrote when they were sorting through her possessions after her death). Moreover, for someone so allergic to households that she asked for divine deliverance from them, Dickinson made precious little effort to escape her own, even in the limited ways that would have been available to her as a society woman. The paradox is summed up nicely by Adrienne Rich. 'Probably no poet ever lived so much and so purposefully in one house,' writes Rich; 'even, in one room.'

The image of Dickinson as a fragile hermit has become widely known. There is, it has to be said, a grain of truth to it. Susan Eilenberg rehearses just a few of the established facts about Dickinson's reclusiveness. 'Increasingly she hid from friends who came to visit, not pretending to be absent but carrying on conversations from behind a door or from the top of the stairs, audible but not visible. Neither doctors nor dressmakers could approach her, nor (after her early daguerreotype) photographers.' These habits intensified across the final decades of her life, when Austin carried on an affair with an overbearing younger woman called Mabel Loomis Todd and used the Homestead as a convenient trysting spot. Perhaps Dickinson's most extreme reclusive episode came in 1874, when she listened to her own father's funeral going on downstairs from the sanctuary of her bedroom. These are not, to put it mildly, the actions of someone who feels at ease in the world, which only compounds Dickinson's tragedy. In effect, the household becomes her only place to go – at once a protective shield and a sexist trap.

I'm convinced that Dickinson's life was, ultimately, a tragedy, though it was certainly not only that. Beyond the constant, wearying effort to stay out of sight when she didn't want to be seen, there were lost friendships, thwarted romances, countless missed opportunities. She had a potentially very rich circle of friends and intellectual sparring partners – her family were well connected: Ralph Waldo Emerson once paid them a visit – and she made fitful attempts to cultivate their society. 'Dickinson was tough but also greedy for affection,' writes Eilenberg, and some of her closest friends and pen pals seem to have shrunk from the demands she placed on them. The prominent author, politician and abolitionist Thomas Wentworth Higginson, who wrote to Dickinson on and off for years and became her editor after her death, found her utterly exhausting on the one occasion they met. 'I never was with any one who drained my nerve power so much,' he told his wife. 'I am glad not to live near her.'

Health worries piled on top of interpersonal stresses. In adulthood Dickinson had dreadful eyesight, and some modern biographers posit that she's likely to have suffered from epilepsy. Though we should approach retrospective diagnosis with caution, it's a condition that would make sense of the many references to eruptions and absence that pepper Dickinson's work, as well as her reluctance to stray too far from home. 'After great pain, a formal feeling comes,' begins one poem. 'The Nerves sit ceremonious, like Tombs'. Whether or not we credit a reading that would frame that 'great pain' as a seizure, and the 'formal feeling' as the sensation of tomb-like blankness that follows it, Dickinson clearly had an acute familiarity with physical and emotional trauma.

Her creative *annus mirabilis* came in 1862, when she wrote no fewer than 227 poems, and it seems to have been triggered by a personal crisis that Dickinsonians have been trying to unravel for decades. Adrienne Rich proves a perceptive critic of this voyeuristic tendency. She attacks the urge to overinterpret Dickinson's art in light of her biography, as if her poetry were just the symptom of a life that tantalizes and fascinates us. At the same time, she articulates how the misogynistic double standards Dickinson had to operate within unavoidably distorted both art and life. 'More than any other poet,' she writes, 'Emily Dickinson seemed to tell me that the intense inner event, the personal and psychological, was inseparable from the universal; that there was a range for psychological poetry beyond mere self-expression. Yet the legend of the life was troubling, because it seemed to whisper that a woman who undertook such explorations must pay with renunciation, isolation, and incorporeality.'

That incorporeality – literally, the lack of a body – has lasted long after the poet's death. Emily Dickinson has become the literary world's favourite ghost story: an eerie

presence haunting the upstairs of her parents' house and, by extension, our imaginations. Partly this has to do with her historical position. She's only the second poet in this book, after Whitman, to have had her photographic likeness preserved, in the daguerreotype alluded to above in the quote by Eilenberg. This makes her tangible in a way that just can't be said of Shakespeare, or even Wordsworth. Unlike the rambunctious Whitman, however, who happily posed for numerous photos that have survived to this day, Dickinson has been frozen forever in that one daguerreotype, produced when she was just 16. (In 2012 a new photo emerged that seemed to depict an older Emily Dickinson sitting with her friend Kate Turner. It's received the green light from scientists and scholars, sparking frenzy among Dickinson enthusiasts, but it hasn't yet entered the public imagination.) Her face in the daguerreotype is appropriately hard to read – sceptical, insouciant, or maybe just gawky in the way of any teenager dressed up in her Sunday best to sit for a snap.

And this in itself is part of the problem, part of the allure: she looks exactly like a teenager. There's little of the historical glaze that sticks to other early photographs. Frank, guarded, vulnerable, with lips slightly parted as if about to speak – she seems so near and yet so far away. 'Most of us are half in love with this dead girl,' snarked the poet Archibald MacLeish in 1960. Sixteen years later, Rich issued a much-needed rejoinder: 'Dickinson was fifty-five when she died.' Despite his condescension, however, MacLeish had put his finger on something important – that in the mind of many readers, Dickinson was younger than that, and always would be.

Not for the first time, then, we are faced with the task of turning around the gigantic oil tanker of a poet's myth and steering to someplace we can read her properly again. Luckily in Dickinson's case, Adrienne Rich has already done a lot of the hard work. The essay from which I've been quoting, 'Vesuvius at Home' (1975), is a visionary act of critical reclamation, one of the finest deep dives on a poet you'll ever read. It laid waste to Dickinson's quirky, lost-girl reputation and blazed a trail for feminist literary studies in the process. On the face of it a travelogue narrating Rich's trip to Amherst in search of Dickinson, it quickly flips the script on that familiar 'walking in the footsteps of greatness' pilgrimage.

The main dragon Rich sets out to slay is the cliché of Dickinson's frailty. Rather than seeing her retreat from the world as a case of weakness, she positions it as an act of feminist strength. Rich suggests that Dickinson 'carefully selected her society and controlled the disposal of her time'. 'Given her vocation,' she continues, 'she was neither eccentric nor quaint; she was determined to survive, to use her powers, to practice necessary economies.' Some 40 years after Dickinson's death, Virginia Woolf would articulate the need for women writers to have 'A Room of One's Own', and in this respect Dickinson was ahead of the game. Rich recounts a reminiscence that Dickinson's niece Martha gave in later life, about a day when she was able to visit her aunt Emily in her bedroom at the Homestead. 'Emily Dickinson made as if to lock the door with an imaginary key,' Rich writes, 'turned and said, "Matty: here's freedom."' I love this story. It cuts against the static daguerreotype image of Dickinson to give us a woman who lived, breathed and made playful gestures to her niece. It also helps us to appreciate her bedroom as a site of 'freedom' rather than an agoraphobe's holding cell (though I wonder, still, about whether it might have been both, to some extent).

Certainly, the freedom Dickinson found in her bedroom enabled her to create some of the most liberated poetry that has ever been written. Here's one of the great 1862 poems, where the boast about freedom is made directly:

I dwell in Possibility –
A fairer House than Prose –
More numerous of Windows –
Superior – for Doors –

Of Chambers as the Cedars –
Impregnable of eye –
And for an everlasting Roof
The Gambrels of the Sky –

Of Visitors – the fairest –
For Occupation – This –
The spreading wide my narrow Hands
To gather Paradise –

Some aspects of this poem will probably feel familiar. The rhythm is steady, even jaunty, an inheritance from the ballad meter of the hymns that Dickinson would have grown up singing. (Lines one, two and four of each stanza have three beats, while the third lines stretch out to an extra fourth beat.) It has an ABCB rhyme scheme, with one nice juicy full rhyme to be enjoyed in the second stanza (eye/Sky). The rhyming pairs in the first and last stanzas, however, indicate just how far from the norm this poem truly is. 'Prose' only rhymes with 'Doors' in the broadest terms; similarly, 'This' and 'Paradise' sound almost nothing like each other besides their final consonants. The first word is hard and definite, with a short vowel sound, while the second has three syllables, ending on a long, rapturous 'I'. It's as if Dickinson is trying to demonstrate her point about 'Possibility' in the very sounds of the poem, urging each syllable to contain more than it normally would.

More than its experiments with rhyme, perhaps the most immediately distinctive feature of 'I dwell in Possibility' is its unconventional use of dashes. They interrupt at startling intervals, creating a suite of choppy pauses – the technical term is 'caesurae' – that complicate the primary rhythm and make the grammar fiendishly difficult to read. The effect carries over to almost every mature poem Dickinson wrote. Once again Rich hits the nail on the head in describing the brazen originality of her style: 'I am thinking of a confined space [i.e. Dickinson's bedroom] in which the genius of the 19th-century female mind in America moved, inventing a language more varied, more compressed, more dense with implications, more complex of syntax, than any American poetic language to date.'

To sound the bottom of this language would be the work of a lifetime. Taken as a whole, the Dickinson corpus has a vortex-like pull. At one level it produces what Danny Karlin calls an 'impression of uniformity, of a metrical average which predominates over local variation'. Once Dickinson found her groove with form, she didn't stray from it: the vast majority of her poems are composed in variations on the artfully corrupt ballad meter we've encountered above. Yet spend time with any single example, and the deviations from the mean become dizzying. Each is a mini kaleidoscope, refracting sense in multiple directions.

For a book about poets thinking, then, perhaps the best way to make inroads into this vast legacy is to look at some poems specifically about the art of thought. Thinking is certainly an art in Dickinson's poems, though it isn't an art we can ever hope to master. The following poem, written in 1863, depicts the process as a beguiling mystery:

A Thought went up my mind today –
That I have had before –
But did not finish – some way back –
I could not fix the Year –

Nor Where it went – nor why it came
The second time to me –
Nor definitely, what it was –
Have I the Art to say –

But somewhere – in my soul – I know –
I've met the Thing before –
It just reminded me – 'twas all –
And came my way no more –

This shares certain qualities with light verse, children's verse and riddles. (I'm reminded of Kay Ryan's point about

Dickinson's work being 'so buoyed by nonsense that it fairly pops out of the water'.) Indeed, in some lights it seems to anticipate 'Antigonish', Hughes Mearns's famous poem about a ghost ('Yesterday, upon the stair, / I met a man who wasn't there / He wasn't there again today / I wish, I wish he'd go away . . .'). 'A Thought went up my mind today' has the same push and pull between presence and absence, except for Dickinson the phantom in the room (literally 'the Thing') is a thought she can't quite put her finger on. The phrasing of the opening line is fascinating, since it attributes all of the agency to the 'Thought' and none to the speaker who experiences it. The Thought becomes an elusive houseguest, tramping up and down the stairs to her mind.

In the example above, the inability to hold on to a thought is presented as a comic predicament. Elsewhere, though, Dickinson reveals how tormenting such feelings of psychic disintegration can be. Here's a short poem from 1864:

I felt a Cleaving in my Mind –
As if my Brain had split –
I tried to match it – Seam by Seam –
But could not make them fit –

The thought behind, I strove to join
Unto the thought before –
But sequence ravelled out of Sound –
Like Balls – opon [*sic*] a Floor –

This poem has a nightmarish quality: it captures the uncanny sensation of things being simple yet impossible, elementary but out of reach. The final image compares thought to that familiar, frustrating task of trying to clutch a set of balls, only to see them spill all over the floor. With its talk of split brains and mental unravelling, it adds weight to the theory that the crisis Dickinson underwent in the early 1860s might have had something to do with epilepsy. Or perhaps the poem just articulates the sensation of a mind cracking under pressure, losing the plot. More than almost any other poet, Dickinson can take us to the brink of madness. It isn't sensationalist or morbid to say so: it's giving her work its due.

Brains are everywhere in Dickinson's poetry. Sometimes malfunctioning and 'split', at other times a space of endless possibility ('The Brain has Corridors – surpassing / Material Place', as one poem has it), the organ turns into a suggestive symbol for Dickinson's fraught relationship with her body, her household, and her culture more generally. In one particularly brain-strewn poem, each of the three stanzas kicks off with a fresh attempt to define the organ. First the brain is said to be 'wider than the Sky'; next, it 'is deeper than the sea'; and finally it ascends to heaven, becoming equal to 'the weight of God'. Clearly, Dickinson was proud of her brain as well as wary of its unpredictability.

If Dickinson had written this insistently about the 'mind', it would have been entirely in keeping with the poetry she knew and loved, from Shakespeare to Elizabeth Barrett Browning. By transposing all this mental imagery to the brain, however, she is making a deceptively radical point. The anatomical reference blurs the age-old dividing line separating the soul from the body (the dualist position, as it is known by philosophers). Barbara Baumgartner suggests that Dickinson's brain obsession may have originated in her state-of-the-art science education. She locates a truly terrifying image from a textbook in the library at Mount Holyoke Female Seminary, where Dickinson spent her final year of schooling at the age of 17. In the diagram, a head has had the skin peeled from its top half, exposing the gross, tangled mass of the cerebellum underneath. (Meanwhile, the bottom half seems entirely unperturbed.) Baumgartner invites us to imagine the impact such an image might have had on a person with Dickinson's curiosity and intellect.

For a woman so familiar with mental unrest, it may have been either terrifying or comforting – or perhaps both – to consider the mind as a material object, prone to going wrong at any moment through little fault of one's own. One way or another, though, she seems to have seen such volatility as the price to be paid for creativity itself. After his nerve-draining meeting with Dickinson, Higginson recorded a few of her choice sayings for his wife. One of them has become famous as a type of motto, held dear by poetry fans who want to bust the art out of its boring old straitjacket. 'If I read a book [and] it makes my whole body so cold no fire ever can warm me I know that is poetry,' Dickinson is reported to have said. 'If I feel physically as if the top of my head were taken off, I know that is poetry.' These are a long way from the polite definitions of aesthetic quality that would have characterized a respectable education, and they point to new, less respectable frontiers in poetic thinking that would become increasingly important in the modern era.

Funny things happen when you take the top of someone's head off. Should the event be understood as a maiming or an epiphany? Either way, the resulting sight should be far more interesting than anything that could be contained by the four walls of a house. 'Ages coil within / The minute Circumference – Of a single Brain,' writes Dickinson, in yet another wrigglingly brainy stanza. These are the awesome vistas of time and space that open up any time we step inside the apparently 'minute Circumference' of one of her poems.

14

How to Think Like Rabindranath Tagore

The 1913 Nobel Prize in Literature went to the first non-European winner of the award, 12 years after the prize had been established. In his will, Alfred Nobel had specified that the award should be given each year to 'the person who, in the field of literature, produced the most outstanding work in an idealistic direction'. With the anointment of Rabindranath Tagore, the Swedish Academy had certainly fulfilled the 'idealistic' part of the brief. In his homeland, Tagore had long been feted as a spokesperson for the new India that was emerging out of the shadows of the British Empire. Yet he was no firebrand preaching from beyond the pale of civilization, as the British would have seen it. In England, Tagore was fast gaining a reputation as a humanist and seer. In 1912, the year before his Nobel win, London had received him as a saintly emissary from the East – a guru who had come to teach the metropole about the land it had conquered.

He'd travelled to England touting an exercise book filled with his first English translations of his own work, adapted from a volume called *Gitanjali* that had appeared in Bengali in 1910. This was a cycle of devotional songs, shaped by a luminous belief in the union between God and creation. In Tagore's archaic English, *Gitanjali* hovers between the author's Hindu faith and an open-ended spirituality that was easily transposed to the West. Unable to render their musical cadences in verse, he set the translations in suggestively biblical prose:

> Life of my life, I shall ever try to keep my body pure, knowing that thy living touch is upon all my limbs.
>
> I shall ever try to keep all untruths out from my thoughts, knowing that thou art that truth which has kindled the light of reason in my mind.

England was enraptured, sending Tagore on his fast-track route to Nobel success. In his prize citation he was praised for 'his profoundly sensitive, fresh and beautiful verse, by which, with consummate skill, he has made his poetic thought, expressed in his own English words, a part of the literature of the West'. By the end of the decade, he would have a fair claim to being the most famous contemporary writer in the world.

Born in Calcutta in 1861, Tagore came from a wealthy landowning family at the heart of Bengali society. Though not from the aristocracy, the family had prospered under the British, particularly Tagore's grandfather, Dwarkanath, who had shown entrepreneurial flair and a talent for collaboration. 'He bought landed property,' writes Biswajit Ray, 'founded a bank, and engaged in opium trading, coal mining, shipping, and indigo planting.' Compared with the swashbuckling Dwarkanath, Tagore's father, Debendranath, was a pious and rather austere man. He divested from the family businesses so that he could devote himself to religious teaching and reform, raising his family off the income from their land.

Rabindranath looked up to his father as an ethical role model while gradually edging away from his exacting spiritual beliefs. On inheriting the family estates, he set out to manage them with an enlightened care for his tenants while pursuing his real interests of educational reform and literature. Tagore took the family ashram – a small plot of rural land named Santiniketan – and developed it into a progressive school whose 'abiding aim', in William Radice's words, 'was to break conventional educational moulds: to develop all aspects of a child's personality rather than merely prepare him for exams and professions'.

This flew in the face of the conventional cultural wisdom. Upper-crust Indian families like Tagore's were supposed to help their children get ahead in a very British world by sending them to Oxford, Cambridge or the Inns of Court before welcoming them back to plum jobs in the colonial administration. His brothers fitted more readily into this mould. The second eldest, Satyendranath, had become the first Indian member of the Indian Civil Service – an irony that would surely not have been lost on his younger brother. Tagore felt thwarted by the expectation to assimilate, and committed himself from a young age to the cause of Indian self-determination. All the while he published poetry, plays, stories, songs and essays, the many genres united by his open-minded, tolerant faith in man and God.

An early poem called 'The *Meghadūta*' articulates Tagore's enchanted though never irrational relationship with his culture. The title refers to a work by the great Sanskrit poet Kalidasa, an epic usually translated in English as 'Cloud Messenger'. At one point, the speaker transplants us to a present-day encounter with the poem:

In a gloomy closed room I sit alone
And read the *Meghadūta*.
My mind leaves the room,

Travels on a free-moving cloud,
Flies far and wide.
There is the Āmrakūṭa mountain,
There is the clear and slender Revā river,
Tumbling over stones in the Vindhya foothills;
There, along the banks of the Vetravatī,
Hiding in the shade of green, ripe-fruited *jambu*-trees,
Are the villages of Daśārṇa, their fences streaming
With *ketakī*-flowers, their paths lined with great
    forest-trees
Whose overhanging branches are alive with the twitter of
    village-birds
Building their nests in the rain.

This rapturous passage is taken from Radice's valuable Penguin Classics edition of Tagore's *Selected Poems*. It harkens to a long-standing poetic tradition known as 'flight of the mind', where the speaker of a poem soars over the earth to gain divine perspective on worldly affairs. What's great about Tagore's flight of the mind is that it doesn't set out to teach us anything. It's purely about the thrill of poetic transportation, an act of levitation that practically goes *whoosh* as the speaker gains altitude. The journey turns into a tour of India's varied landscapes, from mountains and rivers to villages dripping with Monsoon rain.

Tagore's idealism comes to the fore at the poem's close. It's a strange and melancholic passage, a coda to the grand vision that had borne us aloft beforehand. As the speaker struggles to get to sleep, he wonders why there is such a gap between imagination and reality:

Who has cursed us like this? Why this gulf?
Why do we aim so high only to weep when thwarted?

Why does love not find its true path?
It is something not of the body that takes us there [. . .]

For a dreamy, poetic soul, this 'something not of the body' will always trump the material world. The irony, though, is that inner life takes its richness from the scenery we've travelled through in the poem – all those rivers, clouds and 'ripe-fruited *jambu*-trees' that have shone with their proper names, lifted straight out of an atlas of India. Did we bear witness to reality during those stanzas, or just to the mind of the poet? Tagore resolves this doubt exquisitely, by ending on an image of 'the sunless, jewel-lit, evening land / Beyond all the rivers and mountains of this world'. This turns India itself into a semi-fiction: a 'jewel-lit' mirage forever forming and dissolving, and therefore forever out of reach.

Unsurprisingly, such a romantic sensibility set Tagore at odds with the cut and thrust of daily politics in his country. For freedom fighters whose main priority was Indian liberation here and now, it made little sense to look for it in some gilded fantasy drawn from an ancient poem. The role of poetry in the fight for justice was a conundrum that vexed Tagore throughout his career. How to navigate the tension between individual vision and collective struggle? The unique urgency of the political moment only sharpened this dilemma.

Tagore's life sits enclosed, almost perfectly, between two key dates in the trajectory of Indian nationhood. He was born four years after the mutiny of 1857 that led to the country finally being swallowed up by the British Empire after a long period of colonialism-by-proxy. He died in 1941, nine years before India was declared a republic. Though he never knew anything but British rule, he thought actively and creatively about how to bring it to an end. He just disagreed with the way that many of his compatriots were going about it in the meantime.

From the turn of the twentieth century, the leading figure in the Indian independence movement was Mohandas Gandhi. After living for 21 years in South Africa – a country where he refined his vision of nonviolent struggle for 'Swaraj', or Home Rule – Gandhi returned to India in 1915 to lead from the front. One of the first stops he made was at Santiniketan. His meeting with Tagore held great symbolic importance, as the two most famous Indians in the world at that point convened to discuss the future of their nation. Both men respected one another and exchanged honorific titles, with Gandhi bestowing the name of Gurudev – 'divine teacher' – on Tagore, and Tagore reciprocating by calling Gandhi 'Mahatma', or 'Great Soul'. (Not everyone agrees that he was the first to do so: the Mahatma title is such an integral part of Gandhi's legacy that bitter disputes, including at least one court case, have been fought over its lineage.) Despite these spiritual affinities, there were also glaring differences between the two men, some of which popped out to the naked eye.

By this point, Gandhi had started to cultivate the look of humble poverty that is now synonymous with his legend: plain dhoti and khurta clothing a thin body, fuelled by a minimalist vegetarian diet; bare feet; shaven head. In stark contrast, Tagore looked every inch the prosperous zamindar (or landlord) as he welcomed his guest. Corpulent and berobed, with a thick beard and long, flowing hair, he invited Gandhi to join him on a sofa. Gandhi declined, preferring to sit cross-legged on a mat. Whether or not Gandhi intended it, these gestures opened up a fault line, not just between the two men – the ascetic Gujarati on one side, the wealthy Bengali on the other – but between their two approaches to the political questions of the day. In a nutshell, the visual iconography posed the questions, how far are you willing to accommodate the status quo? And what are you willing to sacrifice in order to change it?

It wouldn't take long for these deeper rifts to surface in public. Tagore was a critic of non-cooperation, and wrote a rather moralizing open letter to the English missionary C. F. Andrews opining on the subject. This led to a cool but steely reply from Gandhi published in his own journal, *Young India*. Gandhi gave his article a title that cuts right to the heart of an ongoing debate about how, when and to what extent it might be desirable for poets to get involved in politics – 'The Poet's Anxiety'. Dripping with irony, it begins by skewering Tagore's growing status as 'the Poet of the world'. Far from the figure of respect that this lofty title implies, Gandhi depicts Tagore as a blustering worrywart weighed down by the responsibilities of his global platform.

Above all, Gandhi thought Tagore was overly concerned with how the struggle for Swaraj looked in the eyes of the British. 'He says he has striven hard to find himself in tune with the present movement,' Gandhi deadpans. 'He confesses that he is baffled.' Digging the knife in, he goes on to suggest that Tagore's problem can be put down to his aesthetic refinement and cultured sensibility. 'I have never been able to make a fetish of literary training,' Gandhi writes. 'My experience has proved to my satisfaction that literary training by itself adds not an inch to one's moral height and that character-building is independent of literary training.'

Tagore, of course, was not 'baffled' by Swaraj, any more than Gandhi was an anti-poetry philistine. Such are the exaggerations friends throw at each other when values are at stake. The two men continued to argue in public for several years before they were reconciled in old age. Nevertheless, the duel with Gandhi seems to have made a lasting dent in Tagore's confidence. For a variety of reasons he began to withdraw from social affairs, devoting himself to painting and to Santiniketan, which expanded in 1921 to include a university called Visva-Bharati. Tagore spent years on the global lecture circuit, but eventually ill health started to take its toll. Moreover, the gentle, pacifist strain in his thinking started to feel increasingly out of step with a world gearing up for an existential struggle against fascism.

His final volumes of poetry have a ramshackle playfulness that seems directly to question his public status. At times they border on solipsism, or scepticism about the possibilities of human progress. 'Over the ruins of hundreds of empires,' begins the final couplet of one poem in *Recovery*, 'The people work.' From this all-seeing perspective, Tagore finds a private nook away from the dramas of decolonization. The sentiment exemplifies Tagore's 'antipathy towards both the brutal modernism of imperialism and the claustrophobia of authoritarian nationalism', as Rahul Rao puts it. All empires will eventually lie in 'ruins' – no comfort, then, for the Raj – but in their place Tagore holds out little hope for a utopian future: the people will go on toiling, regardless of who's in charge.

In India, Tagore remains a venerated figure. His poems, many of which have been set to music, are read and listened to by many millions of people. The Indian national anthem, 'Jana Gana Mana' (in English: 'Thou Art the Ruler of the Minds of All People'), was adapted from a hymn Tagore wrote in 1911. Across the West, however, his reputation has never recovered the lustre it had during the decade of his Nobel win. Part of this has to do with piecemeal translation history of his work. Tagore was barely known in the West until he arrived in Europe in 1912 bearing self-translations of *Gitanjali*. With their glut of 'thous' and 'thys' – words that were archaisms even then – these versions have aged about as well over the last hundred years as a ripe soft cheese. Independent translations by the likes of Radice haven't managed to turn the tide in Tagore's favour, yet.

Tagore knew that his literary command of English was idiosyncratic. In fact, he was among the first to admit that he was largely winging it, so much so that he questioned the validity of his Nobel win. In a 1913 letter to his niece, Indira, he took stock of his relationship with his imperial tongue. In a translation of the letter by Rosinka Chaudhuri, Tagore says that the verbs and prepositions of English teem in his subconscious 'like insect colonies', a conflicting image of both occupation and freedom. These English words have infested him, but they also give Tagore license to play with language in a scuttling, poetic way, whenever 'they creep out in the dark and come and do their own work'. Held up to the light, however, they still leave him feeling vulnerable and exposed.

This lack of confidence had a personal story behind it. To a large extent, Tagore's meteoric rise on the London scene was overseen by another great poet, W. B. Yeats. This complicated, unequal association may also have played a part in Tagore's gradual fall from grace. Yeats latched on to Tagore and almost as quickly dropped his interest, in ways that seem rather cringeworthy today. Soon after Tagore's Nobel win, the gaze of modernist London would move on, leaving him a victim of what Amartya Sen has called 'the boom and the bust' of western enthusiasm for eastern culture ('A wonderful thing is imagined about India and sent into a high orbit, and then it is brought crashing down'). By the end of the decade, a jealous Yeats was pooh-poohing Tagore and claiming, quite spuriously, that the English *Gitanjali* was largely his own work.

Cultural exchange is rarely straightforward, particularly when there's a power differential like race in play. For all this, Yeats remains a powerful presence in Tagore's story. He is also closer to the Indian writer in spirit than his ego-tripping advocacy can suggest. As Louise Blakeney Williams has argued, Yeats and Tagore both came from colonies (Ireland

and India, respectively) that had much in common, and both men maintained a similarly ambiguous position within their national independence movements. 'Both authors,' writes Williams, 'condemned the "blood-stained nationalism,"' as Tagore put it, or what Yeats described as "the violence of the mob" that often accompanied extreme nationalism.' Both men, in short, were poets rather than guerrillas. They shrank from radicalism, and valued their own independence of mind as much as, if not more than, the collective independence that could be won at the point of a gun.

Yeats wrote two poems that capture this predicament brilliantly. One is 'Easter, 1916', a collective elegy to the doomed uprising in Dublin that year, crowned by the insight that 'Too long a sacrifice / Can make a stone of the heart'. This has a direct application to the central drama of Tagore's life. He dreaded the many sacrifices that Gandhi called on Indians to make, and worried that they would 'make a stone' of the national heart. No less relevant is Yeats's other great poem of counter-revolutionary ambivalence, 'The Second Coming'. Best known these days for its prophetic third line ('Things fall apart; the centre cannot hold'), the poem carries forward the argument about the rights and wrongs of violent resistance:

Mere anarchy is loosed upon the world,
The blood-dimmed tide is loosed, and everywhere
The ceremony of innocence is drowned;
The best lack all conviction, while the worst
Are full of passionate intensity.

Tagore would never have called Gandhi the 'worst' of anything, yet the contrast between that great man's 'passionate intensity' and his own wavering conviction was plain for all to see.

A Tagore poem that beautifully captures these uncertainties is 'Shah-Jahan'. Addressed to the Mughal emperor who built the Taj Mahal, it reflects on how this grieving widower sought 'To conquer time's heart / Through beauty'. That time itself has a 'heart' is an absorbing idea, one that stretches the bounds of western rationalism, but Tagore is equally eloquent on the state of the human heart. At one point he speaks to it directly, switching the poem's direct address from 'Shah-Jahan' to this endlessly symbolic bodily organ. Radice translates the passage in eddying free verse, filled with half-rhymes and repetitions:

> O human heart,
> You have no time
> To look back at anyone again,
> No time.
> You are driven by life's quick spate
> On and on from landing to landing,
> Loading cargo here,
> Unloading there.
> In your garden, the south wind's murmurs
> May enchant spring *mādhabī*-creepers
> Into suddenly filling your quivering lap with flowers . . .

Ultimately, Tagore's faith lies with the wind and the creepers, natural phenomena that rise and fall with the seasons, bending to time's will. In comparison, human schemes seem so stubborn and small. Perhaps it's the tragedy of idealists to press on regardless and try to make a monument of them. Although Shah Jahan built the Taj Mahal in honour of his beloved wife, Mumtaz, rather than for any higher political end, he still shares the fate of Yeats's self-sacrificing freedom fighters: his heart is translated – almost literally, this time – into stone.

It's a fascinating, tricksy poem, at once pitying the emperor and paying tribute to him, under the guise of a more conventional, hierarchical mode of thought. At one point, though, the speaker dares to be more blunt, calling out the implicit vow the Shah made in building the Taj Mahal ('I have not forgotten you, my love, I have not forgotten you'). 'Lies! Lies!' responds the speaker. 'Who says you have not forgotten?' He scorns the idea that any human heart can escape 'The ever-falling darkness / Of history' or diverge from 'the liberating path / Of forgetfulness'.

And there lies the final, telling contrast with Gandhi and his followers. For radicals and activists, 'forgetfulness' can rarely if ever be a positive thing, much less a source of liberation. One has to stay mindful and alert to win freedom, particularly in the face of an enemy as nimble and all-encompassing as the British Empire. From this angle, Tagore's stance can seem rather privileged and apolitical. Yet in its own way his thinking proved instrumental to the Indian independence struggle, feeding its imagination even as Tagore himself shrank from its harsher demands. Read today, his work teaches us that the human soul can flourish in grey areas of doubt as well as within the hard boundaries of committed action. Sometimes it can be the poet's prerogative to own their anxiety, or to stand on the sidelines and watch.

15

How to Think Like T. S. Eliot

'Let us go then, you and I, / When the evening is spread out against the sky / Like a patient etherized upon a table.' The opening lines of T. S. Eliot's 'The Love Song of J. Alfred Prufrock' (1915) haven't come to mess about. I still remember the lecture hall in Bristol where I first encountered them; the photocopied handout where they sat in a word salad of quotations chosen to illustrate various 'Approaches to Poetry'; the crackle they left in the air, at least in the corner of the room where I was sitting. Who knows what anyone else was thinking? I certainly don't remember a general gasp that broke out over the polite, hungover hush. But maybe that's what I'm getting at here – how there are two types of people in this world, those who get chills from that etherized evening sky, and those who can read these words and then happily get on with their lives. All I can vouch for is my own enchantment. A new part of my brain had been tweaked, some bundle of neurons that got tugged apart and tied back together in a fresh configuration.

I'm not alone in finding a point of origin in 'Prufrock'. 'It has been said of this third line that upon reaching the word etherized the history of modern literature began,' writes

Matthew Hollis in a new book on Eliot, 'so surprising and juxtaposed and electrifying was its introduction.' What's going on here, for Hollis to be able to make such a claim? The element of surprise is crucial. Up until the moment that we reach the patient on the table, the reader assumes that this will be one kind of poem, probably a romantic ode. There is a 'you' and an 'I', setting out together at evening, that most alluring time of day. Who knows what amorous pursuits lie in wait? The poem as invitation puts us squarely in the mode of pastoral, an idealized form of writing that proposes some other-place, usually rural, where the living is simple and the going is good. ('Come live with me and be my love,' begins Christopher Marlowe's 'The Passionate Shepherd to His Love', a classic of the genre.) But Eliot's invitation leads only to the operating theatre.

The very fact that he pulls the rug from under us is a large part of what makes this 'love song' modern. Poetry wasn't supposed to play such tricks on the reader's expectations. Poetry wasn't supposed to go to places like operating theatres at all, for that matter. As recently as 70 years before 'Prufrock' was written, etherization wouldn't have existed. As Christopher Ricks and Jim McCue explain in their gargantuan edition of Eliot's works, this medical procedure would still have been a relatively newfangled invention: 'Use of ether for pain relief was pioneered in 1846 at Massachusetts General Hospital, in the operating theatre later called the Ether Dome.' This breakthrough made previously excruciating interventions bearable, even blissful. The philosopher and psychologist William James – an influence on Eliot – had observed in *The Varieties of Religious Experience* (1902) that etherization might prove a gateway to mystical experience. So the line is at once ominous and heady, only a step away from the *ethereal* atmosphere of traditional verse – but a crucial step, nonetheless.

The poem proceeds from there to a host of other tawdry phenomena: 'one-night cheap hotels'; 'sawdust restaurants'; 'the soot that falls from chimneys'; 'the smoke that rises from the pipes / Of lonely men in shirt-sleeves'. Marmalade, novels, teacups, 'white flannel trousers'. In Wordsworth's *Prelude* and Whitman's *Leaves of Grass*, we likewise see the modern world take shape through recognizable objects and technologies. The new element that 'Prufrock' introduces is the very shapelessness of modernity. We have a recognizable speaker, yet little sense of coherence otherwise. It's a long poem, 131 lines in all, a scope that usually signifies mastery of some kind. But the long, irregular stanzas present an unexceptional person's scattershot impressions, the perspective roaming about 'as if a magic lantern threw the nerves in patterns on a screen'.

That magic lantern simile is another reference to state-of-the-art medical science. As the ever-forensic Ricks and McCue point out, 'just such a projection using "the X-Ray with microscopic attachment" was illustrated beside an article on *Seeing the Brain* in *St. Louis Daily Globe-Democrat* [Eliot's hometown paper] 17 Jan 1897'. We saw in the chapter on Emily Dickinson that a view of the brain as a material object opens up strange – some would say troubling – new territory for poets. In the half-century between her heyday and Eliot's, the human mind had only grown more flesh-like and material. One's very nervous system could now be projected onto a screen for all to see. The result was a body that could be studied and cured as never before, but that had lost some essential mystery or dignity along the way.

If this is what makes the poem 'surprising and juxtaposed and electric', in Hollis's phrase, then we should pay equal attention to the parts that plug it into a deeper tradition.

And indeed there will be time
For the yellow smoke that slides along the street,

Rubbing its back upon the window-panes;
There will be time, there will be time
To prepare a face to meet the faces that you meet . . .

The primary allusion here is to the great passage from *Ecclesiastes* about the cyclical nature of mortal life: 'To every thing there is a season, and a time to every purpose under the heaven: / A time to be born, and a time to die; a time to plant, and a time to pluck up that which is planted.' But behind this common touchstone stalks the ghost of a poem by Andrew Marvell. That poem, 'To His Coy Mistress' (1681), is another example of a poem as romantic invitation, though this time the summons leads nowhere more pastoral than the bedroom. And Marvell's speaker has time – or, specifically, the lack of it – very much on his mind. He practically points to his watch as he tells his mistress, 'Had we but world enough and time / This coyness, lady, were no crime.'

Eliot's Prufrock stands in awe of such resolve. He's modern literature's great young ditherer, badgering his companion with 'a hundred indecisions' and a barrage of questions ranging from the momentous ('Do I dare / Disturb the universe?') to the daft ('Shall I part my hair behind? Do I dare to eat a peach?'). One question splices impotence and importance in a way that sums up the worldview: 'Should I, after tea and cakes and ices, / Have the strength to force the moment to its crisis?' It's a poem haunted, bizarrely but unforgettably, by refreshments. The 'hundred visions and revisions' that Prufrock admits to flash against his mind's eye 'Before the taking of a toast and tea'. I wonder if young J. Alfred has been looking for suitable matches on the marriage market, slogging round the tea rooms making polite conversation with young women and their chaperones. 'In the room the women come and go / Talking of Michelangelo,' goes one refrain, pointing to a more general collapse in values that the poem surveys. High culture has become commodified, middlebrow, commonplace, and the speaker is complicit in this decline even as he bristles against it.

I'd be lying if I said this wasn't a part of the poem's appeal for a young male undergraduate with delusions of intellectual grandeur. Those deep thoughts swirling in a sea of dross; the tinge of romantic failure or loss of nerve. This is likely what kept me reading after the thrill of the opening lines had faded. But it was that initial 'etherized' jolt to the senses that got me through the door, and convinced me I was dealing with something not just relatable, but great.

Remarkably, 'Prufrock' was Eliot's first published poem. He penned it in his early twenties, starting sometime in 1909 at Harvard University, before completing it between 1910 and 1911 during travels to Paris and Munich. As a precocious student, composting the cultural references swirling around his head, and a young man with wanderlust trying to anchor himself on his year abroad, Eliot is perhaps the first poet in this book who really resembles the present-day species. His overeducated and flighty youth preceded a firmly office-bound later life – another common pattern for the modern man of letters. Born in St. Louis, Missouri in 1888, he came from a stolid, modestly wealthy family with roots in the local Unitarian Church. Despite living through two world wars and being the right age to fight in one, he escaped front-line service. Soon after returning from Europe, he commenced graduate study at Harvard and trundled along in that until 1914, when the outbreak of war interrupted his progress. He found himself stranded again in Europe, where he had been moonlighting as a visiting scholar in Oxford and the German town of Marburg.

Eliot moved to London in 1915. On arrival in the English capital, this diffident American couldn't have known that it would become his home for the rest of his life. Nevertheless, a letter to his brother Henry, written a year beforehand, on his first, flying visit to the city, paints a portrait of the Big Smoke that suggests it had captured his imagination. He reports from a city in the first, excitable throes of war, accosted by the noise of 'many babies, pianos, street piano accordions, singers, hummers, whistlers'. 'Ten o'clock in the evening,' he continues, '[and it's] quiet for a few minutes, then a couple of men with late editions burst into the street, roaring: GREAT GERMAN DISASTER!' Xenophobia lurks around every corner. A woman staying in the same boarding house as Eliot complains about a German waiter, demanding 'what's to prevent him putting arsenic in our food?'

However, if Eliot's letter registers knee-jerk bigotry, it also leans into giddy cosmopolitanism. The following sentence, detailing the response to these late-night newspaper vendors, exposes how ridiculous it is to mistrust foreigners in a city like London:

> Everybody rushes to windows and doors, in every costume from evening clothes to pajamas; violent talking – English, American, French, Flemish, Russian, Spanish, Japanese; the papers are all sold in five minutes; then we settle down for another hour until the next extra appears: LIST OF ENGLISH DEAD AND WOUNDED. Meanwhile, a dreadful old woman, her skirt trailing on the street, sings 'the Rosary' in front, and secures several pennies from windows and the housemaid resumes her conversation at the area gate.

This is a brilliantly Eliotic scene. The fragmentary collage of sights and voices; the Babel-like collision of languages; even his sneer at a 'dreadful old woman' singing a popular tune

– it all anticipates his great long poem of 1922, *The Waste Land*. In the poem to come, London would be the crucible of a European order that had been smashed to smithereens by the Great War. Here, Eliot glimpses that war at its inception, before the carnage acquired capital-letter nicknames. But civilization is already tottering on the brink, tilting inexorably towards 'DISASTER!'

In 1917, Eliot joined Lloyds Bank as a clerk in the Colonial and Foreign Department, and by the war's end he'd risen high enough to be entrusted with the job of settling Germany's existing debts with the bank. This role gave him a close, working knowledge of the Treaty of Versailles, the settlement foisted on Germany and her allies by the victorious powers. As Hollis explains, Eliot's circle was influenced by John Maynard Keynes's book *The Economic Consequences of the Peace*. In it, Keynes argued that the Treaty of Versailles represented a 'Carthaginian peace', an allusion to ancient Rome's vindictive treatment of its North African neighbour at the end of the Punic Wars. It was a prophetic tome that predicted further dark days ahead for the European continent, as a humiliated Germany inevitably mounted a backlash. In *The Waste Land*'s climactic fifth section, 'What the Thunder Said', Eliot captures this mood of transhistorical dread in his image of 'cracks and reforms and bursts in the violet air / falling towers: / Jerusalem, Athens, Alexandria, / Vienna, London, Unreal.' This echoes an earlier passage that directly invokes Keynes while tapping into a similarly apocalyptic vibe: 'To Carthage then I came / Burning burning burning burning.'

More prosaically, *The Waste Land* captures the postwar landscape in its portrait of drudging commuters trooping across London Bridge towards an 'Unreal City' of commerce and squalor. Twice the poem conjures this phantasmal cityscape, first 'Under the brown fog of a winter dawn', and next 'Under the brown fog of a winter noon'. That 'brown fog' hearkens back to the pea-soupers doled up in Dickens, and we might recognize some of that novelist's observational genius in Eliot's varied cast of characters. However, where Dickens's London is by and large an English metropolis, Eliot's is a global city through and through. The card-reader Madame Sosostris, 'famous clairvoyante', 'Is known to be the wisest woman in Europe' (not just England). Then there's Mr Eugenides, 'Smyrna merchant', who asks the speaker 'To luncheon at the Cannon Street Hotel / Followed by a weekend at the Metropole' (an invitation delivered 'in demotic French'). Even the poem's beleaguered typist – a London career girl if ever there was one – lays out her undergarments on a 'divan' as she awaits her gentleman caller. 'Divan' is a type of Persian couch, and here the word indicates a certain tacky, wannabe sophistication.

As should be clear from these examples, Eliot's cosmopolitan imagination comes with a grisly dollop of snobbery and prejudice. All the same, there's a porousness to *The Waste Land* that can't help turning towards celebration, even at the poem's bleakest moments. As C. D. Blanton points out, it's always busy 'connecting London to the distant points from which strangers arrive'. This paradoxical mood of welcome and fear is summed up in 'The Fire Sermon', the poem's third part. This section veers towards hopelessness ('I can connect / Nothing with nothing'), but interspersed with the despair are moments of levity and release; scraps of shanties ('The barges wash / Drifting logs / Down Greenwich reach / Past the Isle of Dogs') jumbled in with the otherworldly cries of the maidens from Wagner's *Ring* cycle ('Weialala leia / Wallala leialala'). The Wagner chorus turns the Thames, eerily, into a simulacrum of the

Rhine, reminding readers of the shared European heritage that had been lost in the war. The maidens become refugees from the country whose economy was being shredded by the Carthaginian peace of Versailles.

The aftermath of war was the defining experience of Eliot's generation. For now, though, let's return to that letter of September 1914, sent by a wide-eyed Eliot (aka Tom) to his brother when the fighting was still supposed to be over by Christmas. London's multilingual chaos is one aspect of the letter that reaches forward to the great verse he would write in the future. The next paragraph contains another clue, even more revealing of his emergent preoccupations.

'I find it quite possible to work in this atmosphere,' writes Eliot of London's hustle and bustle. Given the hullaballoo that he's described, this seems counterintuitive – you'd expect a bookish young scholar to be better suited to the library. Yet the next sentence completes the thought, explaining why a racket on the street can be conducive to focus in the mind. 'The noises of a city so large as London don't distract one much; they become attached to the city and depersonalize themselves.'

Depersonalization doesn't sound like a good thing on the face of it. It suggests a draining of vitality, if not outright mental instability. For Eliot, though, it was growing into a key tenet of the poetry that he wanted to read and write. This view is crystallized in 'Tradition and the Individual Talent', the crown jewel in a series of brilliant essays Eliot wrote in the late 1910s. 'No poet, no artist of any art, has his complete meaning alone,' he writes. 'His significance, his appreciation is the appreciation of his relation to the dead poets and artists.' This upends the lazy cliché that the moderns were all about razing the past to the ground. No, Eliot argues, the point of being modern is to negotiate a strong and vital position 'among the dead'.

This is where impersonality comes into play. For how is a poet supposed to find his place among the dead if he's always looking to butt in and draw attention to himself? (It's immaterial to the argument, but in this world the poet is always silently gendered as a 'he'.) Eliot hated the ideal of the Romantic artist looking to spray his unique sensibility over the universe. In particular, he throws shade on Wordsworth, quoting selectively from a famous line in the 'Preface' to *Lyrical Ballads* ('Poetry is the spontaneous overflow of powerful feelings: it takes its origin from emotion recollected in tranquillity'). In Eliot's view, this places far too much store in the power of the poet's feelings, and the starring role he has to play in bringing them to light.

The argument is clinched in a sparkling metaphor. The mind of a poet, Eliot proposes, works in the manner of a catalyst in a chemical reaction. Specifically, he invites the reader to consider 'the action which takes place when a bit of finely filiated platinum is introduced into a chamber containing oxygen and sulphur dioxide'. This is a complicated idea, so we might as well quote Eliot at length as he explains:

> When the two gases previously mentioned are mixed in the presence of a filament of platinum, they form sulphurous acid. This combination takes place only if the platinum is present; nevertheless the newly formed acid contains no trace of platinum, and the platinum itself is apparently unaffected; has remained inert, neutral, and unchanged. The mind of the poet is the shred of platinum. It may partly or exclusively operate upon the experience of the man himself; but, the more perfect the artist, the more completely separate in him will be the man who suffers and the mind which creates; the more perfectly

will the mind digest and transmute the passions which are its material.

In short, chemically speaking, you need the platinum to get the raw ingredients interacting with one another. Once they react and form a compound, the platinum can tactfully get out of the way. As in the science lab, so in the poem: the writer gets to work on the materials he has to hand – which will include some combination of personal experience and his awareness of 'tradition' – but the trick is to create something new and valuable that leaves the catalysing force of the individual mind behind. We don't want to know whom the poet fancies or why they went into therapy; we only want to see the after-effects of that passion and suffering in the finished work. Working as it should do, poetry becomes a process of constant refinement and distillation. As Eliot puts it, condensing the matter as pithily as he can, 'Poetry is not a turning loose of emotion, but an escape from emotion; it is not the expression of personality, but an escape from personality.'

These remarks would take on a new resonance in the years between 'Tradition' and *The Waste Land*. Following a disastrous visit from his mother and brother in the summer of 1921 – their first time visiting England and meeting his wife, Vivienne, of whom they didn't approve – Eliot was plunged into a period of nervous exhaustion. Necessitating a leave of absence from the bank, his condition had the silver lining of granting him the months of concentrated attention that he needed to get back on track with his poetry. While recuperating in Margate and Geneva that winter, he completed the drafts to a sprawling long poem that he'd been tinkering with for months.

The typescripts were soon dispersed among a circle of confidants in various nooks and crannies of Europe as

Eliot solicited feedback. The telling contribution came, unsurprisingly, from Ezra Pound, who had championed Eliot tirelessly since they'd first met in London in 1915. It was Pound who had forwarded 'Prufrock' to Harriet Monroe, the editor of *Poetry* magazine, and convinced her to publish it, with a cover note enthusing that it was 'the best poem I have yet had or seen from an American'. There was more to his advocacy than boosterism, however. A brisk and irritable Tigger to Eliot's gloomy Eeyore, Pound never failed to upbraid his protégé when he suspected him of backsliding or timidity.

Pound's interventions in *The Waste Land* have become the stuff of legend, saved for posterity in the facsimile edition of the poem that was published in 1971. His interjections are great value, sometimes laconic to the point of comedy ('OK' when Eliot has insisted on keeping something Pound doesn't like; 'Echt', the German word for 'genuine', when he hits on the really good stuff). At other points Tigger comes bouncing into the foreground, usually when Eliot's diction has become too indecisive and Prufrockian ('Perhaps be *damned*,' he curses at one point, drawing attention to a hated modifier).

All in all, though, Pound's suggestions amount to a tremendous feat of editorial intuition. He crossed out great tranches of the poem's drafts, encouraging Eliot to winnow and refine. Most notably, he was responsible for *The Waste Land* starting with 'April is the cruellest month', a line that has become so iconic that I heard it on the radio recently teeing up an item on the cost-of-living crisis. Ingeniously, Hollis frames the exchange, and the poem it enabled, as the culmination of Eliot's thinking about impersonality and tradition. 'Like Eliot's example of the catalysing platinum,' Hollis writes, 'a transformation had taken place, a metamorphosis that was particular to the chemical minds of the two men.'

Eliot's poetic mind was never quite as sharp or chemically reactive again. He continued to write good, memorable poems, and to rise in estimation among critics and the reading public. But in later years his thinking about tradition hardened into something more, well, traditional. A key turning point was his reception into the Church of England in 1927, the same year that he became a naturalized British citizen. Soon afterwards he would start referring to himself as a 'classicist in literature, royalist in politics and anglo-catholic in religion'.

These conservative tendencies are to the fore, rather magnificently, in *Four Quartets* (1943). Where *The Waste Land* surveyed the shattered fragments of one world war, this volume offered consolation to a public directly suffering the upheavals of another. In its second poem, 'East Coker', Eliot returned to the theme of time first explored in 'Prufrock'. On this occasion, though, the allusion was firmly in alignment with the sermonizing tone of *Ecclesiastes*.

Houses live and die: there is a time for building
And a time for living and for generation
And a time for the wind to break the loosened pane
And to shake the wainscot where the field-mouse trots
And to shake the tattered arras woven with a silent motto.

One needn't object to the implied politics of this extract to feel that this represents a downgrade on the great Eliot of the 1910s and '20s. Good poems emerge out of many different types of worldview, and this is undoubtedly a Good Poem. What has changed, though – and what holds it back from being a great poem, in my estimation – is the relative inertia of the materials. The poet's mind has become like the chamber in which gases contentedly mingle, rather than the platinum shred that sparks them into something new.

Eliot lived until 1965, long enough to witness the Beatles sweep to stardom peddling a new, optimistic brand of transatlantic pop modernism. His own peculiarly modern imagination had by that point become dusty and well-worn, an avatar of the great tradition that he spent so long imbibing and transforming in his youth. The irony and poetic justice of that outcome would have no doubt delighted him.

16

How to Think Like Langston Hughes

Is there a slipperier topic in all of literature than dreams? For some, they're not a subject writers should stoop to in the first place. 'Tell a dream, lose a reader,' goes the oft-quoted advice for novelists, usually traced back to Henry James. Others put the point less delicately. 'Dreams are boring,' begins a recent *New Yorker* article. 'On the list of tedious conversation topics, they fall somewhere between the five-day forecast and golf.' At the heart of the issue lies a stubborn problem in language: namely, that however vivid, tangible or thrilling the dream might seem to the dreamer, it will inevitably go up in smoke if you try to articulate it in words. Dreams happen to sleeping brains, so translating them into everyday language involves a computational error. It's like going to the post office with an orange and asking for it to be changed into dollars.

This is where poets enter the picture. Dreams have never been off the table for us.

In a while my spirit left the place
where my body slept and dreamed below
and by the grace of God began
its journey to a landscape of marvels.

So spoke the anonymous author of 'Pearl', a Middle English poem about the treasures of heaven, rendered here in Jane Draycott's contemporary translation. Had the 'Pearl' poet listened to Henry James, he'd never have strayed from the earthly garden where he lay down his head. Many poets before and since have found license in the shadow worlds of sleep. In 1797, Samuel Taylor Coleridge was dozing in an opium-addled stupor when he dreamed of a 'stately pleasure dome' in Xanadu belonging to the Mongol ruler Kubla Khan. Of course, he didn't just leave the vision there – he wrote a poem about it.

Despite this rich history, no poet has taken a greater, more persistent interest in dreams than Langston Hughes. Born in Joplin, Missouri in 1902, he grew up Black, poor and ambitious in the Jim Crow–era Midwest, a set of circumstances that turned dreaming into a necessity, if not a means of survival. One poem from his first book tells the reader about a particularly urgent dream.

> To fling my arms wide
> In some place of the sun,
> To whirl and to dance
> Till the white day is done.
> Then rest at cool evening
> Beneath a tall tree
> While night comes on gently,
> Dark like me—
> That is my dream!

('Dream Variations')

This teases out a tension that isn't so clear when one reads 'Pearl', 'Kubla Khan', or any of the other works inspired by fantastical or heavenly visions born in sleep. That's certainly one variety of dream, but not the only one. The word also refers to our deepest aspirations: things we wish and hope to be the case one day, but which aren't now, for whatever reason. At first glance, the dream related in the stanza above could be of either sort. On the one hand, Hughes could literally have fallen asleep one night and dreamed of himself in a hot landscape, whirling, dancing and flinging his arms wide. Or he could be describing his conscious dream of a future yet to come: an achievable but for the time being distant scenario the poem is supposed to bring closer in some way. It's only the present-tense verb of the last line – 'That *is* my dream' – that makes the second interpretation more likely. Whether or not it originated in sleep, this dream has clearly been taken forward into waking life.

But why would such an apparently modest set of desires lie in the realm of dreams? Here's the nub of what makes Hughes's writing so influential. It shouldn't be anyone's 'dream' to enjoy the elementary freedoms described in this poem. Whirling, dancing and resting beneath trees should be open to everyone with an able set of limbs and access to nature. Yet with a few subtle adjectives, Hughes implies why the situation is not like that for people like him. He dreams of performing these actions 'Till the white day is done', a colour choice that could, if we were reading innocently, refer to the sheer 'white' light that characterizes this 'place in the sun'. But we'd have to be pretty oblivious not to notice how the adjective has a racial component too. When he wrote the poem in the 1920s, Hughes and his ancestors had lived through a long 'day' of white supremacy that showed few signs of drawing to a close.

The second stanza varies the themes of the first – arms being flung wide; the command to 'Dance! Whirl!'; a tree offering rest when the 'day is done' – until we get to the last two lines, which take us somewhere else. They conclude the poem with a gesture of release, as the speaker imagines

'Night coming tenderly / Black like me.' If we haven't paid attention to the racial coding so far, then we sit up and take notice now. 'Black like me' clinches the connection between atmospheric conditions and skin colour. Heralding the night, the line also tips the poem over the edge of sleep, back into the other type of dream – the 'Pearl' variety. This is what makes it an exquisitely sad as well as hopeful moment. To imagine a world where Black people are treated 'tenderly', you have to let go of your rational brain and drift into altered states.

Dream on, as the saying goes.

Behind Hughes's dream stands an overarching blueprint: the American Dream. This great phantom was baked into the Declaration of Independence by the words 'Life, Liberty and the pursuit of Happiness'. The existence of that clause means that American writers have always been closer to the idea of dream as desire or objective than as subconscious reverie. When your society has been founded on the promise of freedom and happiness for all, it sets you on a collision course with that promise, whether you like it or not.

For Black American writers of Hughes's generation, the American Dream demanded to be addressed. At best an enigma, at worst a barefaced lie, it continued to provoke millions of Black citizens who had supposedly been granted equal access to those 'inalienable rights' in the aftermath of the American Civil War. The Fifteenth Amendment to the Constitution, ratified in 1870, prohibited the denial of the right to vote 'on account of race, color, or previous condition of servitude'. In other words, southern states that had gone to war to defend their right to hold slaves were at a stroke obliged to defend the right of those former slaves to participate in democracy. This led to a period of backlash culminating in the so-called Jim Crow laws, which allowed individual states to pursue a policy of 'separate but equal'. Any Black American would have told you that the 'equal' part of that formula was a sham. In practice it meant legal segregation, and it persisted well into the twentieth century.

In 1939 Hughes turned his attention to this state of affairs in a speech given at the Carnegie Hall in New York. The occasion was the Third American Writers' Congress, which convened at the beginning of June, just three months before the Second World War erupted in Europe. Hughes had already got up close and personal with fascism when he'd travelled to Spain in 1937 as a war correspondent, to cover the plight of Black American soldiers fighting for the International Brigades in the country's civil war. At the Writers' Congress, as a mark of respect, he read the names of 45 writers across the world who had lost their lives in fascist countries. 'The audience stood with bowed heads as the roster of the dead was read,' reported the *New York Times*. But Hughes wasn't finished with this sombre ovation. If the audience wanted to relax and give itself a pat on the back for not living in a fascist country, his speech was set to jolt them out of their complacency.

'All the problems known to the Jews today in Hitler's Germany,' Hughes announced, 'we who are Negroes know here in America.' The speech articulates a damning indictment of the racism at the heart of American democracy. There is only one key difference between the situation facing Black Americans and the victims of Nazi oppression, Hughes suggests:

Here we may speak openly about our problems, write about them, protest, and seek to better our conditions. In Germany the Jews may do none of these things. Democracy permits us the freedom of a hope, and some action towards the realization of that hope. Because we live in a democracy, tonight I may stand here and talk to you about our common problem, the problem of democracy and me.

Later in the speech he tells the story of a friend of his, 'a well-known Negro novelist' who was invited to talk about his new book 'before a large women's club at their clubhouse'. This celebrated author couldn't get past the doorman. He had 'to go to the corner drugstore and telephone the ladies that he was on the sidewalk waiting to appear before them'. Hughes's mordant wit shows how absurd the logic of segregation had become, over 40 years since the *Plessy v. Ferguson* Supreme Court case had affirmed the legal basis of 'separate but equal'. Where was the equality to be found in someone being forced to elbow his way into his own event, as if he were a feckless hotel guest who'd lost his key? Meanwhile, the humiliating separateness of his condition was all too obvious. A 1920s cultural boom had led to well-heeled Whites enjoying jazz clubs and Black writers (as Hughes knew from first-hand experience), making situations like this one par for the course. The 'Negro novelist' was in demand, yet that's where the similarities with his White counterpart ended. 'Black authors, too, must ride in Jim Crow cars,' notes Hughes.

At this point, with the main argument nailed down, there's a gear shift. Hughes's restraint leaves him as he enters the call-to-action phase of the speech. The catalyst is that familiar, troublesome but inescapable idea at the core of their democracy. 'We are all Americans,' he urges.

We want to create the American dream, a finer and more democratic America. I cannot do it without you. You cannot do it omitting me. Can we march together then?

He goes on to suggest that his audience, and by implication the wider writing community of the nation, 'put [their] heads together and think and plan – not merely dream – the future America'. With this appeal to a co-ordinated plan of action, Hughes gets to the root of the problem with dreams. A dream's no good to anyone if it's left to wither in an individual mind. To give it half a chance of coming true requires collective will. 'We want America to really be America for everybody,' the speech concludes. 'Let us make it so!'

It's a fine speech, offering a snapshot of Hughes at the end of his most politically committed decade. In 1932 he had travelled to Soviet Russia as one of '22 African-Americans who had been hired to act in a Soviet film about race relations and labor disputes in the American South', as Jennifer Wilson relates. With the benefit of hindsight, this decision to participate in a piece of cultural propaganda produced by Stalin's regime seems less than wise, but we should be clear about the opportunity that the USSR represented to many Black Americans of the interwar era. 'I feel like a human being for the first time,' said the actor, singer and activist Paul Robeson when he arrived in Moscow to develop a film about the Haitian Revolution with the director Sergei Eisenstein.

The scale of Stalinist brutality was not yet apparent, nor the shallow expediency of the dictator's anti-American antiracism. Hughes would go on to repudiate his communist affiliations, notoriously, in testimony provided to Joseph McCarthy's House Un-American Activities Committee (HUAC) in 1953. In some circles, liberal and reactionary alike, he stood condemned by his association with the Soviet Union. In others – notably, and painfully, his own community – it was the capitulation to McCarthy that left the stain on Hughes's reputation. He was damned either way, it seemed.

Bonnie Greer makes the HUAC appearance the central drama of her biography, *Langston Hughes: The Value of Contradiction*. It represented a turning point in his career, she argues, fatally wounding his status among young Black Americans who had fought in World War II, earning hard-won concessions to equality. This generation was 'vocal and standing up for [its] rights, in housing and jobs, in the courts and in the streets'. 'To them,' Greer continues, 'Langston was old-fashioned. To others, by going to the senate, he was a traitor to the cause.'

There's a paragraph break at this point that emphasizes the generational chasm.

'And they cast him out of their minds and their hearts.'

Such were the almost biblical stakes at play in the struggle for civil rights that was about to enter its crucial phase.

This, to be sure, was a long way for Hughes to fall. For many years he had been the pre-eminent Black writer in America. The first to earn his living exclusively from his work as a speaker and author, he enjoyed a wide readership that crossed racial lines. Hughes's childhood had been tough – not exceptionally so by the standards of the time, but itinerant and precarious, overshadowed by the breakdown in his parents' marriage. As Greer points out, he was descended from a prestigious African American lineage. His grandfather was the abolitionist Charles Henry Langston, who had been tried and sentenced for crimes against the 1850 Fugitive Slave Act after participating in a daring rescue mission in Oberlin, Ohio. Despite his conviction, Charles Henry went on to have a successful career as an activist, community leader and educationalist. His wife, Mary Patterson, had been the first African American woman ever to graduate with a BA degree, and his brother, James

Mercer Langston, had been the founding dean of Howard Law School.

The family's story, in other words, was one of unqualified Black excellence – and yet by the time Charles Henry and Mary's bright, artistic daughter Carrie came of age, many of their hard-won advantages had been eroded. Carrie was reduced to travelling around the country in search of work, leaving her son, Langston, in the care of his grandmother. Mary Patterson was a formative influence on Hughes, regaling him by turns with tales from the Brothers Grimm and the family's abolitionist history. What she imparted above all, however, was a steely resolve and a mistrust of sentimentality. 'Nobody ever cried in my grandmother's stories,' Hughes would recall in his memoir *The Big Sea*.

> They worked, or schemed, or fought. But no crying. When my grandmother died, I didn't cry, either. Something about my grandmother's stories (without her ever having said so) taught me the uselessness of crying about anything.

This refusal to cry would always temper the idealism of his published writings.

These days Hughes is best known as an avatar of the Harlem Renaissance, the movement in Black art that flowered in north Manhattan during the 1920s. He certainly gave life to the music scene that pulsed through the neighbourhood in that decade. 'The rhythm of life / Is a jazz rhythm, / Honey,' begins a poem in his debut collection, *The Weary Blues* (1926). However, anyone tempted to read this in a simple, hedonistic light can't be paying attention. Look at the shortness of the lines, and the rhythm-defying placement of 'Honey' as a stand-alone word. 'The gods are laughing at us,' declares the next line, underscoring that this is a world of hard knocks and bitter fate.

'What happens to a dream deferred?' This is the key question that Hughes poses in 'Harlem', the poem at the heart of *Montage of a Dream Deferred* (1951). Perhaps his most experimental work, the volume belies any notion that Hughes suddenly turned 'old-fashioned' in the postwar era. It shows him at his sharpest, and least willing to cry, as he looks back on the broken promises of the jazz age.

Riffing on his central question, the speaker of 'Harlem' cycles through a series of possible outcomes for this neglected dream. 'Does it dry up / like a raisin in the sun?' he begins. 'Does it stink like rotten meat? / Or crust and sugar over— / like a syrupy sweet?' At this point he seems to shrug, tiring of his parlour game: 'Maybe it just sags / like a heavy load.' This grudging admission turns out to be a momentary truce, however. There follows a brief pause – the flash of a stanza break – before Hughes delivers his mule kick of a final line:

Or does it explode?

This, in a nutshell, was the dilemma of civil rights. Bearing the load, or making things explode? Always a handy rhymer, Hughes excels himself here. For a moment he makes it seem as though there's some sort of etymological link between these two unrelated words – a 'load' lurking in 'explode', waiting to be blown apart.

By framing these different pathways as questions, he also manages to place himself above the fray. Peaceful or violent resistance? Revolution or gradual reform? All options are on the table, and perhaps it's more than a poet could hope for to negotiate between them. Hughes had tried being explicit in a series of fairly blunt political poems published across the '30s and '40s that had only served to land him in hot water. (One, titled 'Goodbye Christ', had led to his condemnation in the pages of the *Saturday Evening Post* and eventually served as evidence for the prosecution in the HUAC hearing.) Today these folk tirades read like agitprop, making it hard to escape the conclusion that poetic thinking emerges at the point where overt political speech runs out of steam. As we've seen in the chapter on Rabindranath Tagore, Hughes wasn't the first poet to feel torn between his conscience and his writerly vocation, and he wouldn't be the last.

Another parallel between the two writers can be found in the fact that Hughes made an outsized impact on one of the iconic freedom fighters of the twentieth century. Dr Martin Luther King Jr. was a civil rights activist and Baptist minister from Atlanta, Georgia, who learned directly from the example of Tagore's friend and sometime sparring partner Mahatma Gandhi. King was also a keen reader and occasional practitioner of poetry, and in 1959 he wrote to Hughes to voice his esteem. 'My admiration for your works is not only expressed in my personal conversations,' he wrote, 'but I can no longer count the number of times and places, all over the nation, in my addresses and sermons in which I have read your poems. I know of no better way to express in beauty the heartbeat and struggle of our people.'

A recent study by W. Jason Miller excavates the full scale of the inheritance: 'Langston Hughes's poetry hovers behind Martin Luther King's speeches and sermons the way watermarks show through bonded paper when it's held up to light,' he writes. Of all King's debts to Hughes, his visionary riffs on dreams and dreaming are the most recognizable. 'King redeemed metaphors from Hughes's poetry,' argues Miller, using a theologically charged verb ('redeemed') that implies a form of sacred fulfilment in the preacher's adaptations from the poet.

King's masterpiece, of course, is the speech delivered at the March on Washington on 28 August 1963, now known universally by its most famous line: 'I have a dream.' This is a text now firmly ingrained on the collective soul – recognition levels reach as high as 97 per cent among American schoolchildren – but Miller reveals how much of its theme and structure was inherited from Hughes. One of King's favourite poems, 'I Dream a World', was originally part of the libretto for *Troubled Island*, an opera Hughes wrote with the composer William Grant Still. It's easy to trace what King would take from it:

> I dream a world where man
> No other man will scorn,
> Where love will bless the earth
> And peace its paths adorn.

These high-minded dreams of peace and brotherhood became part of the turn-off for Black readers who favoured the militant, Malcolm X approach to liberation. Despite his distaste for sentimentality, Hughes always prized simplicity, resonance and universality – virtues that would translate readily to the pulpit, King's natural habitat.

It was having such language stored in his memory that gave King the confidence to shoot from the hip in front of some 250,000 people at the Lincoln Memorial. 'I Have a Dream' was not a prepared speech. It's now part of the folklore surrounding this era-defining moment that it nearly didn't happen at all. With his planned address stalling for momentum, King heard a nearby voice imploring him to change tack. 'Tell 'em about the dream, Martin, tell 'em about the dream!' yelled the gospel singer Mahalia Jackson, alluding to a sequence she remembered from previous King speeches. The rest is history, though what's less widely known is that the torrent of wisdom and verbal wizardry that followed would have been unthinkable without the poetry of Langston Hughes. This is one occasion, then, where – Henry James be damned – we can be very glad that a writer had both the courage to tell the dream, and faith that he wouldn't lose his audience.

17

How to Think Like Pablo Neruda

In October 1943, Pablo Neruda rode to the top of Machu Picchu on a mule supplied by the Peruvian government. As he ascended the craggy slopes and surveyed the ruins, Neruda did what many tourists to the abandoned Inca city have done before and since, and had an epiphany. Here is how he describes the moment in his memoir, published 31 years later.

> At the top, I saw the ancient stone structures hedged in by the tall peaks of the verdant Andes. Torrents hurtled down from the citadel, eaten away and weathered by the passage of the centuries. White fog drifted up in masses from the Wilkamayu River. I felt infinitely small in the centre of that navel of rocks, the navel of a deserted world, proud, towering high, to which I somehow belonged. I felt that my own hands had laboured there at some remote point in time, digging furrows, polishing the rocks. I felt Chilean, Peruvian, American. On those difficult heights, among those glorious, scattered ruins, I had found the principles of faith I needed to continue my poetry.
>
> (Translated by Hardie St Martin)

Improbable though it may seem, Neruda only slightly exaggerates the importance of his pilgrimage. He was, and remains, one of the few people whose spiritual and artistic awakenings merit this level of attention. His memoirs were published posthumously following his death in 1973, by which point he was a Nobel laureate with the status of a secular saint across much of the Spanish-speaking world and beyond.

At the time of his midlife journey to Machu Picchu, some thirty years before then, he was only a middle-ranking diplomat with several poetry collections to his name, but there were already auspicious signs of the global fame to come. He had travelled to Peru as the third stop on a triumphal tour as he made his way back home from Mexico, where he had been working as Consul General of Chile. From Mexico City to Lima, his every movement had been tracked by local newspapers and greeted by excited crowds. No wonder, then, that his trip to Machu Picchu had the feeling of a homecoming. Neruda was still Chilean, to state the obvious, but also in some respect Panamanian, Colombian, Mexican, Peruvian. Increasingly it made sense to refer to him using his favoured, transcontinental epithet – American.

Nowadays, in most parts of the world, that word denotes a single American nation dominating global affairs from its North Atlantic perch. It's one of Neruda's many gifts, then, that he scatters our attention from the United States and asks us to read America across the full length of the continent, from Alaska to Tierra del Fuego.

I am here to tell the story.
From the peace of the buffalo
to the pummeled sands
of the land's end, in the accumulated
spray of the antarctic light,

and through precipitous tunnels
of shady Venezuelan peacefulness . . .

This is from 'Amor America', a prologue poem to Neruda's magnum opus, *Canto General* (rendered here in its classic English translation by Jack Schmitt). We've seen such sweeping continental visions before, from the great poet of the North American landmass, Walt Whitman. Neruda was conscious of this inheritance, addressing his spiritual ancestor at a later point in *Canto General*: 'Walt Whitman, raise your beard of grass, / look with me from the forest, / from these perfumed magnitudes. / What do you see there, Walt Whitman?'

If his ascent of Machu Picchu at the age of 39 represented a rebirth of sorts, it's worth stepping back to consider where he had come from. Born in 1904, Neruda grew up in a particularly damp and windswept corner of the Americas, almost at the diametrically opposite end of the continent from Whitman's Brooklyn. His childhood hometown was Temuco, a rough frontier settlement in what he called the 'Far West' of Chile. In his introduction to a new edition of Neruda's *Twenty Love Poems and a Song of Despair*, the Argentinian poet Leo Boix sums up the austere beauty of this South Pacific region. 'It is an ethereal landscape of ancient black pine forests, silver gulls and towering sea waves usually surrounded by fog and oceanic winds and framed by the foothills of the southern Andes and vast starry night skies.' As Neruda sat down at Machu Picchu and surveyed the jungle spread before him, it must have pleased him to consider how he was hiking through the same mountain range that had loomed over his childhood, almost 4,000 kilometres to the south.

Neruda commemorates his midlife pilgrimage in 'The Heights of Machu Picchu', a 12-part poem that forms one of 15 sections in *Canto General*. As if to imitate the long trek to the summit, the poem circles through a range of vertigo-inducing topics – love, anthropology, nature, violence – before opening out into a more literal travelogue in section VI. We can almost feel the altitude change, the foliage falling away as the ruins come into relief:

And so I scaled the ladder of the earth
amid the atrocious maze of lost jungles
up to you, Machu Picchu.
High citadel of terraced stones . . .

Neruda goes on to address the ancient site in a series of one-line stanzas that emphasize the close, nurturing relationship between landscape and speaker: 'Mother of stone, sea spray of condors'; 'Towering reef of the human dawn'; 'Spade lost in the primal sand'. In the passage from Neruda's memoirs quoted at the start of this chapter, these tender, maternal descriptions are reconfigured in the phrase 'navel of rocks [. . .] navel of a deserted world'. It's a brilliant image, casting Machu Picchu as the remnant of something fundamental and life-giving: a stub left over from one's umbilical cord, no less. This is the depth of connection that had sprung up between the poet and his beloved continent, America.

Neruda speaks of his encounter at Machu Picchu offering 'the principles of faith I needed to continue my poetry'. This is interesting, since it implies that his faith had faltered somewhere along the way. If it had, then it couldn't be out of a sense of failure or neglect. His writing up to that point had enjoyed great success. When it was published in 1924, *Twenty Love Poems and a Song of Despair* had established the 19-year-old Neruda as a force in Latin American literature. It was composed in Santiago, where he had moved from

Temuco to study. Soon after landing in Santiago, he became a fixture on the city's bohemian scene, haunting late-night cafés in his trademark broad-rimmed hat and cloak. It's difficult to think of a poetry collection that better captures the texture of adolescent love; harder still to point to one that does so without descending into juvenilia. Readers were entranced, earning Neruda a faithful band of disciples who trailed him around the city in matching cloaks.

Though it was written in balmy Santiago, Boix is right to identify *Twenty Love Poems* as a product of the chilly, fog-drawn landscape of Neruda's southern Chilean childhood. Here's a passage from 'White Bee', translated by W. S. Merwin:

> Here is the solitude from which you are absent.
> It is raining. The sea wind is hunting stray gulls.
>
> The water walks barefoot in the wet streets.
> From that tree the leaves complain as though they were
>   sick.

These lines are drenched in climate and terroir, yet there's no sense of the land as a commonwealth as there would be in Neruda's later work. Here, nature and the elements are significant only insofar as they hold up a mirror to the heartsick lover and the object of his affections. As Boix observes, it's a strikingly aquatic collection. 'The speaker regularly appears immersed or even made of water, be it the sea, rain, dew or a river, all elements essential to Chile, a country with nearly 4,000 miles of marine coast and over 380 lakes and 560 rivers.' A uniquely Chilean collection, therefore – though we might wonder whether Neruda would have expressed similar passions in poems of skyscrapers and manholes if he were from New York, or of sheep and terraced houses if he were Welsh. He's using what he has to hand, though not yet speaking directly *to* Chile, much less the wider community of the Americas.

This would change, gradually, as Neruda saw more of the world. His diplomatic career began in the mid-1920s as a means to an end, a way of setting out on adventures and earning a crust. Early postings took him to Burma and Ceylon (as they were then known), humid and lonely places from which he sent haranguing letters to former girlfriends, imploring them to drop their lives in Chile and join him abroad. At the same time he carried on a prolific sex life with local women, in one case establishing an intense sexual liaison with his Burmese secretary, Josie Bliss. Eventually tiring of the attachment, Neruda ghosted Bliss and decamped to Ceylon, only for her to track him down to his new seaside home on the outskirts of Colombo. 'She arrived,' writes Neruda's biographer Adam Feinstein, 'laden with a rug, a sack of rice and some Paul Robeson records, to which she and Neruda had loved listening during their life together in Rangoon.' Neruda soon packed Bliss back off home, but the encounter stayed with him till the end of his life. In his memoirs, he called her 'a love-smitten terrorist, capable of anything'.

The love affairs of poets rarely make for edifying reading – salacious and vicariously enjoyable, perhaps, but almost never in ways that reflect well on the person or the work. In Neruda's case, there's a particularly stark gulf between the gravity and human courage displayed in his poetic and political careers, and an attitude to romance that can seem trivial, childish, self-serving, cruel. At best, Neruda doted on women and leveraged his charisma to get them to dote on him. There's a particularly jaw-dropping story from the time he spent living in hiding from the Chilean government in the late '40s, when he would routinely ask his host, Lola Falcón – someone who had already taken great personal risk on his behalf – to cook him hard-to-source delicacies, including eels in garlic, langoustines and beef with béarnaise sauce.

At worst, though, Neruda's womanizing had a darker tinge. In recent years a growing Chilean feminist movement has campaigned to re-evaluate his status as national hero. The key indictment is an admission in Neruda's memoir about an episode of sexual violence, committed against his Tamil servant. ('It was the coming together of a man and a statue,' he recounts. 'She kept her eyes wide open all the while, completely unresponsive. She was right to despise me.') As with all such reckonings, the question of what we do with this knowledge involves fraught calculations about impact, intention, contrition, patterns of behaviour, ongoing artistic value, and the extent to which a person's wrongdoing distorts their art. In Neruda's case, these questions are less settled than they've ever been, though it would be wrong to present them in a simplified light; wrong, equally, to ignore them altogether. All one can say with conviction is that poets are involved in the greater web of human violence, and that their behaviour may disgust us.

Part of the reason that Neruda continues to warrant study, in my view, is that his life and work tell a story about violence that is complex and humane. In a later diplomatic posting to Spain, he became embroiled in the country's civil war and saw fellow writers and friends like Federico García Lorca and Miguel Hernández perish at the hands of Franco's fascist forces. He would later recall that the experience of Spain had turned him into a Communist, claiming that 'the physical destruction of all these men was a drama for me. A whole part of my life ended in Madrid.' He had lived there in a lovely mountain-facing apartment that came to be known as the Casa de las Flores (House of Flowers), and it's the horrible violation of domestic harmony that he evokes in one of several great poems he wrote about the war, 'I Explain Some Things'.

My house was called
the house of flowers, because everywhere
geraniums were exploding: it was
a beautiful house
with little dogs and little kids.

(Translated by Mark Eisner)

Those 'exploding' geraniums are a risky touch in a poem that leads towards the real devastation of a morning where 'everything was burning' and 'fires / were shooting out of the earth'. But the risk is what makes it worthwhile, by drawing attention to the queasy proximity of life and death: how beauty and destruction both rely on the unleashing of hidden energies.

Neruda didn't rail against fascism only in his verse. In his diplomatic office, he led a logistically complicated mission to migrate 2,000 Spanish refugees to Chile in 1939. As a wartime consul in Mexico he was a victim of Nazi street violence, and as a postwar Chilean senator he vociferously opposed his country's increasingly authoritarian president, Gabriel González Videla. The latter confrontation resulted in a 14-month period of internal exile, starting in January 1948, during which time Neruda was harboured in a network of safe houses across Chile before finally being helped to escape in a dramatic horseback flight across the Andes into Argentina.

If anything, the need for material resistance to fascism made Neruda susceptible to political repression from the left. For too long he was an apologist for Stalin's Soviet Union.

Through it all he remained committed to the important role that poetry had to play in the struggle. The problem was that poetry required freedom of thought, whereas politics entailed obligation. 'You will ask why his poetry / doesn't speak to us of dreams, of the leaves, / of the great volcanoes of his native land?' ponders the penultimate stanza of 'I Explain Some Things'. The speaker's reply to this anticipated demand is blunt: 'Come and see the blood / In the streets!'

These are similar dilemmas to those that vexed Rabindranath Tagore and Langston Hughes. In a later chapter, we'll see how they played out in the life of Aimé Césaire. This generation of anticolonial and nation-building writers assumed the mantle of spokesperson with varying shades of reluctance, fully aware of the cost that figurehead status could have for their art. I believe this gets us close to what was going on at Machu Picchu that day, when Neruda felt his faith in poetry rekindle. His imagination had for too long been forced into hard ethical clarity by the urgency of events. With his discovery of the ancient ruins, he found a more ambiguous symbol of strength and liberation that transcended the political strife of the age.

The hardening of Neruda's political mind is ironic because, left to his own devices, he had a particularly sensuous and surreal imagination. His work abounds with roses, roots, fires and moons: symbols that escalate in intensity and diminish in clarity the more you encounter them. They become like musical notes, plucked out to strike a particular tone or mood, more than concrete nouns designed to latch on to things in the world. In the midst of this shadow language lurk brilliant, highly specific images like 'melted pianos', 'sad, chalky tombstones' and the 'shadow of a wet wing shielding my bones' (to take just three examples from

'Ode with a Lament', translated by Forrest Gander). In 'Ars Poetica' (translated by Stephen Kessler) Neruda speaks of feeling many improbable things at once, 'like a humiliated waiter, like a bell gone a bit hoarse, / like an old mirror, like the smell of an empty house / where the guests come back at night hopelessly drunk'. The poem closes with 'a banging of objects that call without being answered, / and a restless motion, and a muddled name'.

There is no better poet of restlessness and muddle than Neruda. At times he seems scared of the very act of thinking, as if it takes too much effort and commitment to be a sustainable part of life.

I don't want to go on like a root in the shadows,
hesitating, feeling forward, trembling with dream,
down down into the dank guts of the earth,
soaking it up and thinking, eating every day.
('Walking Around', translated by Forrest Gander)

At other times, thinking is the only thing that keeps him going.

I'm thinking, isolated in the vastness of the seasons,
dead center, surrounded by silent geography:
a piece of weather falls from the sky . . .
('Oneness', translated by Stephen Kessler)

Either way, though, the thinking mind is an autonomous and unpredictable presence. It can also be intimately connected with companionship and pleasure, virtues that this gregarious hedonist prized as highly as any. 'I love the light of a bottle / of intelligent wine / upon a table / when people are talking,' he writes in 'Ode to Wine' (translated here by Mark Eisner). I can think of no better tribute to the joy of sharing a bottle with friends. This is an experience that can easily get relegated to the margins of life, as something that we do when we're off the clock, not really present in our minds at all. Neruda's trick here is to attribute intelligence to the wine itself, the slant of the light as it catches the bottle. Thinking isn't only something done by humans.

In later years Neruda became a full-on dignitary, hobnobbing with Picasso, honoured across the globe. He was nominated to be a candidate in the Chilean presidential election of 1970 but stepped aside in favour of his friend and ally Salvador Allende. When Allende unexpectedly won, becoming the first democratically elected socialist head of state in Chile, one of Neruda's first responses was to ask for a diplomatic posting to France. His second (and, despite it all, enduring) marriage, to a woman named Matilde Urrutia, had run into trouble when he fell in love with her niece, and he needed an escape route. Even in his elder-statesman phase of life, certain appetites – and instincts for satisfying them – remained undimmed.

Neruda's health began to decline, and he was diagnosed with prostate cancer in 1971. In a tragic final twist, the illness entered its terminal phase as Allende's government fell apart under pressure from General Augusto Pinochet's right-wing military forces. The coup d'état duly came in September 1973, leading to the cloak-and-dagger death of Allende. For Neruda, it must have felt like he was reliving the purges and assassinations of the Spanish Civil War all over again, on his home soil.

At the time of the coup, he was working on his memoirs in his beloved home in Valparaíso. On the morning of 14 September, just as he and Matilde concluded work on the final section, a troop of soldiers from the new military government turned up on their doorstep. Whatever they'd been tasked with doing to the country's literary hero and chief surviving leftist, their courage deserted them on being brought face to face with the man himself. Neruda stared at the inexperienced commander and said, 'Look around – there's only one danger for you here – poetry.' The young man mumbled his apologies and called off the search, leaving Neruda to die in peace.

18

How to Think Like Elizabeth Bishop

In May 1969, Elizabeth Bishop was waiting to give a reading at New York's Guggenheim Museum. By then she was almost 30 years into her literary career, so this was a perfectly natural habitat for her, a platform befitting her status as one of America's greatest living poets. That same year saw the publication of her *Complete Poems* – rather a statement of intent from a writer who by that point had only published three fairly slim volumes, released at leisurely intervals, each one arriving a decade after the last. *The Complete Poems* went on to win that year's National Book Award, and Bishop would pick up a host of other gongs and garlands in the otherwise sad and troubled final decade of her life.

Introducing her that evening was her close friend and correspondent, the equally, if not more, renowned poet Robert Lowell. The key phrase Lowell used to sum up her talents had a peculiar, creepy resonance. He called Bishop 'the famous eye', no doubt alluding to a body of work that had won plaudits for its terrific powers of observation. Yet there's something slightly demeaning and competitive in the phrasing, too, a sense that Lowell isn't just singling out this 'famous eye' for praise, but is reducing Bishop to the accolade, turning her gift into a mere body part. This is what makes her quick-witted response all the funnier, and sharper: taking the stage, Bishop began her reading by saying, 'The "famous eye" will now put on her glasses.'

This ironic reversal is typical of Bishop. Time and again in her work, we are lulled into looking at something familiar, only to find that the expected object, creature or landscape is hardly what we thought it to be at all. 'Love Lies Sleeping' is an uncanny dawn poem, or aubade, from Bishop's first collection, *North & South* (1946). In it, the speaker looks out from her window to see 'an immense city, carefully revealed, / made delicate by over-workmanship'. In the final two stanzas, the speaker projects this cityscape into the head of another character, a male. Focusing on the physicality of his sight, she writes that 'the image of // the city grows down into his open eyes / inverted and distorted'. After all, whenever a person looks at something, their brain is working overtime to flip the upside-down image printed on their retina into something that appears correct to them – the right way up, so to speak. Trees grow from brown-bark trunks into leafy-green foliage. Cities fade up from pavements to buildings to sky. Strictly speaking, this might count as a distortion, but it's also a bona fide everyday miracle, and the final lines of 'Love Lies Sleeping' do justice to that. In another typical Bishop manoeuvre they take the form of a self-correction, as she rows back from her previous claim that the man sees the city 'inverted and distorted'. 'No,' she says, gaining confidence. 'I mean / distorted and revealed, / if he sees it at all.'

Bishop's 'famous eye', as imagined by Lowell, seems to correspond to some sublime faculty, a kind of X-ray poetic vision. Call it omniscience, if you like. It's a deeply Romantic way of thinking about the role of the poet, one that dates back to Wordsworth and his daffodils, which 'flash upon [his] inward eye' when he recollects them later in tranquillity. With her insistence that the world stands 'distorted and revealed' by human sight, then, Bishop is pushing back on the weight of that tradition and inviting us to join her on a more slippery slope. Revelation is intimately bound up with distortion. The world comes filtered through our wayward senses. The daffodils hit your retina with their trumpets at the base and their stalks reaching upwards towards the soil. And in a world like that, it can be little wonder that a famous eye might need her reading glasses.

This deep, physical fascination with eyes surfaces in 'The Fish', one of Bishop's most famous poems. Written in Key West – an island community on the southernmost tip of Florida where she lived for ten years, on and off, from 1938 – the poem dramatizes a moment aboard a fishing boat when the speaker is brought face to face with her catch. She regards his lice-infested body and his 'grim, wet, and weaponlike' mouth with a similarly grim yet rapt attention (and make no mistake, Bishop's pronouns very much establish the fish as a *he*, not an *it*). After a long, meticulous description the poem ends abruptly, as some mysterious mixture of disgust and delight – or is it respect? – compels the speaker to 'let the fish go'.

Before that moment of release arrives, however, the speaker has to look the fish directly in the eye. It's worth quoting the passage in full:

> I looked into his eyes
> which were far larger than mine
> but shallower, and yellowed,
> the irises backed and packed
> with tarnished tinfoil
> seen through the lenses
> of old scratched isinglass.
> They shifted a little, but not

to return my stare.
—It was more like the tipping
of an object toward the light.

Again, what's striking here is Bishop's fascination with the eye as a physical organ, rather than as a grand metaphor for vision (a 'famous eye'). She looks intently at the fish's eyes and notes their depth, colour and density. There's power in this position – literally, in the sense that she could kill it if she liked, and rhetorically, in the sense that she's speaking – but does the fish care? Not a bit: his eyes 'shifted a little, but not / to return my stare'.

It's this willingness to deal with nature on its own terms that has given Bishop's work new resonance in a time of ecological crisis. Had Wordsworth met the same fish, he would have ransacked it for symbolism, trying to turn it into a metaphor for the human condition. Bishop treats it as, well, an ugly but captivating animal (in the first line she calls it 'tremendous'). She builds her description methodically, even scientifically, as if ticking off every surface inch. Because she's a human being herself, her terms of reference can't help but be human as well. The eyes are both 'larger' and 'shallower' than hers, and the irises can only be captured using the metaphor of 'tarnished tinfoil'.

That word 'tarnished' shows that although nature exists on its own terms, there's nothing particularly sentimental about it. Everything is a little bit spoiled, a little bit lousy – but wonderful too. From the tinfoil of his irises to the 'shiny entrails' she imagines beneath the fish's skin, to 'the pool of bilge / where oil had spread a rainbow / around the rusted engine' of the boat, the poem dances between grime and glittering light. It's that familiar combination of revelation and distortion. There is no purity in nature, only non-human

219

beings living in the midst of other creatures and ecosystems, some of them human, some of them shaped by humans, some of them nothing to do with humans. The environment can be beautiful or awful, or both at once. It depends on who's looking, and through what eyes.

In some ways, Bishop led an uneventful, exemplary writer's life. She was born, she moved from place to place with her family, she went to college, she inherited wealth – not enough to buy her an ivory tower, quite, but certainly enough to give her a comfortable start. She received a lucky break through her early friendship with Marianne Moore, the spiky doyenne of American modernism. Moore endorsed her work from the off and put Bishop in touch with the editors of her first publications. From here, she published regularly in *The New Yorker*, developed a modest body of increasingly celebrated verse, taught when the right opportunities came along, and lived more or less where she chose to otherwise. She corresponded with the great and the good and hobnobbed at literary soirées whenever she happened to be in town. Gradually the awards and honorary degrees rolled in.

It's a very mid-twentieth-century version of a writer's life. Politics remains largely offstage, material comfort is assured, and beyond the odd bit of teaching there are no major professional or vocational distractions – soldiering, say, or religion, or nation-building. (During World War II she did work for a short while grinding optical lenses for binoculars in a US Navy shop – it's hard to think of a more appropriate occupation – but only lasted five days before her own poor eyesight and eczema forced her to quit.) Never lacking a room of her own, to borrow Virginia Woolf's famous prescription, she experienced few of the traditional obstacles facing female writers, apart from the occasional sexism and condescension of male peers. As an out and fairly proud lesbian, she was even spared the notorious 'pram in the hallway' that Cyril Connolly once called the 'enemy of good art' (Connolly thought it the duty of the artist's wife to keep the baby out of earshot).

But these are merely surface details, barely hinting at the real depths of Bishop's life. Beneath this smooth veneer, she knew great confusion and upheaval, and no small amount of tragedy. Born in Worcester, Massachusetts, Bishop had no memory of her father, who died of Bright's disease in the year of her birth, 1911. Her mother, Gertrude, moved Bishop at the age of four to Nova Scotia in Canada, to be nearer her maternal grandparents, the Bulmers. Just a year later Gertrude was hospitalized with a severe mental illness, the exact nature of which remains uncertain. In effect this orphaned Bishop, condemning her to a childhood spent shuttling back and forth between her beloved grandparents in Nova Scotia and her aunt Maude and uncle George back in Massachusetts. With the recent release of letters written by Bishop to her analyst, Dr Ruth Foster, it's come to light that she suffered six years of sexual abuse at the hands of Uncle George, from the age of 8 to 14.

Her adulthood was no less fragmentary, though this time the disruptive influence was love. The central relationship of her life was with the Brazilian architect Lota de Macedo Soares, a bond that would split Bishop's universe decisively along a North–South axis. When they first met in 1942 Lota was in a relationship with another woman, and there was a delay of almost ten years before she and Bishop fell in love, in Lota's homeland.

It was a cashew fruit that brought them together. Bishop had recently travelled to Brazil and suffered what she described in a letter to Marianne Moore as a 'an attack of a fearful and wonderful allergy' after trying this local delicacy. Lota nursed her back to health and it quickly became apparent that Bishop wouldn't be returning to North America anytime soon. They lived together in the city of Petrópolis for the next 13 years.

We catch a glimpse of their early relationship, and its roots in mutual care, in a gorgeous poem called 'The Shampoo'. This closes the sequence of new work, titled *A Cold Spring*, that Bishop published in a compound volume with *North & South* in 1955. With the quiet swagger of a Metaphysical poet, Bishop boasts that their relationship will last as long as lichens grow on rocks. Emboldened by this, she twists the familiar Metaphysical argument that time is running out (and, hence, let's get it on) by claiming that 'Time is / nothing if not amenable.' And with the pressure off, she lets herself really enjoy the features of her beloved, praising the 'shooting stars in [her] black hair' twinkling 'in bright formation'. The final gambit – the great Metaphysical ask, we could call it – focuses on that gorgeous hair, and is much more erotic than any of the usual sex acts could hope to be. 'Come,' she says, 'let me wash it in this big tin basin, / battered and shiny like the moon.'

If Bishop's love life could have been preserved in that moment, she might have been happier. Unfortunately, though, she didn't just have John Donne's love of a ravishing conceit; she also shared some of his roving habits as a lover ('I've never met a woman I couldn't make,' she once bragged to Lowell). Fifteen years after Bishop's arrival in Brazil, Lota died, and by all accounts her death was firmly linked to the deterioration of their relationship. Their final year together had been practically messy and psychologically harrowing. The turning point came in 1966, when Bishop took up a teaching post at the University of Washington, in Seattle – the cold Pacific Northwest, diametrically distant from Lota on the tropical South Atlantic coast. Here she met a younger woman named Roxanne Cumming and the two embarked on an affair. On finding out about this, an already ill and depressed Lota was devastated. Against her doctor's advice she travelled north to be with Bishop, but on a final trip in September 1967 the strain grew to be too much. Following an overdose of the sedative Nembutal, Lota died in New York City.

This is one of the key traumas that underlies Bishop's most famous poem. 'One Art' is a villanelle, a highly wrought French form that relies on the circulation and repetition of two key refrain lines. The first such line in 'One Art' has become famous, perhaps the closest thing modern poetry has to a quotable pop hook, ready to be printed on tea towels and posters (albeit very sad tea towels and posters): 'The art of losing isn't hard to master.' This travels through the poem in the expected way, returning three times with only a slight variation in the final stanza ('[is] not too hard' for 'isn't hard').

It's in the second refrain where Bishop works her magic. It isn't a line so much as a single word that gets repeated: 'disaster'. By naming it, of course, Bishop drags the spectre of disaster into the poem, even though she takes pains at every step to banish it: 'no disaster'; 'None of these will bring disaster'; 'it wasn't a disaster': the denials mount up, though we can just about buy the speaker's argument so long as the misplaced items are possessions or trivialities – keys, watches, former houses, even forgotten names. Yet as the screw of the villanelle tightens, the losses become impossible to write off. In the fifth stanza they extend to 'realms', 'two rivers' and 'a continent'. What could be bigger than that? The following stanza provides an answer, in the shape of an unnamed lover that we know now to be a woman called Alice Methfessel. Losing Alice and her 'joking voice, a gesture / I love' – surely that would be too much to bear? This wasn't an idle fear at the time of writing (though Bishop and Methfessel were reconciled after a painful separation).

At this late stage in Bishop's life – 'One Art' was written in the winter of 1975, four years before she died – Brazil was just a memory. She never visited again. We feel the suppressed ache as she casts off her second continent, with the feigned coolness of a snake shedding its skin. By this point in the poem we know she isn't even fooling herself, yet still the tough, understated voice that has guided her through four decades of writing tries to deflect the agony. '[T]he art of losing's not too hard to master,' she asserts for the final time, before conceding, at last, that 'it may look like (*Write* it!) like disaster.'

That italicized command reveals a lot. It's the sound of someone whose only truly successful identity has been as a writer trying to come to terms with misfortunes that leave writing in the dust. The kicker is that she might be less prone to the art of losing were she less obsessed with this art of language. And yet it's only by setting the disaster down plainly on the page that it can finally be acknowledged and absorbed.

There's something incongruous about the fact that 'One Art' has become Bishop's calling card in recent years. As a poem, it cuts against many of her usual instincts. From the beginning of her career she'd shown great talent for manipulating rhyme and set forms, so it isn't the artifice exactly. It's more the lack of specificity. All of the nouns are generalities: 'places, and names, and where it was you meant / to travel', as if such significant entities were interchangeable. 'Lose something every day,' begins one line, settling for an empty word like 'something' that would surely have provoked Bishop the famous eye to get her red pen out in earlier years.

This, of course, is the whole point. It's a poem about forgetting and losing, so a key part of its genius lies in how it imitates absence of mind. These qualities have given it a new lease of life in recent years as a poem that speaks poignantly to the experience of dementia. In *Still Alice*, a 2014 film about a linguistics professor coming to terms with her diagnosis of early-onset Alzheimer's, a powerful scene sees the eponymous Alice build a speech around the opening line of 'One Art'. Julianne Moore's performance is exquisite. Using a yellow highlighter to guide herself, line by line, through the written script of her speech, she trembles and keeps the tears at bay with a level of control that embodies Alice's claim that she is 'not suffering' but 'struggling'. Bishop's words are doing a lot of work here to bolster her resolve, proving that there is an *art* to losing one's identity – an art that must be mastered, no less.

It takes a major gift to write a poem like this, one so resonant that it chimes with a situation completely different from that which the author was writing about. Yet I still can't help but feel that it takes us away from Bishop at her absolute best. For that, we have to return to those landscapes, creatures and objects that draw her in with their particularity – the 'bright green leaves edged neatly with bird-droppings' in the mangrove swamps of Florida ('Seascape'), say, or the Canadian bus journey described in 'The Moose',

on red, gravelly roads,
down rows of sugar maples,
past clapboard farmhouses
and neat, clapboard churches,
bleached, ridged as clamshells,
past twin silver birches [. . .]

And so it continues, through a vivid northern sunset that sees 'the windshield flashing pink, / pink glancing off of metal'. As ever, Bishop tunes in to the harmonies that strike up between the man-made and the natural environment. Her ability to notice things, and to call them to our attention, is astonishing.

When we read the passage above, we don't just see silver birches; we see a particular set of '*twin* silver birches'.

In a famous letter to Anne Stevenson from 1964, Bishop rhapsodizes about one of her all-time heroes, Charles Darwin. Bishop was a devoted reader of his journals, which described the voyages to the Galápagos Islands that contributed to the formulation of *On the Origin of Species*. For Bishop, this was much more than a merely scientific text:

> I can't believe we are wholly irrational – and I do admire Darwin! But reading Darwin, one admires the beautiful and solid case being built up out of his endless heroic observations, almost unconscious or automatic – and then comes a sudden relaxation, a forgetful phrase, and one feels the strangeness of his undertaking, sees the lonely young man, his eyes fixed on facts and minute details, sinking or sliding giddily off into the unknown. What one seems to want in art, in experiencing it, is the same thing that is necessary for its creation, a self-forgetful, perfectly useless concentration.

There can be no higher tribute to this supreme poet of observation than to say that she succeeded in creating such an art of 'self-forgetful, perfectly useless concentration'.

19

How to Think Like Aimé Césaire

Martinique is a territory of France located in the Caribbean Sea. It forms part of the Lesser Antilles, a chain of islands curving towards South America, away from the bigger land masses of the northern Caribbean (Jamaica, Cuba, Hispaniola). The French have owned it in one way or another since 1635, when an adventurer named Pierre Bélain, sieur d'Esnambuc led an expeditionary force that wrested control of the island from the native Carib population. More brutal displays of power soon followed. In 1660, a failed Carib revolt resulted in the elimination of that people from Martinican soil, through either expulsion or extermination. Over the next 200 years Martinique was turned into a lucrative asset for the French state, powered by the transatlantic slave trade. Cotton, coffee and sugar cane pumped money eastwards across the Atlantic, while the forced labour required to produce these crops flowed in the opposite direction, from the west coast of Africa.

Slavery was finally abolished across the French Empire in 1848, paving the way for Martinique's absorption into the 'normal' political culture of the mainland. These days it sends representatives to the French parliament and enjoys a high standard of living relative to other Caribbean nations, due to wages and social benefits being linked to those of metropolitan France. Meanwhile, the BBC cosy-crime drama *Death in Paradise* is filmed 200 kilometres up the road on the island of Guadeloupe, another French-Creole overseas territory with close links to Martinique. That programme's fictional island of Saint Marie is a handy surrogate for what many foreigners assume life to be like in this jolly and easy-going – if disproportionately murder-strewn – corner of the Caribbean.

For Aimé Césaire, born in the Martinican town of Basse-Pointe in 1913, his homeland was anything but a postcard paradise. Death, however – or the idea of death – was in plentiful supply. Here is one of the many furious landscapes contained in Césaire's masterwork, *Cahier d'un retour au pays natal* ('Journal of a Homecoming'). The translation is by N. Gregson Davis:

> At the close of foreday morning, this inert town with its hinterland of lepers, of consumption, of famines, of fears cowering in gullies, of fears perched in trees, of fears buried in the ground, of fears drifting in the sky, of accumulated fears and their fumaroles of anguish.

To state the obvious, this is nowhere that you'd like to set up a tourist trade. Simultaneously motionless and blasted by misfortune – disease, starvation, a host of unnamed 'fears' lurking in gullies and treetops – Césaire's Martinique resembles nothing less than a circle of Dante's Hell.

This extract gives a good indication of the general style of *Cahier*, a mini-epic largely made up of prose fragments with periodic eruptions of free verse. Davis describes it as a work of 'uneven, spasmodic [. . .] progress, temporary setbacks, twists and turns, divagations'. In this the form imitates, or rather dramatizes, its content. 'Homecoming' often involves disturbing moments of déjà vu, which are evoked in the poem's chant-like repetitions and refrains. It's that sense of knowing somewhere like the back of your hand yet feeling doomed to return to it, each time as if for the first time.

Césaire wrote *Cahier* in the late 1930s, when he was a young man living a long way from home. In 1931, as one of the most gifted students in Martinique, he'd been awarded a scholarship to complete his schooling in Paris, the capital of the empire. Distinguishing himself, he soon graduated to one of France's most prestigious institutes of higher education, the École Normale Supérieure (ENS). For a young scholar from a ferociously education-oriented background, this must have seemed like a moment of vindication. Césaire was not just any clever kid from the colonies, however, and his immersion in the French educational establishment produced not gratitude or careerist ambition, but disgust for the racial power structures that had shaped his upbringing.

At the ENS, Césaire met other high-achievers from downtrodden outposts of the empire, notably the Senegalese student Léopold Sédar Senghor. Césaire and Senghor would establish a long-standing friendship, with both men playing key roles in the postwar anti-colonial struggle and rising to the highest political office in their homelands. (In 1960 Senghor became the first president of Senegal, where he presided over an increasingly authoritarian regime until 1980.) At the time of their meeting, they were two young and footloose intellectuals bent on fomenting ideas, reading up on African history, and immersing themselves in the works of Harlem Renaissance authors like Claude McKay and Langston Hughes. They found their place at the heart of a growing Black counterculture based around short-lived journals like *L'Etudiant Noir* ('The Black Student') and *Légitime Défense* ('Justifiable Self-defence').

At some point in these heady years, a new concept emerged that would define the rest of Césaire and Senghor's lives. Nobody knows the exact origins – who was the first to utter it around a café table or commit it to paper – but the word itself was unmistakable: *Négritude*. The meaning of this term in English is hard to pin down: 'Blackness' would be a blunt starting point, though the later American concept of Black Pride might be closer to the mark. 'Negritude' – the term is often anglicized nowadays – has a sardonic edge, however. As Davis explains, the word is brilliantly two-faced: 'On the one hand, the final syllable . . . is formed by analogy with Latin-derived abstract nouns ending in the suffix -*tudo*; on the other, the syllable *negr-*, though ultimately derived from the Latin *niger* ("black," in a value-neutral sense) had come close to acquiring, in French, the semantic cargo of a racial slur.' In short, the word presents a head-on collision between the respectably European – it almost sounds like 'rectitude' – and the racialized reality of Blackness.

Césaire's *Cahier* was the first book to introduce negritude to a wider readership. The concept bubbles up, as if from nowhere, with the light-bulb flash of an epiphany. Yet for all its brightness, it's an epiphany that lacks any of the certainty that one might expect from a manifesto. Here's what Césaire has to say about his big new idea:

My negritude is not a stone, its deafness heaved
against the clamor of day
my negritude is not a film of dead water on the dead eye
of earth
my negritude is neither a tower nor a cathedral
it delves into the red flesh of the soil
it delves into the burning flesh of the sky
it digs through the dark accretions that weigh down its
righteous patience

All these things that negritude is not – 'a stone', 'a film of dead water', 'a tower', 'a cathedral' – threaten to shoot the word down before it's had time to get off the ground. As the stanza develops, though, it gradually starts to consolidate the positive meanings of the term. Davis points out that the key change is grammatical, a switch from nouns to verbs (namely, 'delves' and 'digs'). 'The shift to verbs strongly indicates that négritude is not to be regarded as a state,' he writes, 'but an activity – an activity of self-exploration, of "delving" into the psycho-social subconscious.'

This may sound like a niche argument about syntax, but the point is vital. Demagogues and populists might try to turn negritude into an object, a programmatic thing to be wielded like a club. For a poet like Césaire, however, it can only make sense as a process: something that you *do*, and which is therefore as prone to change as the person doing it. In this way, negritude – like all of the most durable ideas, one could argue – factors in the prospect of its own evolution and renewal.

There's still something prodigious and unfathomable about *Cahier d'un retour au pays natal*. It's an explosion of a poem, a megaton blast that makes pretty much everything else you read feel puny in comparison. In an obituary written after Césaire's death in 2008, the Martinican writer Édouard Glissant wrote that Césaire 'caused [the poem] to spring forth, as if by dint of a powerful stamping of the foot on the still distant land'. That sudden, far-reaching movement of a foot is important. In exposing the violence, waste and stupidity of racial imperialism, the poem kicks and punches like a street fighter. The *Cahier*'s second sentence in French is '*Va-t-en*', which Davis translates in a rare moment of delicacy as 'Buzz off'. 'Go to hell' feels more like it, as Césaire sends an array of colonial mediocrities packing, from 'law-and-order lackeys' and 'hope-infesting termites' to priests.

For a poem about home composed several thousand miles away, *Cahier* contains precious little nostalgia. 'A disgrace, this Straw Street,' the speaker spits at one point, turning his attention to a particularly grim thoroughfare on the island: 'an obscene appendage, like the private parts of the village'. Everything festers, simmers, erupts: Straw Street is the place where 'the youth of the village fall into debauchery', where 'the sea disgorges its refuse, its cadavers of dogs'. It also becomes a symbol of Césaire's seething mind. He was influenced by the surrealist movement, which championed the use of bizarre, juxtaposed images as a means to unlock the hidden forces of the subconscious. The *Cahier* couldn't be imagined without these strategies, though it works by pummelling surrealism in the face and forcing it to contend with the wretched, real-life weirdness of colonial life. The dead dogs and rubbish form a collage more vivid than anything Salvador Dalí could devise.

The turmoil of the poem, in other words, is the turmoil of Martinique. Yet it could also relate, at some level, to tribulations in the life of its author. F. Abiola Irele points out that the poem was written at a time 'when Césaire himself was going through a period of stress', referring to his increasingly complicated personal affairs. In 1937, Césaire married Suzanne Roussi, a fellow Martinican studying in Paris who was introduced to him by Senghor. It was a marriage of minds – Suzanne, like Césaire, was an editor for *L'Etudiant Noir*, and went on to become an important writer and thinker in her own right – but family commitments sat awkwardly with Césaire's intellectual development. Suzanne soon became pregnant, a factor that Irele speculates might have had something to do with Césaire dropping out from ENS just before the agrégation, his final examination.

Senghor would later confirm that 'Cahier d'un retour au pays natal was delivered in suffering.' Mounting family and academic pressures played out against a backdrop of rising military tensions in Europe. Fascism was on the march, an ideology whose white supremacism would have posed a direct existential threat to colonial subjects like Césaire. These stormy undercurrents finally came to a head in September 1939 with the outbreak of the Second World War. Just a month beforehand – the same month that the earliest version of Cahier was published in a small journal called Volontés – Césaire had boarded a ship heading back to Martinique. Europe was no longer a safe place for him and his young family. This reality would have been hammered home when France fell to Nazi Germany a year into the war and the collaborationist Vichy government assumed control of Martinique.

Circumstantial details like these are more than enough to account for Senghor's claim that the Cahier was 'delivered in suffering'. It seems likely, though, that the poem was as much a product of things going on inside Césaire as it was of things going on around him. Quite simply, reckoning with racism has a cost, and this was a reckoning that possessed Césaire throughout his twenties. The thrilling intellectual pressure cooker of interwar Paris – that laboratory of negritude, where he'd found his soulmates and his purpose as a writer – was also a psychological ordeal. Again, Senghor offers a clue as to what was going on behind the scenes. Carrying on his childbirth analogy (that of a work 'delivered in suffering'), he claims that the poem's 'mother nearly lost her life, I mean reason'.

It's difficult to know how literally to take this phrase, whether it refers to a specific psychiatric episode or to a more general malaise. True or not, at one point in the *Cahier* Césaire appears to agree with Senghor's stark assessment:

How mad of me to dream up a marvelous caper above the
 degradation!
For sure the Whites are great warriors.
Hosanna for the masters and the castrated blacks!
Victory! Victory, I tell you: the vanquished are happy!
Delightful odors and songs of mud!

Over the last hundred years, activists and sociologists have developed a sophisticated language to describe the feelings of nervous exhaustion experienced by people of colour forced into the work of anti-racism. For Césaire, there was no recourse to concepts like emotional labour or battle fatigue. Instead, the exhaustion spills over into the fabric of the poem, through 'mad' outbursts and exclamations, 'Delightful odors and songs of mud!'

If one side of the *Cahier*'s dynamic is negative, however, the other is ultimately hopeful. The poem builds to a rousing, mystical finale, as the speaker learns to balance the inherited traumas of his existence – his negritude – with some measure of grace and transcendence. In the final movement, he summons a great 'Dove', bidding it to 'ascend / ascend / ascend': 'ascend to lick the sky,' he continues, 'and the great black hole wherein I longed to drown myself the other moon / that's where I now long to fish out the night's malicious tongue in its sweeping stillness!' Where Blackness used to be a vortex goading the speaker to drown himself, it is now a pool that invites him to go fishing in its depths. The activity of negritude goes on, expanding into the world beyond the final page of the poem.

Césaire lived for six decades after the publication of *Cahier*, making him the first poet in this book to see the new millennium. These were 60 action-packed years spent at the cutting edge of Caribbean and global affairs. As soon as the dog days of World War II were over, Césaire threw himself into the democratic politics of his homeland. Standing on a Communist Party ticket, he became mayor of Fort-de-France and a Martinican deputy to the French National Assembly. He wasted no time getting on with the job, either, and refused to shy away from the sharp choices that political office requires. Notably, in 1946 he sponsored a bill that made Martinique a fully fledged department of France alongside Guadeloupe, French Guiana and Réunion. This conferred the rights of citizenship on Martinicans, albeit at the cost of closer integration with and governmental oversight from mainland France.

Did this amount to a new charter of equality for the island, or was it a continuation of colonialism by other means? For many Caribbean radicals, particularly of the younger generation, it was a brazen sell-out. Throughout his life Césaire remained unrepentant, despite increasing evidence that departmentalization had proved to be a 'double-edged sword', to use H. Adlai Murdoch's phrase. Talking to Françoise Vergès shortly before his death, Césaire stressed the simple political aims of the original policy:

The Martinican people didn't care about ideology, they wanted social transformations, the end to troubles. The official position stated: 'You are French.' Never had a law been more popular: by becoming fully French, we would

have the benefits of family allocations, paid leaves, etc. . . .
We wanted to be Europeans.

This is a long way from the radical voice of the *Cahier* that announces, 'Europe has for centuries gorged us with lies and bloated us with afflictions.' One wonders what the young Césaire would have made of the state funeral his country gave him in 2008, an occasion attended by no less a pillar of the French establishment than its right-wing president, Nicolas Sarkozy.

In defence of Césaire, one might respond – a little glibly, but I don't think without reason – that it's easy to be a poet, and hard to be a politician. This is not to say that poetry is frivolous or easy to do well, just that it's a vocation where you follow your own instincts or else don't bother. Particularly in the modern era, the art form has self-appointed limits and rules. Politics, on the other hand, is an art of brute possibility and incremental gains. Increasingly in the neo-liberal era it requires ideological compromise and self-censorship. It commits one to speak in what Aneurin Bevan called 'the language of priorities' rather than the boundless language of the creative mind. The exception to this state of affairs lies in authoritarian regimes, where the exercise of political power becomes all too easy, and creative freedom all but impossible.

This was a prospect that Césaire intimately understood. We see his wariness about revolutionary tyranny in his 1956 resignation from the Communist Party – a protest against Stalinism – and the prophetic trilogy of plays he wrote in the 1960s, which diagnose the perils of establishing a polity in post-liberation Africa and the Caribbean. Glissant's analysis of the tragic dynamic in these works is illuminating: 'the formerly colonized adopts the manners, strategies, and injustices of the former colonizer; the passion for power suffocates him and turns him against his people, in Haiti as in the Congo: tragedy is aware of that'. By accommodating himself and his Martinican homeland to the French system, Césaire might have avoided this particular form of tragedy. (The contrast with his former comrade Senghor tells its own story here.) But the negotiation of ideals has tragic potential, too, and it's at least an open question whether this great thinker and theorist of Black autonomy ended up giving too much away.

The place where those ideals live on, then, is in Césaire's poetry. Perhaps the best way we can think about his legacy is to embrace what Mireille Rosello calls 'the perceived distance between the poet's violence and his political moderation', and avoid trying to bridge it in any coherent way. Real-world violence, after all, is without exception terrible (a truism that sets to one side the question of whether violence might, in certain circumstances, be justified). The violence of ideas, meanwhile, could be beautiful and liberating, throwing up new perspectives in the clash of opposites.

In this, Césaire remained a committed surrealist. He expounds upon such a philosophy in 'Poetry and Knowledge', an essay that remains his most enduring artistic statement:

> What presides over the poem is not the most lucid intelligence, or the most acute sensibility, but an entire experience: all the women loved, all the desires experienced, all the dreams dreamed, all the images received or grasped, the whole weight of the body, the whole weight of the mind. All lived experience. All the possibility.

Remarkably, Césaire unveiled these ideas for the first time at a meeting of philosophers in the Haitian capital of

Port-au-Prince in 1944: a moment towards the end of the war when one might expect the great minds of the colonial world to have been focused on the defeat of fascism and on national liberation rather than on poetry. But for Césaire this wasn't a zero-sum game. He presents poetry as a force that imparts its own brand of knowledge, as indispensable and world-shaping as any in the realms of science or politics. To build a nation worthy of the name, one needs access to its language of 'possibility'. Anything else would lead only to new forms of bondage and oppression in place of the old.

20

How to Think Like Dylan Thomas

This one's personal. Dylan Thomas bestrides modern Welsh poetry like a chubby-cheeked, shabby-blazered colossus. Any Welsh poet who tries to be modern therefore has to pass through him first, whether they want to or not – myself included. It's hard even to get off first name terms with him, so I'm afraid that's what we're going to be stuck with here. Dylan made the weather, and now the rest of us can choose either to get drenched in it, bring an umbrella or head somewhere else altogether.

Fifty years ago the critic Harold Bloom put forward a famous theory, 'The Anxiety of Influence'. Bloom's basic idea was that poets since the Enlightenment have always been writing in the shadow of their forebears – Homer, Dante, Shakespeare. The best, or 'strongest', modern poets turn that inferiority complex into an asset. They take the lead in a dynamic confrontation that produces fresh new work. But however successful they might be in that struggle, the writing process remains fraught with angst:

> For the poet is condemned to learn his profoundest yearnings through an awareness of *other selves*. The poem is *within him*, yet he experiences the shame and splendor of *being found by* poems – great poems – outside him.

Dylan Thomas is that titanic other, rambling in the background of Welsh literature. Reading him down the years, I've been 'found' by all manner of familiar insights and strange music relating to my country, a place Dylan memorably called 'the loud hill of Wales'. Often now, when I pick up a pen or sit down at my laptop, I see his nonchalant, slightly dumbstruck face staring back at me. There he is, propped up on an elbow in the grass, tie bunched haphazardly under his cardigan. There he is, supping a pint in the corner of a Fitzrovia pub, playing up to his role as court bard – or court jester – of the bohemian London scene.

Or here he is, in a 1950 letter to the American poet John F. Nims and his wife, conjuring a better, more colourful self-portrait than anything I could come up with:

> Remember me? Round, red, robustly raddled, a bulging Apple among poets, hard as nails made of cream cheese, gap-toothed, balding, noisome, a great collector of dust and a magnet for moths, mad for beer, frightened of priests, women, Chicago, writers, distance, time, children, geese, death, in love, frightened of love, liable to drip.

I'll go out on a limb and say there's never been a funnier citizen of the Republic of Verse than Dylan. This bravura list contains many of his characteristic comic tics: riddling sound play, riffs on slang and proverbial phrases, semantic switcheroos. On its own, 'hard as nails' would be a sarcastic quip, but throw in 'made of cream cheese' and the cliché opens onto complexity. Maybe this is a person who presents one way – tough, bristling, imperturbable – to cover up the fact that he's really nothing like it. Get too close and he could turn to a squidgy mess in your hands. His public image is 'liable to drip'.

Other true words are spoken in jest. There's the withering snapshot of the poet's prematurely ageing body, hammed up for effect, but only in the way a good cartoonist will exaggerate their subject's features to nail a likeness. By this point in life – he was 36 – Dylan's youthful, floppy-haired charm had started to coarsen along with the blood vessels in his nose. He was growing in international fame as a writer, broadcaster and speaker, but acquiring just as big a reputation as a bon viveur. Ask anyone who knew him a little, and they'd likely tell you he was the life and soul of the party, 'mad for beer', and not to be counted on if you lent him a tenner. Those who knew him better might point to his sporadic fits of generosity, his deceptively industrious working habits, or the shyness that afflicted him between bouts of drink-fuelled bravado – but they were just as likely to be stood up by him or left out of pocket.

It's a good job, then, that his words were beautiful. The opening stanza of 'Fern Hill' is as good an advert as any for the joys of reading Dylan at his best:

Now as I was young and easy under the apple boughs
About the lilting house and happy as the grass was green,
    The night above the dingle starry,
       Time let me hail and climb
    Golden in the heydays of his eyes,
And honoured among wagons I was prince of the apple
    towns
And once below a time I lordly had the trees and leaves
       Trail with daisies and barley
    Down the rivers of the windfall light.

'Fern Hill' commemorates the Carmarthenshire farm where Dylan spent childhood summers, 30 miles away from Swansea, his industrial hometown. The poem was written deep into the Second World War and comes saturated in rose-tinted technicolour. The real farm had been rough as old boots – in a rather more realistic story, Dylan wrote that it 'smelt of rotten wood and damp and animals' – but here it blossoms into an al fresco paradise. I can think of no work that better captures the great delusion of entitlement that a happy childhood brings: how the loved and carefree boy becomes a 'prince of the apple towns', romping around his domain. You don't have to have grown up near a farm with 15 acres and an orchard to know how that feels.

The sound of the thing is as important as its meaning. In fact, you could argue that sound is as integral to meaning as the definition of any particular word or phrase. The poem's rhythms skip and tumble where others plod. There's an abundance of muted syllables, giving everything a gambolling, lamb-like gait. ('Happy as the grass was green' is an example of what I mean: you'd only really stress '*happy*', '*grass*' and '*green*', so the other four syllables rush along, excitedly filling the gaps.) No single line is quite the same, rhythmically, as any other.

At the same time, set beside these subtle variations, Dylan assembles a rigid design scheme. Each of the poem's six nine-line stanzas conforms to a pattern of syllables per line. (The pattern, if you want to count, goes 14, 14, 9, 6, 9, 14, 14, 7, 9 in stanzas one, two and six, and 14, 14, 9, 6, 9, 14, 14, 9, 6 in stanzas three, four and five.) In effect, this arrangement blows a raspberry at the great poetic tradition he's inherited. If we think of the history of English verse as, essentially, the history of iambic pentameter – the ten-syllable, ti-tum-ti-tum-ti-tum meter that we've met in Chaucer, Shakespeare, Milton and Wordsworth – then this is a gorgeous way of doing anything *but* iambic pentameter. The 14-syllable lines expand lushly beyond that mark. The six- and seven-syllable lines fall laughingly short. The nine-syllable lines, on the other hand, flirt with iambic pentameter while always just eluding it – the lopped-off extra syllable quite literally knocks that meter off its feet.

I see all this as a form of Welsh jazz. 'Fern Hill' has the same combination of technical wizardry and offhand swagger that defines the music of Duke Ellington and John Coltrane. A set structure provides a road map, allowing the artist to vary their theme while never straying far from home. On top of rhythm there are the individual notes that form the melody, and Dylan pays just as much attention at this level. Throughout the poem, vowel calls out to vowel – 'boughs' to 'towns', 'barley' to 'starry' – in a riotous sonic display. (The poetic term for these meshing vowels is *assonance*.) Key words repeat from stanza to stanza, such as 'green' and 'time', which fuse at the end in the magnificent phrase 'Time held me green and dying'. Given such virtuosity, it comes as no surprise to learn that Thomas bashed through some 200 drafts of the poem, fine-tuning a work he knew was shaping up to be his masterpiece.

First published in the literary magazine *Horizon*, 'Fern Hill' reached a wider audience when it appeared in Dylan's postwar volume, *Deaths and Entrances* (1946). Almost immediately, readers latched on to it as an elegy to childhood innocence, delivered amid the rubble and ash. His attunement to the public mood had been hard-won. After failing an army medical in 1940, he entered into a type of wartime service writing propaganda scripts for the Ministry of Information. First in London and then in Swansea, he witnessed the ravages of the Blitz first hand, and several of his poems from the time pay tribute to life and death on the Home Front. The most ambiguous and beautiful of these is 'A Refusal to Mourn the Death, by Fire, of a Child in London'. Rejecting any easy consolation, the speaker vows not to 'blaspheme down the stations of the breath / With any further / Elegy of innocence and youth'.

Perhaps the most significant development of Dylan's war years came with another type of service he was able to offer. Starting in 1937, but ramping up in the early '40s, he became a regular presence on BBC radio stations. He chipped in for the Beeb with lectures on a variety of literary and autobiographical themes, from 'Life and the Modern Poet' to 'Persian Oil'. The 1940s were 'the great age of radio', according to William Christie, and Dylan 'would become one of the kings of the virtual castle'. Apart from being a vital outlet for reliable information during wartime, the BBC provided continuity in the intellectual life of the nation. As with the cinema boom of the early twentieth century, writers were given more or less free rein to invent a new medium for a mass audience, and Dylan's talents rose to the occasion. In his hands, the wireless flowered into a glorious playground for language – a place to be demotic, offbeat and lyrical, all without leaving the listener behind.

This happy relationship would eventually result in *Under Milk Wood*, quite probably the most original radio drama of all time, and the zenith of Dylan's writing about Wales. Once heard, the goings-on in Llareggub – a fictional Welsh everytown, whose name was conjured from 'Bugger all' spelled backwards – are impossible to forget. As is Dylan's uncanny manipulation of intimacy over the airwaves:

Come closer now.

Only you can hear the houses sleeping in the streets in the slow deep salt and silent black, bandaged night.

Only you can see, in the blinded bedrooms, the combs and petticoats over the chairs, the jugs and basins, the glasses of teeth, Thou Shalt Not on the wall, and the yellowing dickybird-watching pictures of the dead. Only you can hear and see, behind the eyes of the sleepers, the movements and countries and mazes and colours and dismays and rainbows and tunes and wishes and flight and fall and despairs and big seas of their dreams.

From where you are, you can hear their dreams.

On the page, a phrase like 'slow deep salt and silent black, bandaged night' looks ungainly, a ridiculous mouthful; on the radio, the warp and weft of those six strung-out adjectives is magical. Here and in several of his greatest poems, Dylan makes the avant-garde sexy and immersive like no one else.

Before he got to Llareggub, however, he earned his stripes as a chronicler of his real-life home patch. Swansea emerged as the main subject of no fewer than four radio talks, a number that increases if you include his wider west-Wales hinterland of the Gower, Carmarthenshire and the Aeron Valley. Of these homeward-looking broadcasts, 'Reminiscences of Childhood' has justifiably become the most famous, mainly for the following sentence:

I was born in a large Welsh industrial town at the beginning of the Great War: an ugly, lovely town (or so it was, and is, to me), crawling, sprawling, slummed, unplanned, jerry-villa'd, and smug-suburbed by the side of a long and splendid-curving shore where truant boys and sandfield boys and old anonymous men, in the tatters and hangovers of a hundred charity suits, beachcombed, idled, and paddled, watched the dock-bound boats, threw stones into the sea for the barking, outcast dogs, and, on Saturday summer afternoons, listened to the militant music of salvation and hell-fire preached from a soap-box.

What a panorama, what a sound. 'Ugly, lovely town' is the hero phrase, a reverse-pride motto that nowadays you'll find blazoned across Swansea landmarks. At a literal level, it captures the grit and beauty of the place, but more than that it's a genius piece of sound play. Trust Dylan to tap into the hidden connection between two apparently opposite words. The identical vowel sounds nudge us into an important realization. So often in Wales, ugliness and loveliness go hand in hand; slag-heap greys are smeared against rolling greens and 'splendid-curving shore[s]'. This is assonance lifted to the level of social commentary, proving once and for all that the music of language didn't just decorate Dylan's verse – it structured the very contours of his thought.

As with all good anxieties of influence, my feelings about Dylan are decidedly mixed. A surprising amount of his poetry leaves me lukewarm or cold. Endlessly pyrotechnic and thick with symbols, it can quickly become dry and airless. Recurring motifs of life and death – wombs, worms, milk, hearts, graves, grass – vibrate with the relentless energy of a fridge. The intensity of his music overheats: not so much the syncopation and swing of jazz, as the grinding groove of industrial techno. Take 'Altarwise by Owl-Light':

Death is all metaphors, shape in one history;
The child that sucketh long is shooting up,
The planet-ducted pelican of circles

Weans on an artery the gender's strip [. . .]

And so it continues, each line surging further and further into the red, across ten sonnet-length sections. Dylan understands the risks of his chosen style. 'Death is all metaphors' keys us into the abstract nature of the poem – how each apparently concrete noun stands for something bigger than itself – but it doesn't make the end result less risky or hard to fathom. (If anyone can shed light on 'planet-ducted pelican of circles', send answers on a postcard to the usual address.) Risks can be wonderful when they pay off, but I'm not sure Dylan's always do.

These feelings are embarrassing to me because they lump me in with a long line of snobs and philistines. As John Goodby points out, 'Thomas was resented by many during his lifetime for his combination of stylistic exuberance, roaring boy reputation and common touch.' For an example of this condescension, Goodby points to George Steiner's characterization of him as 'an "impostor" peddling bardic excess "with the flair of a showman to a wide, largely unqualified audience [which] could be flattered by being given access to a poetry of seeming depth"'. 'Unqualified audience' is a particularly noxious insult. Dylan was a grammar-school boy whose diverse tastes and flair as a writer were largely self-taught. What's more he was Welsh – a double novelty – and his poetry seemed to answer an appetite for something primitive and mystic in the interwar mood. The fact that it was scrupulously measured, and influenced by everything from Freud to French Symbolism to Thomas Hardy, hardly counted. Dylan became everybody's favourite noble savage, until the tides of taste moved on and he found himself an 'impostor'.

The mercy was that this didn't happen, fully, until after his death. The death part came prematurely, in 1953, and its circumstances have been ramped up into rock 'n' roll legend. What we know for certain is that it happened in New York City, at the tail end of one of several American speaking tours that he embarked on for money and adventure from 1950. He claimed to hate America and to miss his wife and children terribly whenever he was away from them. But if he travelled to the States against his will, then he did a good job of fooling the acolytes, girlfriends and barflies he palled around with while he was there. He tore into the boozy East Coast literary circuit with nervous relish, blotting out money worries, marital strife, and unresolved grief over his father's death in 1952.

The most tenacious aspect of the Dylan death myth concerns his final words. On Sunday 8 November, he had a big drinking session at the White Horse Tavern in Greenwich Village. (The bar's still there today, doing a brisk trade on Dylan's name.) After being rushed to the emergency room of St Vincent's hospital in the early hours of Monday morning, he's supposed to have said, 'I've had eighteen straight whiskies – I think that's a record!' before giving up the ghost. (In some versions of the story, he's receiving a scrub bath at the time of death, watched over by the poet John Berryman.) As his granddaughter Hannah Ellis argues, it's 'highly likely that he did' speak these words, yet 'very doubtful' that the alcoholic numbers would have added up like that. (People who have done their homework place the whisky tally more in the region of six to eight.) On a cursory inspection of Dylan's medical notes, it becomes clear that he was a very unwell man by the autumn of 1953, battling a host of undiagnosed respiratory problems. The drinking made matters worse, but didn't poison him to death.

No matter: the boozehound story quickly elbowed out any complicating factors. Dylan rose phoenix-like from his ashes to become the poster boy for a generation of beatniks, dropouts and moody students. The American poet Kenneth Rexroth summed up his allure when he eulogized Dylan alongside another tragic genius who blew himself out in the mid-1950s. 'Like the Pillars of Hercules,' Rexroth wrote, 'like two ruined Titans guarding the entrance to one of Dante's Circles, stand two great dead juvenile delinquents – the heroes of the post-war generation: The saxophonist Charlie Parker, and Dylan Thomas.' Parker was a visionary and uncompromising musical stylist who pioneered the experimental postwar jazz style known as bebop. A heroin user, he was also a drug addict on a different scale from Dylan. The comparison domesticates Parker's rage and alienation – much of which came down to racial prejudice – while burnishing Dylan with a wild-boy reputation he only half deserves.

This questionable legacy has proved, paradoxically, to be the guarantee of Dylan's ongoing celebrity. To this day he remains one of the few genuinely box-office poets, forever in print and depicted on screen and stage by a parade of actors including Alec Guinness, Anthony Hopkins and Matthew Rhys. Meanwhile, in Poetry Land, his stature as a serious writer has pretty much collapsed. His verse sounds overly rich and pretentious next to the stripped-back social realism that ruled the roost in British poetry for many years. In Goodby's words, 'Thomas is a kind of embarrassment on just about every level of the mainstream poetry world. His work is powerful and won't fade away, and it appears that something needs to be said about it; but, for some reason, it cannot be made to fit the standard narratives and so nothing gets done.' That situation may be changing, but Dylan's wayward reputation and mythic death remain obstacles to any proper appreciation of his writing.

My own burdens of anxiety are connected to all this. I said that a Welsh poet trying to be modern has to pass through him, and I think that's true. Dylan still represents the pinnacle of a certain type of Celtic noise. Mellifluous, muscular, turbo-charged by scripture and fireside banter, it's an incredible sound. I tune in to his music from time to time and find it hard to escape. (If this chapter were about me or my poetry, I'd list examples.) To push that music further would result in chaos; to backtrack, as many Welsh poets did in the decades following his death, too often leads to a music-free dead zone on the outskirts of prose. A happy medium is hard to find.

Why should this national psychodrama be of interest to anyone outside Wales? Maybe it isn't, but I flatter myself to think that it might be. The story of Dylan is a story of big talent, scurrilous gossip, silliness, grift, technological and social change, and excellence thriving quietly in plain sight while the rest of the world goes doolally for a myth. It tells us a lot about celebrity culture and the shifting sands of cultural taste. None of this means anything, of course, next to the glow of recognition I get from walking the Welsh coastline and turning to salute the 'heron / Priested shore' ('Poem In October'). The shore was there long before Dylan named it that – but Dylan gave me the words to call it my own.

21

How to Think Like Frank O'Hara

Frank O'Hara died on 25 July 1966, two days after being run over by a dune buggy on the beach resort of Fire Island. He was only 40, and at the time, at least among the bourgeois world, known less as a writer than as a curator for New York's Museum of Modern Art (MoMA), where he moonlighted on weekdays in a suit and tie. This imbalance is reflected in the subheading to a somewhat sniffy *New York Times* obituary published the day after his death: 'Exhibitions Aide at Modern Art Dies – Also a Poet'.

For after-hours drinking sessions at the Cedar Tavern, or weekend escapes from Manhattan, O'Hara favoured a more buttoned-down look of workshirts, chinos, sweaters and sneakers. These were the clothes in which he consorted with painters and fellow poets, not as a fluffer of egos or convenor of shows, but as a sparkling, waspish interlocutor. He was a man with a genius for friendship and provocation, as recalled by the poet James Schuyler: 'His conversation was self-propelling and one idea, or anecdote, or *bon mot* was fuel to his own fire, inspiring him verbally to blaze ahead, that curious voice rising and falling, full of invisible italics, the strong pianist's hands gesturing with the invariable cigarette.'

Over the decade and a half since his arrival in the city, O'Hara had established himself as a de facto court poet to the New York art scene. Known to almost anyone who was anyone, but with a special closeness to figures such as Larry Rivers, Jane Freilicher and Joan Mitchell, he flitted in and out of artists' studios and drinking holes, gathering conversational data to be set down in his work. This privileged, access-all-areas relationship is directly dramatized in a poem from 1957 called 'Why I Am Not a Painter'. It starts in the painter Michael Goldberg's studio, where the speaker has dropped in to find Goldberg tinkering with a new composition.

> 'Sit down and have a drink' he [Goldberg]
> says. I drink; we drink. I look
> up. 'You have SARDINES in it.'
> 'Yes, it needed something there.'
> 'Oh.' I go and the days go by
> and I drop in again. The painting
> is going on, and I go, and the days
> go by. I drop in. The painting is
> finished. 'Where's SARDINES?'
> All that's left is just
> letters, 'It was too much,' Mike says.

It's worth reflecting on the different inflections of 'go' in this stanza. The first arrives straight after Goldberg offers his disarming non-reason for working sardines into the painting ('it needed something there') and O'Hara gives his suitably disarmed reply: 'Oh'. The speaker *goes* straight afterwards, without any follow-up questions or even so much as a toodle-oo. The elementary verb conveys chance, spontaneity, continuity – *on*goingness, we might say – as if the movement in and out of people's company is an involuntary action. It brings to mind gaseous particles spreading to fill a space, just as 'the days go by' in our lives. As with people, and time, so with art: while the speaker is coming and going, 'The painting / is going on.' (Note the weird, phantom grammar of that sentence: not 'Mike is painting a picture', but '*The painting* is going on.') It's the great achievement of this poem to bring everything into such casual equilibrium. By adopting an almost confrontationally stop–start and unpoetic register, O'Hara hacks into the poetic rhythm of life itself.

As with much of O'Hara's work, there's a voraciousness in 'Why I Am Not a Painter', a *joie de vivre* – but one doesn't have to travel far to glimpse its opposite. In the third and final stanza, the speaker reports on his own artistic endeavour, a poetic sequence called 'Oranges' that quickly balloons beyond an initial line about the title colour.

> Pretty soon it is a
> whole page of words, not lines.
> Then another page. There should be
> so much more, not of orange, of
> words, of how terrible orange is
> and life. Days go by.

Suddenly the days going by don't seem so innocent or thrilling; instead, they have been implicated somehow in the realization that life, like orange, can be 'terrible'. The desire to capture something precise and beautiful runs into the impossibility of truly grasping anything at all. These are the minor notes that underpin all great O'Hara poems, even the most apparently ebullient.

A similar melancholy relationship with time emerges in one of the most widely quoted O'Hara passages of all, from 'Mayakovsky':

> Now I am quietly waiting for
> the catastrophe of my personality

to seem beautiful again,
and interesting, and modern.

The character Don Draper intones this in voiceover during the closing scene of 'For Those Who Think Young', an episode of the US TV drama series *Mad Men*. That episode is the first instalment of a season that culminates in the Cuban Missile Crisis, and 'Mayakovsky' seems to bottle the mood of enervated dread. Underneath his own gravelly voiceover, reciting lines about a nameless country that is 'grey and / brown and white in trees', Don strides along the empty suburban street, walking the dog to a mailbox where he posts a copy of O'Hara's *Meditations in an Emergency* to an unknown recipient. He lights a cigarette in close-up, before the camera swirls overhead, and Don chews on the final stanza of the poem:

It may be the coldest day of
the year, what does he think of
that? I mean, what do I? And if I do,
perhaps I am myself again.

A moment of gorgeous, heavily stylized synergy – and it's to the credit of *Mad Men*'s showrunner, Matthew Weiner, that he singled out the downbeat drag in a poet who is often miscast, or simplified, as a bubbly flâneur.

O'Hara suffered from periods of depression throughout his adult life, as well as fits of manic, self-destructive drinking. It's hard, and probably misguided, to pinpoint exactly where or when such tendencies emerge. We do, though, know that he experienced formative losses and traumas, and that these in turn fed into more complex feelings of independence or excitement. He captures this sense of painful but necessary growth in 'Ode to Michael Goldberg ('s Birth and Other Births)', a long autobiographical poem O'Hara wrote in 1958, reflecting on his Depression-era childhood and subsequent service in the US Navy towards the end of the Second World War:

> wonderful stimulation of bitterness
> to be young and to grow bigger
> more and more like cells, like germs
> or a political conspiracy
>
> and each reason for love always
> a certain hostility, mistaken
> for wisdom
>   exceptional excitement
> which is finally simple blindness
> (but not to be sneezed at!) like
> a successful American satellite . . .

During the war, O'Hara served on the USS *Nicholas*, a destroyer that formed part of the covering force in the Okinawa campaign, America's final assault on a beleaguered Japan. It was a posting that involved a lot of waiting, though never in idle detachment. Everything seemed to be pointing towards an invasion and subsequent land battle, until that prospect was suddenly cancelled by the savage, conclusive violence of the Hiroshima and Nagasaki bombings.

These events haunted O'Hara, first surfacing in a wartime memoir called 'Lament and Chastisement' that he produced five years later for a writing class in Harvard: 'we killed the great Japanese architect the great German scientist the great Italian musician dropped death on Hiroshima killed killed killed and yes I hate us for it killedkilledkilled'. Apart from anything else, this essay serves as a reminder that the Cold War angst evoked in *Mad Men* would have held entirely real memories for O'Hara. He knew that 'quietly waiting' could lead to moments of decisive, and deadly, action – moments that seem to circle endlessly, like 'a successful American satellite', until suddenly they rain death from the sky.

For the next 20 years, interludes of blank anxiety continued to recur in O'Hara's life. Friends remember him entering one such listless mood in the months before his death, almost as if he had a premonition that something was drawing to a close. The poems had dried up. His work at MoMA was increasingly absorbing and demanding – he was gearing up to direct a major Jackson Pollock retrospective – yet something was amiss. His professional and creative lives were out of joint, as were several key friendships and love affairs, relationships that increasingly seemed to be running out of steam, blowing gaskets. People recall him speaking about a desire to emulate Keats, Shelley and Apollinaire, three poets who blazed brightly and died before life could make them ugly or irrelevant – an ominous but fitting development for O'Hara, who had long been fascinated by James Dean.

The accident that killed O'Hara took place in the early hours of the morning, at the end of a Saturday night he'd spent with friends at the Pines dance bar. Wired and tired, he finally called it a night at around half past two, heading to the beachfront to hail a cab with the writer J. J. Mitchell. The jeep rattled along, its backseat filled with partygoers and stragglers, until a few minutes into the journey a rear tyre blew. As the passengers got out and waited for a replacement, O'Hara drifted away to stare at the Atlantic. Not long afterwards, a young man came joyriding with his date along the strand and swerved to avoid the broken-down cab, colliding with O'Hara. Medics were called, and a perfunctory police investigation conducted, before the stricken O'Hara was rushed to the only available hospital nearby, the small and short-staffed Bayview General in Mastic Beach.

To this day, an air of freak tragedy hangs over the incident. O'Hara didn't die on Fire Island, in a blaze of nihilistic glory. He succumbed to internal injuries two days later, slipping fitfully in and out of consciousness – though, in a bitter irony, he might well have survived had his liver not already sustained so much self-inflicted damage. O'Hara's biographer, Brad Gooch, weighs up the evidence that O'Hara might have allowed or even willed himself to be run over, as the apotheosis of some romantic death wish, before finally dismissing it. O'Hara may have flirted with veneration for James Dean and Jackson Pollock – two 'archetypal, tragic, suicidal, American geniuses', in Gooch's words – but in his work he modelled an aesthetics of cracking on, tending always towards the mode of comedy. This is the pragmatic pulse of daily living that carries through his self-described 'I Do This, I Do That' poems, as they glide or skip or otherwise forge ahead through the maelstrom of New York.

In one famous example, the speaker is so busy rushing around and living that he practically trips over a newspaper headline reporting that a Hollywood actress is in trouble:

Lana Turner has collapsed!
I was trotting along and suddenly
it started raining and snowing
and you said it was hailing
but hailing hits you on the head
hard so it was really snowing and
raining and I was in such a hurry
to meet you but the traffic
was acting exactly like the sky
and suddenly I see a headline
LANA TURNER HAS COLLAPSED!

To my knowledge, O'Hara is the only poet to have used the phrase 'trotting along', and he will likely remain so. He owns it now. It's not just that O'Hara's poems so often emerge from the act of walking through the city, at a quick enough clip that 'trotting' seems the only word for it; it's the fact that, after a fashion, he makes everything else *trot along* around him as well. Here, the sky is thick with movement, discharging rain and snow, and it's a similar situation on the roads, where the traffic is 'acting exactly like the sky'. Against such a kinetic backdrop, the sudden arrest of movement in Lana Turner – and the blunt exclamation nailing the headline flat against the newsstands – comes as a rude shock, an insult that the poet springs into action to overrule.

The end of the poem conjures a beautifully funny, and sad, diminuendo:

> there is no snow in Hollywood
> there is no rain in California
> I have been to lots of parties
> and acted perfectly disgraceful
> but I never actually collapsed
> oh Lana Turner we love you get up

There's yearning and affection in that celebrated closing line – both signature traits of an O'Hara poem – but also the less acknowledged quality of stoicism. Get up, Lana, it says, your work here isn't done. Life may be terrible, but it sure as hell beats the alternatives. Tapping into this mood, O'Hara's friend Tony Towle sent a note up to the intensive care unit in Bayview General shortly before O'Hara died. 'Frank,' it read, 'we love you. Get up.'

O'Hara's premature death – one of the most publicly witnessed, and elegized, in modern literary history – presaged an afterlife of strange and lasting celebrity. In recent years, he's been reborn a thousand times on social media. Famously quotable, his poetry lends itself to being snapped and papped and posted on Instagram – quite literally, in the case of Jennifer Lawrence, who was photographed in 2018 holding what seemed to be a copy of O'Hara's *Lunch Poems*, until this slender volume turned out, in fact, to be a $1,500 Olympia Le-Tan clutch bag.

A minor cottage industry has sprung up debating the rights and wrongs of O'Hara's latter-day role as an influencer *avant la lettre*. In one corner stand the sceptics who resent how his poetry has been reduced to frothy soundbites, or taken as a template by excitable millennials. In the other stand those who call out these narratives of decline as tin-eared and condescending – a form of cultural snobbery that the defiantly omnivorous O'Hara would have had no truck with at all. As Sinéad Stubbins wrote in a 2019 *Guardian* think piece, 'I don't think Frank O'Hara would think it was silly that I discovered his work on a social media app that is primarily designed for empowering bikini selfies and laxative tea advertisements. He would probably think it was funny.'

Stubbins cites several lines from O'Hara's 'Naphtha' that lend credibility to her thesis: 'I am ashamed of my century / for being so entertaining / but I have to smile.' This complex note of celebration and enjoyment – undercut by just the faintest sniff of superiority – can be traced to 'Personism', a poetic anti-manifesto O'Hara tossed off in 1959. In this essay, O'Hara levels the brilliantly democratic defence of popular art, 'Nobody should experience anything they don't need to, if they don't need poetry bully for them. I like the movies too. And after all, only Whitman and Crane and Williams, of the American poets, are better than the movies.'

I like the movies too. Here, if one were needed, is a rallying cry and point of origin for poetry in a multimedia age, when slim lines of verse have to vie for our attention with cinema, TV, comic books and billboards, to say nothing of the Twitter/X threads and Insta stories that have gleefully sucked O'Hara into their vortex in recent years. Food and drink is another element in this grand cacophony, and – not coincidentally – O'Hara is about the most gourmet poet of the twentieth century. 'Light   clarity   avocado salad in the morning' runs the opening line of one gorgeous poem, as if calling to a future where everybody's favourite stone fruit would be as lovingly and frequently photographed as Lana Turner. O'Hara would have been tickled by the hypermodern rise and rise of the avocado – its journey from elite fad to mainstream basket-filler; the way it's become a symbol of generational inequality, with reactionaries frothing at the mouth about how young people prioritize guacamole over house deposits.

In other words, I am firmly in the camp of Stubbins et al. Let's continue to celebrate the ephemeral, bodily, pleasure-driven O'Hara that has become such a defining pop-art mood of the twenty-first century. O'Hara loved mass culture as much as anyone, and if his passions feed directly into an annoying, over-caffeinated modern brunch aesthetic, then it only goes to show how ahead of the game he was. As with his smart-casual sartorial choices, O'Hara may have become a victim of the ubiquitous taste that he in some way helped to shape – but that shouldn't detract from how bracing and progressive those tastes were in the context of his time.

One would sound only a small note of elitist caution. Actually, it's not elitist at all, since the joyous embrace of 'high' and 'low' art is precisely the point – but all the same, we should be careful not to flatten O'Hara into an all-purpose alibi who lets us 'drink too much coffee / and smoke too many cigarettes' and slump in front of Netflix in our cultural pyjamas (even if his much-Instagrammed poem 'Steps' offers a ready-made excuse for the coffee and the cigarettes, at least). After all, the movies may be great, and although the majority of poets can't hold a candle to them, Walt Whitman, Hart Crane and William Carlos Williams most certainly can. In fact, they're *better* than the movies, in O'Hara's estimation, and one could also throw Stravinsky into the mix, along with a range of other icons of challenging modernist art.

'Having a Coke with You' is the O'Hara poem that encapsulates the full spectrum of his cultural enthusiasms. Another deceptively offhand love poem, it starts with a barrage of praise for the beloved, in which the speaker casually declares that having a Coke with them 'is even more fun than going to San Sebastian, Irún, Hendaye, Biarritz, Bayonne / or being sick to my stomach on the Travesera de Gracia in Barcelona' – again, with that keen nose for quality, ranking this everyday but fulfilling experience above a jaunt through the most fashionable tourist spots along the Basque and Catalan coasts. The second stanza widens the comparative lens from travel to art:

I look
at you and I would rather look at you than all the portraits
    in the world
except possibly for the *Polish Rider* occasionally and
    anyway it's in the Frick
which thank heavens you haven't gone to yet so we can go
    together for the first time
and the fact that you move so beautifully more or less
    takes care of Futurism
just as at home I never think of the *Nude Descending a
    Staircase* or
at a rehearsal a single drawing of Leonardo or Michelangelo
    that used to wow me

This is not a poem that is shy in its hyperbole. The object of the speaker's affections 'more or less takes care of' the last six centuries of art, from Futurism back through Duchamp's *Nude Descending a Staircase* to the Renaissance masters 'that used to wow' him. In the midst of this grand catalogue, however, he spares a single artwork from the sword of his passion – Rembrandt's *Polish Rider*, which he begs leave to visit in the Frick gallery from time to time.

Transported by the pell-mell rush of the syntax, we'd be forgiven for thinking the *Polish Rider* might be a Pop extravaganza to match the tenor of the speaker's feelings. Googling it, though, we'd find something decidedly different: a gorgeous but imposing man staring back at us on horseback, under dark and variegated skies. His smile is inscrutable, and one hand sits cocked on his hip, holding an axe above a sheath of arrows. Love and fizzy drinks couldn't be further from the scene. It's a typical O'Hara twist to unleash these brooding atmospheres on the diner where he's sitting with his boyfriend, having a glass of Coke, many thousand miles away in space and time from this Cossack patrolling Europe's eastern borders. Suddenly we're closer to the landscape of 'Mayakovsky', and that troubled world that is 'grey and / brown and white in trees'.

Maybe half a dozen times now, I've taught 'Having a Coke with You' to teenagers – kids in sixth form, usually, who are far enough along in their romantic careers to tap into the mood, and willing enough as budding intellectuals to take on the helter-skelter challenge of the references. Contrary to popular belief, O'Hara isn't easy. The stream of his consciousness pelts thick and fast down the page, and it often isn't intended for you, as such. He wrote for particular audiences – sometimes audiences of one – that could rely on their intimacy with the author to make sense of the gaps and leaps in his thinking. To scaffold 'Having a Coke with You' as an accessible learning experience, one needs a slide show full of paintings and a rudimentary map of Europe. It's a lot of heavy lifting to do for a supposedly spontaneous poem issued straight from the heart.

Yet for all these obstacles, they get it – oh, how they get it. They get the fact that 'fun' has been invoked by the end of the first line, and bottled in a symbol that may be bad for them but tastes so good. They get the video of him reading the poem in a sassy but tender monotone, a cigarette dangling from his lightly gesturing right hand. And most of all, they get the fact that these apparently arcane references could be endlessly expanded to fit the texture of their lives – that each of us has our own version of romping from San Sebastian to Barcelona and getting sick to our stomach from excitement, or our own peerless masterpiece that only the sexiest, most thrilling people will bear comparison to.

This is O'Hara's gift to us, from one entertainment golden age to another. He helps us to read the pleasures and anxieties that flash across the surface of each individual day, and to write ourselves into the poem of his life. And every time we do that, in some small but meaningful sense, we go a long way to writing the poems of our own lives, too.

22

How to Think Like Sylvia Plath

Her suicide haunts us. I remember when I first came upon the facts of Sylvia Plath's death. I was reading Janet Malcolm's *The Silent Woman: Sylvia Plath and Ted Hughes* for a class on literary biography. Malcolm performs a surgical investigation into the bitter dispute over Plath's legacy and estate that had rumbled on for decades at the time the book was published in 1994. But she also attempts to reconstruct the poet's final days, during which Plath cared for her young children, alone, while battling a fierce bout of depression in a bitterly cold English winter. (Her husband, Hughes, had been having an affair, leading to the couple's separation.)

There's a sentence that still rattles around my mind, telescoping the agonizing details of the day when she ended her life. 'Whatever Hughes might have undone or redone in his relationship to Sylvia Plath,' Malcom writes, 'the opportunity was taken from him when she committed suicide, in February 1963, by putting her head in a gas oven as her two small children slept in a bedroom nearby, which she had sealed against gas fumes, and where she had placed mugs of milk and a plate of bread for them to find when they awoke.' That final act of care knocks the wind out of me – the bereft tenderness, the rationality.

For a fuller sketch of the life and myth of Sylvia Plath, we can turn to Elaine Showalter:

> We all know the story. A brilliant, neurotic young American woman poet, studying on a fellowship at Cambridge, meets and marries the 'black marauder' who is the male poet-muse of her fantasies. Doubled and twinned [. . .] they launch on the hard labour of poetic careers, supporting themselves on writing prizes and intermittent teaching jobs. She dreams that they will divide the kingdom of poetic fame; she will be 'The Poetess of America', as he will be 'The Poet of England and her dominions'. But the marriage frays. Tied down to their two babies, frustrated at the slowness of success, she discovers that he is having an affair, and they separate. In the following months, she writes the greatest and angriest poems of her life, perhaps the greatest of her generation: but they are rejected by literary editors as 'too extreme'. In the coldest winter of the century, at the age of 30, she commits suicide by gassing herself.

'We all know the story': yes, indeed, and isn't this part of the problem? Plath was an astonishing writer, yet her public image tapers dreadfully towards that February day in a north London kitchen.

'Lady Lazarus' is one of those 'greatest and angriest' of poems that she wrote towards the end of her life, gathered in the posthumous collection *Ariel*. It's a poem about attempting suicide that uncannily predicts the voyeuristic future that awaited the author when her attempts finally proved successful. With a bracing lack of decorum, Plath imagines the 'peanut-crunching crowd' that will come barging in to see her in her shroud, before they 'unwrap me hand and foot— / The big strip tease'. By this point in her writing life – and it pays to remember that she was only 30 – Plath had whittled her craft down to a fearsome music, half oracle, half nursery rhyme. 'Do I terrify?' she asks at one point, and we can assume the answer is supposed to be 'yes'.

The irregular three-line stanzas screech around various hairpin bends – short lines, queasy sing-song rhythms, and rhymes so wrong they come out sounding weirdly right.

Dying
Is an art, like everything else.
I do it exceptionally well.

I do it so it feels like hell.

It's a poem that seems always to be on the verge of saying the unsayable. It flirts with a strange Nazi iconography that critics have traced to Otto Plath, the overbearing German-born father who died when Plath was eight.

Those Oedipal storms are raging on the surface of *Ariel*, but so is an otherworldly calm: a sense, in the words of 'Edge', that 'The woman is perfected' in pursuing her death. The passive voice in that line is truly chilling ('perfected' by whom, for whom?). No less memorable are the lines that follow, signalling a final sigh of contentment: 'Her dead / Body wears the smile of accomplishment, / The illusion of a Greek necessity.'

Plath was clearly aware of how her life and death could fit into a tragic mould. 'Greek necessity' gestures to Aristotle's theory of tragedy, where he talks about the 'pity' and 'fear' that an audience experiences watching a great figure's inevitable demise, leading to a moment of catharsis where they feel purged of these emotions. In fiction we willingly embrace this arc. There isn't a real person to worry about behind the story, so we can enjoy the cathartic release without feeling bad about the consequences. The hero's fall is inevitable because it was written that way.

It's part of what makes *Ariel* so complex and unsettling that Plath seems to invite us to believe in that inevitability before pulling the rug away. We lean into the air of 'Greek necessity', forgetting that this is just an 'illusion'. There's a real person lurking behind the speaker's fictional pose – and neither her life nor her death were preordained, or made for our consumption.

What did Plath think about poetry? More interestingly, how did she do her thinking in poetry, and how did it relate to her wider understanding of the world? These are the questions that should occupy us in a book like this. I want to approach them in a slightly roundabout way, by looking at the single novel that she wrote in her lifetime.

The Bell Jar has gone on to become a multimillion-selling phenomenon. It's an intriguing, raw and in many ways gripping novel about a young woman named Esther Greenwood's mental breakdown and recovery. Set in New York, Boston and suburban Massachusetts in 1953 – 'the summer they electrocuted the Rosenbergs' – it fictionalizes Plath's real-life hospitalization after she attempted suicide through an overdose of sleeping pills. The book has become a token of precocious, alienated young womanhood, a phenomenon that Janet Badia explores in a witty survey of the novel's many on-screen cameos in films and TV shows ranging from *Natural Born Killers* to *Family Guy*. Predictably, this popularity and the demography of its assumed readership has led to the novel being routinely dismissed as a 'potboiler'; pap for teenage girls.

In recent years its critical reputation has caught up with its pop-cultural celebrity. Analysis tends to focus on the themes of feminism, psychiatry and sex, or on its cultural context as a Cold War novel. (The Rosenbergs were alleged Soviet spies, caught up in America's Red Scare of the early '50s.) Less remarked upon, perhaps because it's so obvious to say of a story based on Sylvia Plath's life, is Esther's identity as a budding poet. Badia nods to this when she talks about her as a woman who enjoys a plethora of life choices based on 'her success as a student'. 'In one of the central metaphors of the novel,' she explains, 'Esther imagines these choices in her life as a green fig tree branching out before her, with one fig representing "a husband and a happy home and children", another fig representing "Europe", others representing an academic career, publishing, poetry; and "beyond and above these figs were many more figs [she] couldn't quite make out".' This is true as far as it goes, though it sucks poetry into the morass of possibilities, as just another option a listless high achiever could turn her hand to if she tried.

There's more to be said for Esther's poetic vocation. Admittedly, Plath frames it as something that other characters casually demean, and Esther has internalized this condescension, seeing poetry as a goofy little hobby. But that in itself tells a story. Our first glimpse of a real-life versifier comes in chapter three, when Esther goes to lunch with her boss – she starts the novel doing a placement at a fashion magazine in New York – and 'a famous poet'. He's a classic bohemian, turning up at the smart restaurant dressed in 'a horrible, lumpy, speckled brown tweed jacket and grey pants and a red-and-blue checked open-throated jersey', before proceeding to eat his salad 'with his fingers, leaf by leaf, while talking to me about the antithesis of nature and art'. Despite his flagrant lack of manners, this is a guy whose whims and theories the world is happy to indulge. 'Nobody giggled or whispered rude remarks,' Esther says. 'The poet made eating salad with your fingers seem to be the only natural and sensible thing to do.'

Esther, meanwhile, has to cram poetry into the cracks of her life as a model student. At college, she's required to take classes across the sciences as part of her English major. She does well in botany but finds physics to be a drag (or a form of 'death', to go with her own dramatic phrasing). 'What I couldn't stand,' she says, 'was this shrinking everything into letters and numbers. Instead of leaf shapes and enlarged diagrams of the holes the leaves breathe through and fascinating words like carotene and xanthophyll on the blackboard, there were these hideous, cramped, scorpion-lettered formulas in Mr Manzi's special red chalk.'

This brings us close to the inside of Esther's imagination, and by extension Plath's. She hates abstraction and constraint, the 'shrinking' of a vivid world into letters, numbers and formulas. One thinks here of Wordsworth's famous line dismissing the sciences ('We murder to dissect'), which could connect Esther to a deeper philosophical lineage, if she cared to take on the mantle of a Romantic. The irony, though, is that she quite likes some of the surface trappings of science – its parade of 'enlarged diagrams' and jazzy vocabulary – and so hits on a handy scheme to get the best of both worlds.

Duping the college into letting her sit in on the chemistry class for no credit, and thereby ticking the science box without getting examined on it, she finds a regular, undisturbed window for writing poems. There's a lovely moment where all the pieces slot into place. 'Mr Manzi stood at the bottom of the big, rickety old amphitheatre, making blue flames and red flares and clouds of yellow stuff by pouring the contents of one test-tube into another, and I shut his voice out of my ears by pretending it was only a mosquito in the distance and sat back enjoying the bright lights and the coloured fires and wrote page after page of villanelles and sonnets.'

As she sits back and enjoys the light show, scribbling her verses, Esther is almost daring us to dismiss her. Who is this superficial young lady, so clearly out of her academic depth? But her dilettantism is also the key to her talent as a poet. By being able to tune out the noise and associate freely, she succeeds in describing the world in a unique and vivid way. When Esther looks at the UN building, she doesn't see a symbol of politics or international brotherhood, but 'a weird, green, Martian honeycomb' jutting into the New York skyline. In these moments of lurid vision, the slippage between Esther Greenwood, naïve young poet, and Sylvia Plath, mature literary artist, is hard to distinguish. A similar taste for audacious metaphors emerges in the great poems in *Ariel*, which are set in motion by the opening line of 'Morning Song' and its address to a newborn: 'Love set you going like a fat gold watch.'

'Fat' is a particularly Plathian adjective. It can signify disgust, abundance, or often both at the same time. It shows up regularly across *The Bell Jar*, usually in routine body-shaming comments, such as an idle thought Esther has about her boss lying in bed 'with her fat husband', or her encounter with a 'tall, fat medical student'. Yet elsewhere we get 'a grey sky' the morning after Christmas, 'fat with snow', or 'the fat blue china cream jug with the white daisies on it' that accompanies breakfast in the mental hospital where she convalesces. To be sure, these aren't straightforwardly innocent images, but they complicate fatness by connecting it to familiarity, generosity, care. These various associations come woozily together when a nurse leans over Esther in bed and 'her fat breast muffled my face like a cloud or a pillow'.

I'd go further, though, to suggest that fatness underscores Plath's entire relationship with poetry. The tree that represents her future may be wholesome and green, but the fruit at the end of every branch is more troubling, 'a fat purple fig'. This lures a keen Plath reader back to one of her finest poems, 'Blackberrying', where the fruits are depicted 'Big as the ball of my thumb, and dumb as eyes / Ebon in the hedges, fat / With blue-red juices.' Something about the mixture of blackness and fecundity, ripeness and rot, fires Plath's imagination like nothing else.

Both these dark fruits, the figs and the blackberries, call out to another, more frightening image at the climax of 'Daddy'. This is the poem that throbs in the background of all Plath's mature work, a snarling minotaur at the heart of the labyrinth, where she confronts her authoritarian father head-on. In the final stanza, the speaker practically cackles in triumph: 'There's a stake in your fat black heart / And the villagers never liked you. / They are dancing and stamping on you.'

Daddy as a slain vampire; the future as a glut of figs that have fallen, withered, to the floor – in these metaphors of wastage, ecstasy and violence, we see Plath's muse in full flight.

It would be a mistake to disinvent this darkness, out of fear of sensationalizing Plath. In its rhetoric, themes and imagery, her work requires us to take darkness seriously. In her life, though, Plath was many things – a seasonal farm worker in the summer holidays, a keen cook, a handy draughtsperson – and not all of her identities should be filtered through the lens of trauma. She was by all accounts funny and charismatic, qualities that show up richly in her writing.

A recent radio documentary, written and presented by the contemporary poet Emily Berry, brings these different sides of her character together. Titled 'My Sylvia Plath', it interviews people who knew her, alongside younger admirers who have only their cherished impressions to go by. The production weaves their words together alongside those of Plath herself as she crisply reads and discusses her work in footage from the BBC archive. (Her voice! That's a part of the puzzle that deserves an essay in its own right – this grand, ironic New England drawl, sounding so much older than the three decades of life that shaped it.) One of Berry's interviewees is Plath's newest biographer, Heather Clark, who set out explicitly to revise the many accounts of her life that placed her death at the centre, as some sort of awful black hole drawing everything towards it. 'I wanted to try to reframe her life as one that was moving forward,' she tells Berry.

Nobody speaks more movingly, or with greater complexity, about the tension between life and death in this legacy than Berry, who was seven when her mother died, also by suicide. Berry reflects on Plath as another daughter left reeling by a parent's early death (in Plath's case Otto's, when she was eight). 'In Sylvia Plath,' she says, 'the two sides of my mother's death seemed to merge into one person: the mother who had died, and the child who had been left behind.' Another enigma comes to light when Berry considers that of the two surviving friends of Plath she interviews, 'one never saw her happy' and 'one never saw her sad'. This sets up a gorgeous meditation about the value of life at even its lowest ebbs.

> A friend of my mother's once told me how she herself had coped with the intense unhappiness that she experienced for seven years after her husband's death. She told herself, 'Well, I don't have to be happy in order to live.' This wasn't news but it struck me as a revelation – to think that there is as much value in an unhappy life as a happy one. That unhappy people can, in fact, go on. When one feels beset,

when one feels colonized by unhappiness, as Sylvia Plath presumably did in the last months of her life, the thought that there is something very wrong – that one is misusing one's life in being unhappy – just adds to the suffering. If only it were easier to feel that happiness and unhappiness are completely equal, or that they aren't rivals; that to be unhappy is not to have failed at life but just to be living, for the moment, in one of the many ways people live (and, of course, many people live unhappily). And who is to say what wild and miraculous energies might not be released, what immeasurable power the thoughts of an unhappy person might have, what shining starlit epiphanies during those dark nights of the soul?

These are the questions that I'll be carrying forward through the many years of reading Sylvia Plath I hope to enjoy in the future.

23

How to Think Like Audre Lorde

This is the first chapter where the title feels like a presumption. The ruse that has structured my project so far – that there might be clear, transferable ways for anyone to think *like* a given poet – runs into trouble in the case of Audre Lorde, the self-declared 'Black, lesbian, mother, warrior, poet' whose ideas have fundamentally shaped the fight for social justice in recent decades. 'If you are a feminist with a social media account in the 21st century,' writes Reni Eddo-Lodge, 'you'll have come across Audre Lorde's work.' High recognition is one part of what makes the task absurd. (How to improve on the startling clarity of well-known lines like 'Your silence will not protect you', or 'The master's tools will never dismantle the master's house'?) But my identity is, of course, an added layer of audacity, given that for every one of Lorde's first three epithets (Black, lesbian, mother) I would have to insert the opposite (White, straight, father). How can a person like me hope to be a reliable witness to Lorde's thought, much less the author of a how-to guide?

It's the remaining two words in her list that provide some kind of entry point. 'Warrior' and 'poet' are more porous; no longer innate characteristics, but inhabitable roles. They open up space for common cause. This, I believe, is part of Lorde's purpose in listing identities in the first place: not to put up barriers between people but to locate points of connection and invite solidarity on that basis. The barriers will exist in any case and Lorde's formula helps us to think about how they are constructed. The listing also invites us to consider our own status within a culture where people are stratified in this manner – and to sign up for the project of dismantling and rebuilding the culture if it strikes us as unjust.

Lorde was a guiding spirit in the evolution of intersectionality, the modern theory of how privilege and disadvantage cut across social groups. First labelled by the legal scholar Kimberlé Crenshaw in 1989, intersectionality holds that different forms of marginalization overlap and reinforce one another. A poor White single mother faces many of the same struggles as a poor Black single mother, yet by not having to contend with racism on top of her financial and family pressures, the White single mother navigates the world differently. Conversely, the Black single mother has every experience of poverty compounded by the fact that she also has to wade through the obstacles of race. This might seem only to state the obvious, but it hasn't stopped many irate commentators from lamenting about how intersectionality amounts to a non-stop 'Oppression Olympics'.

Lorde had no need of the term 'intersectionality', but she lays out a groundwork for the theory in her essay 'There Is No Hierarchy of Oppressions'. The title alone explains, if any explanation were needed, why the trolls have got this 'Olympics' idea all twisted: this isn't about ranking or gloating about oppressions; rather, it's about mapping them out so they can be understood more clearly and abolished. None is intrinsically greater or worse than any other. Coming of age intellectually in the New York feminist movements of the

1960s and '70s, Lorde grew infuriated by the subtle racism she experienced at the hands of would-be White allies. Meanwhile, fellow travellers from the Black liberation movement were often embarrassed about her status as a queer woman in an interracial relationship.

This is how she frames the issue, with a transparency that not even a puce-faced panellist on *Question Time* could misconstrue:

> Within the lesbian community I am Black, and within the Black community I am a lesbian. Any attack against Black people is a lesbian and gay issue, because I and thousands of other Black women are part of the lesbian community. Any attack against lesbians and gays is a Black issue, because thousands of lesbians and gay men are Black.

We make an error, in other words, when we treat Blackness or queerness as isolated phenomena, as if people were siloed in one of those identities without also being the other (or, for that matter, carers, employees, landlords, welfare claimants, degree holders, sufferers of depression – you name it). 'I simply do not believe that one aspect of myself can possibly profit from the oppression of any other part of my identity,' Lorde contends. It makes no sense to pick and choose which fights to back because all forms of persecution derive from the same sources: fear of difference, scarcity, the desire for domination. As soon as someone aligns themselves with the oppressor out of personal convenience, they sell themselves down the river – because with an arbitrary change of mood or circumstance, the same forces could just as easily be aligned against them. Or, as Lorde puts it: 'I know that my people cannot possibly profit from the oppression of any other group which seeks the right to peaceful existence.'

These words ring out with visionary precision in an era so bitterly polarized and misinformed as ours, when divisions are often cynical smokescreens created by those with power to divert the powerless from forming effective coalitions. As the old Latin phrase has it, *cui bono?* Who benefits? Unless in some real sense you can say that everyone does, the chances are that you don't either.

When we read these ideas laid out in Lorde's essays and speeches – meticulously, with due regard to complexity but zero tolerance for bad faith and distractions – it can all appear so simple. Simple to grasp, that is, not to bring into being: if nothing else, Lorde reminds us how entrenched injustice is, and how difficult it is to disentangle from our daily lives.

It isn't simple to understand, of course – neither the problem itself nor her diagnosis of the solutions. Underneath its lucid surface, Lorde's nonfiction disguises years of hard, intricate thinking. She arrives at conclusions and calls to action where many writers would throw up their hands and wallow in ambiguity. But that doesn't erase the long road it must have taken to get there.

What of poetry, though? Cast your mind back to the introduction of this book, where I discussed John Keats's view that '[w]e hate poetry that has a palpable design on us', meaning poetry that tries to tell us what to think. If we go along with that, then where does that leave Lorde, a poet with a unique gift for persuasion who seems to have exactly such a 'palpable design' on changing our minds? I don't want to spend time with a poet who uses language merely as a means to an end, a rhetorical tool designed to convince us of this or that position. On the other hand, I don't want to read poetry cut off from the realities that Lorde explores in her work. I want ethically engaged poetry that can help me to see things in a new light, without going so far as to bludgeon me over the head. But when the chips are down and we're dealing with something urgent, like racism or police violence, do any of these niceties really matter?

The first thing to say here is that Lorde understood these tensions intimately. Here is the start of 'Power', the opening poem in her 1976 collection, *Between Our Selves*:

The difference between poetry and rhetoric
is being ready to kill
yourself
instead of your children.

Poetry and rhetoric are not the same thing, then. The two forms of speech have separate properties and address different needs. That's about as much as I can clearly say when trying to interpret this stanza. It's fiendishly difficult to parse, casting doubt from the start on any certainty the reader might be tempted to hold on to. No sooner has the opening line set up a crisp distinction ('The difference between a mammal and a reptile', it sounds like) than it unravels in a web of metaphor. Which type of language corresponds to 'being ready to kill / yourself' and which, by implication, to killing 'your children'?

I showed this to my colleague Bohdan, and asked him how he read it. (Such are the everyday water-cooler conversations in creative writing departments, believe me.) Bohdan pointed out something that I'd passed over, which is that from a strictly grammatical point of view, poetry must be killing yourself and rhetoric must be killing your children. That's the order of phrasing and, objectively speaking, I can't argue with it. For some reason, though, I find it tricky to swing behind this conclusion. Maybe it's because the whole thing just feels so counterintuitive. Reading Lorde, we're used to encountering systems of oppression that are violent, even fatal. But this interpretation brings the killing in-house, laying it at the door of writing itself. Whichever mode you pick – poetry or rhetoric – it will have blood on its hands.

Here Bohdan bravely had a go at a paraphrase. The rough sense might be (and here I paraphrase Bohdan) that poetry requires us to be brutal with ourselves, to go to dark places within our psyches that we'd prefer to avoid – which, in a manner of speaking, it *kills* us to acknowledge – whereas rhetoric means getting your hands dirty, going out into the world, and being unafraid to hurt those closest to you if that's what it takes. (It reminds me of the common advice in writers' workshops to 'kill your darlings' – that is, take a scalpel to the bits of a story or poem that you're most attached to just because they sound pretty or clever.) It felt like we were getting somewhere.

Yet the rest of the poem continues to destabilize us. The second stanza draws us into the dreamworld of the speaker, where a 'dead child' can be seen 'dragging his shattered black / face off the edge of my sleep'. Has he been killed by her own subconscious? By the poem? Certainly, as far as the reader is concerned, he'd have no existence either way if the poet didn't mention him. This lends some support to Bohdan's tentative reading, only this time it's poetry, not rhetoric, that appears to be the perpetrator – the medium that makes children die – perhaps in order to cope with grief and violence in the world beyond the poem.

But then we're flipped around again. The next stanza confronts us with a child murder that unequivocally did take place, in the real world, in a way that seems to be nothing to do with poetry. This time the culpability lies with a 'policeman who shot down a ten year old in Queens' and 'stood over the boy with his cop shoes in childish blood', saying, '"Die you little motherfucker"'. To head off any doubts, Lorde adds that 'there are tapes to prove it'. It isn't hard to see why her work speaks to a social media age, when we are constantly being asked to negotiate the difference between uploaded footage, fake news, editorial context and personal response.

'Power' enacts the drama of activism and moral choice in a messy, fucked-up world. It serves as a kind of workbook, a space in which all the clashing thoughts and sensations of Lorde's political imagination can mingle and collide. After all, we don't form our political opinions in some kind of pristine vacuum: we do it while contending with newspaper headlines, dreams, the flashing images on our screens, and all the emotional, irrational hunches that have to inform our morals, even if we don't let them have the final say. Poetry is a medium that can be true to that wider force field, in stark contrast to rhetoric, which has to sweep all the uncertainty aside in favour of a sleek, articulated position.

And this is where I came to my third, or fourth, or twenty-fifth reading of that opening stanza. Until this point it had seemed to be saying that there are these two necessary forms of writing (poetry and rhetoric) that involve two necessary forms of violence (figuratively speaking, killing yourself and killing your children). You reach for one in some circumstances and for the second in others. But what if we looked at this in a different way, as though the meaning of the metaphor was that you kill yourself precisely to *avoid* having to kill your children? (Think of a bomb about to go off: which parent wouldn't jump on it?) That's certainly one available nuance of what 'instead' could mean in that sentence.

And that got me thinking again about rhetoric, and how so often it's just another way of saying 'manipulation' or 'propaganda'. Empty rhetoric. What if poetry was the form of writing we did to avoid falling into that trap – not so much the flipside of rhetoric as its antidote? Maybe, I thought, we write poems to stay in touch with the chaos of reality, so that when the time comes to clear our minds and get our considered viewpoints down in prose, what emerges isn't the bogus promise of rhetoric, but something closer to wisdom. This is the impression that I get from Lorde in her finest essays and speeches. 'Take me or leave me,' she seems to say, 'but here is where I stand. This is what liberation could look like. Now – will you join me?'

Lorde was born in New York City in 1934, the daughter of Barbadian and Grenadine parents who had emigrated to the USA ten years earlier. After graduating with a master's in library science from Columbia University in 1961, she embarked on a career in that field in New York's public schools. In 1962, she married a legal aid lawyer named Edwin Rollins. Since Rollins was himself queer (and White), Lorde considered the marriage to be a 'social experiment', albeit one that delivered them two children. Whatever the relationship was like, it held until their divorce in 1970, after which Lorde set up home in Staten Island with their children and her new partner, Frances Clayton. Lorde died in 1992 after a long, intermittent battle with cancer, which she wrote about unsparingly in works like *The Cancer Journals* (1980).

She had her first poem published while still in high school, in an issue of *Seventeen* magazine, but it took her until the age of 34 to publish a full volume of poetry, *The First Cities* (1968). This was a pivotal year, since it also saw Lorde move to Jackson, Mississippi to become poet-in-residence at Tougaloo College, a historically Black institution. Here is where she met Clayton, a psychology professor, and where she developed a passion for education in the course of running a poetry workshop. 'The ways in which I was on the line in Tougaloo . . .' she recalled to Adrienne Rich in 1979. 'I began to learn about courage, I began to learn to talk. This was a small group and we became very close. I learned so much from listening to people. The only thing I had was honesty and openness.'

On her return to New York, she brought this spirit of honesty and openness to bear on a new, more polemical style of writing pioneered in her second volume, *Cables to Rage* (1970). The collection opens with 'Rites of passage', a poem dedicated to Martin Luther King Jr that reads like a tough-minded epitaph to the dialogue on dreams that had developed between King and Langston Hughes in the decade or so before their deaths (Hughes's in 1967, King's in 1968). 'Once we suffered   dreaming', Lorde says, before evoking the image of children playing. This would ordinarily be a symbol of innocence, except these are children who 'follow the game / without winning'. Perhaps, then, they are Black children, learning how to find a sliver of freedom and contentment in a world that's rigged against them. The final two lines strike a note of hope – 'we are growing / through dream' – though after counting the cost of all the death and failure this short poem packs in, it seems to be a very qualified sort of hope.

Another *Cables to Rage* poem is important here. 'Poem for a poet' is an elegy to Randall Jarrell, one of the key writers and critics of the American postwar era. It continues a conversation with him in the wake of his 1965 death, when he was hit by a car while walking along the highway, in an incident many suspect to be a suicide. Lorde had met Jarrell not long before his death, at a weekend-long spring festival held at the North Carolina Women's College. ('He had the flavor of someone who had retreated, who had performed a final action,' she later recalled in an interview with Karla M. Hammond.) It was a positive, formative occasion, during which Lorde said, 'I learned much about myself.' Jarrell was an encouraging presence, 'a good experience of my trip South'.

This feeling of fondness and respect carries over into 'Poem for a poet', though Lorde's address to Jarrell also confronts something that had been missing in their earlier encounter. In hindsight, Lorde remembers the festival as 'a coffin's retreat / of spring whispers   romance   rhetoric' – a reminder that rhetoric isn't just something that people do from podiums and newspaper columns, it's something they do in poems too. All those centuries of (mainly White and male) poets talking in 'spring whispers' about affairs of the heart come spooling out in a messy heap. Lorde exposes how historically privileged that type of writing is, and how insulated it is from the struggles that so many people face. The poems read at the festival lacked any awareness of the ongoing civil rights campaigns still roiling across the South at the time: 'nobody mentioned the Black Revolution / or Sit-Ins   or Freedom Rides   or SNCC / or cattleprods in Jackson Mississippi'. By implication, Lorde's is the poetry that will fill this gap, and already we can see that it requires a much messier, more open form to make sense of these realities.

This is a changing-of-the-guard moment, though for many years afterwards it would have been hard to tell that anything had changed at all, at least if you surveyed the poetic mainstreams of Britain and America. Political poetry waxed and waned in popularity, as it always does, though White men continued to win prizes and dominate the publishing scene. From today's vantage point, the extent to which this situation has changed could be debated – I think most people would agree that positive, though incomplete progress has been made in recent years – but what seems clear to me is that the most exciting work of the twenty-first century takes its cues from Audre Lorde. It continues to write into the apolitical absence that she detected in North Carolina at that spring festival in the '60s, often in forms that sit suggestively on the borderline between verse and prose. Claudia Rankine, Anne Carson, Ocean Vuong, Anthony (Vahni) Capildeo, Danez Smith, Layli Long Soldier, Bhanu Kapil, Terrance Hayes: these are the poets at work now who are keeping the (English) language fresh, agile and in touch with current events. And those are just the blockbuster names. The list leaves out dozens of excellent lesser-known poets likewise working in Lorde's slipstream.

But politics, like slang, can date a poem faster than a time stamp. On its own, it's never enough to be topical or committed. Lorde understood that her work needed deeper roots to build a sustainable alternative to that dead old mode of 'spring whispers   romance   rhetoric'. One way she nurtured these roots can be found in *Zami: A New Spelling of My Name* (1982). Today we might call this 'biomythography' an example of autofiction, the title given to the contemporary genre where a story's plot and protagonist link closely, if waywardly, to the life of the author (famous exponents include Sheila Heti, Ben Lerner, Rachel Cusk and Karl Ove Knausgård). Whoever the narrator of *Zami* is exactly, and whatever relationship she bears to the real-life Audre Lorde, her coming-of-age story tells us a lot about how poetry could be reimagined in her image. This is a story that begins not with the narrator but with her mother, Linda, and the type of knowledge that she brought with her from the Caribbean to a cold and indifferent New York.

'There was so little that she really knew about the stranger's country,' Lorde writes. What she does know amounts to a set of basic survival skills, conditioned by her immediate surroundings: 'How the electricity worked. The nearest church. Where the Free Milk Fund for Babies handouts occurred, and at what time.' As the narrator develops the litany, however, we get closer and closer to the source of her mother's inner mind.

> She knew about mixing oils for bruises and rashes, and about disposing of all toenail clippings and hair from the comb. About burning candles before All Souls Day to keep the soucouyants away, lest they suck the blood of her babies. She knew about blessing the food and yourself before eating, and about saying prayers before going to sleep.

More revealing, even, than these close-held bodily rituals and beliefs is Linda's 'special and secret relationship with words'. Lorde explores this bone-deep idiolect in a section of *Zami* titled 'How I Became a Poet'. Here she summons old phrases like 'next kin to nothing' (used to describe someone's skimpy, unsuitable attire) and 'from Hog to Kick 'em Jenny' (a measurement for 'impossible distances' derived from the names of reefs in the Grenadines). These half-remembered idioms mingle with memories of her mother's body in bed, 'the morning smells soft and sunny and full of promise'. There's a telling snapshot as her mother applies petroleum jelly to the narrator's scalp, a moment of everyday care that evokes *'the rhythms of a litany, the rituals of Black women combing their daughters' hair'*. These are rhythms, we intuit, that have nothing at all to do with iambic pentameter.

'I am a reflection of my mother's secret poetry as well as of her hidden angers.' This realization offers a radical new way of grounding a poet's education. Rather than steeping herself in a literary canon that has no interest in who she is or where she's

come from, Lorde reorients her art, quite literally, towards her mother culture. This approach chimes with a passage in her essay 'Poetry Is Not a Luxury', where she laments a 'european mode' of thought that sees the world 'only as a problem to be solved', a kind of prison where 'we rely solely upon our ideas to make us free'. Her next paragraph shapes the alternative:

But as we become more in touch with our own ancient, black, non-european view of living as a situation to be experienced and interacted with, we learn more and more to cherish our feelings, and to respect those hidden sources of our power from where true knowledge and therefore lasting action comes.

Her mother is one such hidden source of power. By shining a light on her in *Zami*, Lorde aligns poetry with a deeper literary canon – not the parade of educated, famous, mostly 'european' men whose work has been passed down to us in print, but the anonymous millions whose wisdom has been scattered on the wind. Her mother could very easily have become one of them, had Lorde not recalled her to the world. Heeding the lessons of her work, then, it becomes our responsibility – as readers, writers and lovers of poetry – to make sure such a loss is never allowed to happen again.

24

How to Think Like a Contemporary Poet

As a creative writing teacher, I'm used to students coming to class with set ideas about poetry – what it is, what it should be. Many of those ideas have roots buried deep in history. That it has to rhyme is the big one, though nowadays most people are wise to my agenda when I broach the topic. ('No, Dai, it doesn't *have* to rhyme,' they concede. 'It's just nice if it does!') Good modern poetry can rhyme, of course, as anyone who's read A. E. Stallings or Paul Muldoon will confirm, though usually it doesn't. It tends to be written in the loose, endlessly adaptable mode that we still call 'free verse', for want of a better term. Alas, that label essentially describes everything and nothing in an era when a very high percentage of poetry is 'free', in the sense that it steers clear of rhyme, meter and set forms. It would be quicker to count the people who still go in for iambic pentameter than those who don't.

We need to remind ourselves that this is a pretty big change from the historical norm. Free verse (or 'vers libre') originally sprang up as a necessary term to describe a radical minority of French writers around the 1880s: poets like Jules Laforgue who, in his *Derniers vers* (Last Verses), chucked the rule book out the window and composed without constraints. Spreading to English-language poetry through the modernists – Pound, Eliot, H.D., Wallace Stevens – it quickly became standard practice. So familiar was free verse by the 1930s that Robert Frost could quip that he'd rather play tennis with the net down than write in that style. It's a good analogy, witty and to the point, though of course it loads the dice by suggesting that poetry can only be fun and rewarding if we abide by the rules. That works for sport, but I'm not sure it's true at all when it comes to literature. In fact, one could say that the history of modern poetry is a history of people learning to live, feel and write in a universe without any rules.

Nevertheless, teaching creative writing I sometimes feel like a tennis coach trying to enthuse people about the virtues of playing without a net. They've turned up fully prepared, sweatbands on their foreheads, racquets at the ready, and the first thing I get them to do is rally back and forth on an empty court. To keep our spirits up, I point to something lovely that Carl Sandburg once said in response to Frost ('I have not only played tennis without a net but have used the stars for tennis balls'). At first this goes down well, until we try to play a game in the Sandburg spirit and realize that we don't have any stars. Metaphors are tricky like that, and they often seem to be the only thing that poets have to hand.

I exaggerate a little. (Only joking – I exaggerate a lot. Come do a class with me! It'll be fun.) But the substantial point remains that poetry in the twenty-first century is a strange – and I think very wonderful – form of creativity without rules. It can be this, it can be that, but it's more likely to be something else. If the person who wrote it calls it a poem, then it's a poem. That can be a hard thing to explain without resorting to mysticism. (Think back to those great lines from

Emily Dickinson: 'If I read a book [and] it makes my whole body so cold no fire ever can warm me I know that is poetry. If I feel physically as if the top of my head were taken off, I know that is poetry. These are the only ways I know it. Is there any other way?') What I'm most interested in, I tell my students, is not poetry as a literary form or genre, necessarily, but rather a way of seeing and relating to the world – a way of thinking.

'But what does that *mean*?' they ask.

And it's a fair question. So I try to go back to the root of things, in the hope that by sifting through all the old ideas about poetry, we can emerge with a clear-ish picture of how poets think today.

I start with Alexander Pope, and a quote we've already met in the chapter on William Wordsworth:

True wit is nature to advantage dress'd,
What oft was thought, but ne'er so well express'd,
Something, whose truth convinc'd at sight we find,
That gives us back the image of our mind.

This is cheating a bit, since Pope is talking about 'True wit', not poetry. In fact, he sets up wit as a rival to poetry, not as its ideal definition. (The lines just before this go: 'Poets, like painters, thus, unskill'd to trace / The naked nature and the living grace, / With gold and jewels cover ev'ry part, / And hide with ornaments their want of art.' By which he means that poets don't have the talent or confidence to let plain, unadorned reality – 'naked nature' – shine through their work. The scallywag!) I keep it in, though, because Pope is bitching on poetry in a poem, so the quote ends up serving, ironically, as a handy definition of the type of poem that he aspires to write. Poetry à la Pope will converge on the profoundest insights;

truths so arresting when we encounter them that they seem self-evident. In short, this is the perfect capsule definition of the Enlightenment poem.

This sparks a chain reaction that spans the next three centuries. Flicking from slide to slide on my PowerPoint, I run the class through a series of theories and provocations from a gallery of famous poets. Each idea, I suggest, presents itself as an advance on what's come before.

Lights, please!

SLIDE 1
'Poetry is the spontaneous overflow of powerful feelings: it takes its origin from emotion recollected in tranquillity . . .'

Because what contradicts Pope better than a little William Wordsworth? This nugget from the preface to *Lyrical Ballads* is my ground zero of Romanticism. It sets up poetry as a kind of divine outpouring, originating in the dignity and strength of the poet's 'feelings'. Emotion is firmly in the driving seat and Reason can take a hike. We see these words blazoned on top of a portrait of Wordsworth with a hand to his temple, head slightly bowed, presumably weighed down by the burden of all those powerful feelings. It could double as a profile pic for a spoof social media account called Generic Poet from Times of Yore.

Click!

SLIDE 2
'I wish our clever young poets would remember my homely definitions of prose and poetry; that is, prose,— words in their best order; poetry,—the best words in their best order.'

Now, this is from Samuel Taylor Coleridge, Wordsworth's buddy and fellow Romantic. Coleridge was always a spikier intelligence than Wordsworth, and these words – a scrap of dinner-table conversation, preserved by his nephew, Henry Nelson Coleridge – gently mock the pretentions of 'young poets'. This can be read, if you like, as a Pope–Wordsworth hybrid. 'Best words in their best order' lends a bit of backbone to the Romantic cult of the emotions. It elevates poetry to a special pedestal, similar to the one it occupies in Pope's 'Essay on Criticism'. We're back to poetry as the art of hitting the nail on the head, putting one's finger on the truth, articulating 'What oft was thought, but ne'er so well express'd' – only this time with an added spritz of Romantic sensitivity.

Click!

SLIDE 3
'A poem should not mean
But be.'

This jumps forward a good century from the last slide. These lines are from Archibald MacLeish's poem 'Ars Poetica' (1926), and they crystallize a view that starts to bubble up at the end of the nineteenth century. 'Art for Art's Sake' is the slogan, and it became a rallying cry for freethinkers, bohemians and aesthetically minded gentlemen who hated the bossy moralism of the Victorians. The basic idea is that literature should serve no purpose but its own. It doesn't need to edify or instruct, only provide an experience in language. MacLeish takes this a step further to say that poetry shouldn't even try to *mean* anything in the traditional sense. Funnily enough, he expresses this thought in a poem that looks suspiciously like it's trying to mean something. Nevertheless, the idea itself becomes more and more important as poetry gets weirder, and less conventionally 'meaningful', throughout the twentieth century.

Click!

SLIDE 4
'To make two bald statements: There's nothing sentimental about a machine, and: A poem is a small (or large) machine made of words. When I say there's nothing sentimental about a poem I mean that there can be no part, as in any other machine, that is redundant.'

When William Carlos Williams floated these 'bald statements' in 1944, he was taking aim at everything else on my slide deck – poetry as truth; poetry as heightened emotion; poetry in its Sunday best, or as an object of art. That's all just so much 'sentimental' hokum, in Williams's view. A poem is simply a contraption, a word-mechanism where all the cogs fit together. This drags poetry into the modern age, where our lives are likewise governed by machines. At the same time, it refines the stately promise of Pope and Coleridge, buffing up the poem as an orderly design. It's just that now we don't expect the poem to be anything more than that. Meaning is relegated to the sidelines in favour of the design itself – the poem as a functional model, a *thing* 'made of words'. Williams was part of a school called the objectivists, and you can see why.

At this point we take a break. The energy's dipped; the room's got a little sweaty from all those dead folks shouting their opinions. When we reconvene, we talk about the elephant in the room – namely, that all those dead folks are also White and male. (William Carlos Williams was half-Puerto Rican, so this isn't a cut-and-dried matter – but we can generalize.) No coincidence, obviously, when you consider the history of literature. No coincidence, either, that this identity generates self-assurance in expression. All of these definitions are assertive and categorical. Poetry *is* this, or – more normative again – a poem *should* do this, not that. This is the language of people who are used to having their voices heard.

It's with the next slide that (finally!) we jump out of the past and approach the contemporary moment.

SLIDE 5
'Poetry is an egg with a horse inside.'

I first came across this line while doing my own master's in creative writing, thanks to one of my teachers, the late, great American poet Lucie Brock-Broido. With her torrent of auburn hair and quizzical smile, Lucie had a unique physical presence and an equally distinctive approach to poetry. If she believed anything, it was that poems should be possessed of something that García Lorca called *duende* – a type of intense energy, comparable to the striking movements of a flamenco dancer. Generations of poets passing through her classes imbibed Lucie's personal poetics, embodied in a chunky, ring-bound volume of photocopied pages that remains one of my treasured possessions. The poems inside exemplified what she was looking for: *duende*; the real deal; a chill so cold that no fire can warm you – call it what you will. Lucie's favourite descriptor in English, as the only word that came close to *duende*, was 'feral'. She urged us all to be feral, in our own ways.

If all this sounds a bit melodramatic, then it was – but it was also playful, tender and nurturing, which is where the egg with a horse inside comes into it. This was a semi-mythical phrase, first attributed to a third-grade student (so an eight- or nine-year-old) that some poet had gleaned on a school visit and spread by word of mouth. Lucie's eyes lit up whenever she thought about the image: the poem as something delicate and perfectly balanced, with this stampeding, feral life force inside. We were asked to come up with our own imagistic definitions, but none of us could improve on it.

Matthea Harvey is another poet who encountered the phrase in a class, introduced by her own teacher, Henri Cole. Harvey has written a lovely essay considering this phrase as a tool for teaching children poetry – or, more specifically, teaching them 'about the transformative swing door of simile, the rabbit hole of metaphor, and how poetry can be or do anything they want it to'. To illustrate the point, she plays along with her own game:

> Poetry is a peacock in a pea coat. Poetry is a UFO made of marshmallows. Poetry is a bowlful of dead bees [. . .] If poetry is all these things, what *can't* it do?

It's that last question that signals the big shift of contemporary poetry. Though less noticeable at first glance, it's a shift as profound as the sea change from formal to free verse that happened in English around a hundred years ago. The modernists may have cast off the shackles of rhyme and meter, but they continued to coin definitions of poetry that tried to limit and distinguish what the art could do. (Pound: 'Poetry is news that stays news.' Stevens: 'The poem must resist the intelligence / Almost successfully.') To enter a world where 'poetry can be or do anything [we] want it to' is to pass from one element to another – the singular to the plural, fire to air.

Armed with our third-grader's definition, we're free at last to leave behind centuries of high-and-mighty thinking about poetry. No more is the word 'poet' a form of value judgement, an exclusive mark of culture, education and taste. As my students can see as well as anyone, that model churned out poets who look exactly like the people in power across western society – my parade of White blokes in dowdy suits.

It isn't that we have to purge that hall of fame. Much of the old work remains essential, and the canon has never been quite as one-dimensional as it seems. Rather, the challenge of contemporary poetry is to step into a new paradigm – one defined not by exclusion, but by expansion and permission. In this new world, a poem can be anything from a peacock in a pea coat to a printout of the BBC home page with every third word erased. It can riff on anything from Hegel to Monica from *Friends*, Stormzy to Fibonacci. It can be high or low, deadpan-ironic or ardently sincere, a spray of isolated fragments or a block of crystalline prose.

It can even rhyme, if you want it to.

But all of this is still to talk about poetry from the wrong end of the telescope, as something to be theorized and talked about rather than enjoyed. How does this newfangled paradigm translate to the kind of thinking that poets are doing on the ground, so to speak – in their poems?

To answer that, we have to start from the premise that contemporary poetry isn't just one thing, but a glorious, many-headed beast. It's the sum total of all the thinking done by the poets in this book, and much more besides.

It's Kate Kilalea writing the freest of free verse in a poem called 'Hennecker's Ditch'. 'I stood at the station like the pages of a book / whose words suddenly start to swim,' it begins, teasing us with this image of language on the brink of turning liquid. Then comes the third line, solid as a nail: '*Wow. The rain. Rose beetles.*' Contemporary poetry means entering side by side with the poet into the privacy of her mind, close enough to hear her say *Wow*. It's raindrops as fat and iridescent as rose chafer beetles. (Elizabeth Bishop would be all over that line.)

It's Danez Smith in 'summer, somewhere', conjuring a counterfactual afterlife for Black boys killed too soon on earth. In this paradise regained, the boys shoot hoops, kiss, and mingle with the landscape. Their causes of death can be seen dimly out of the corner of the reader's eye, in the poem's allusions to guns, branches, and a 'world of laws [that] rendered us into dark / matter'. But here there is also resurrection, of a kind Langston Hughes could scarcely dare to dream of:

someone prayed we'd rest in peace
& here we are

in peace   whole   all summer

Contemporary poetry happens in the space between words, at the edge of the page. It's the different kind of thinking allowed in the long gaps between 'peace' and 'whole' and 'all summer'.

It's the energy of the slam, that arena of performance poetry so long banished to the margins of polite society. Page versus stage: that's how the dichotomy has traditionally been framed, often with an implicit slant from the 'page' camp, a superiority complex, if you will. Smith (pronouns they/them) is just one poet who's shown up the poverty of that split in recent years, their practice having been honed onstage – or in 'the dark bars of slam', as they put it in a recent interview – before blooming into something hybrid and fully itself, equally distinctive on the page. Apart from being ignorant of the sheer skill it takes to pull off a performance poem – the stamina, the presence, the physical coordination of tongue, voice and body – the Anti-Stage Brigade shows remarkable forgetfulness. Poetry's deepest roots lie in oral culture, from the bards of Europe to the griots of West Africa, travelling wordsmiths who would bring the news to people in verse, singing for their supper.

'Griot' is the only job description that Benjamin Zephaniah felt comfortable with, ultimately. As I was getting to the end of writing this book, this great British-Jamaican poet died of a brain tumour, far too young. It's a strange thing to say of someone so widely loved in life, but the poetry world never knew quite what to do with him. A bona fide national treasure – and someone who famously resisted the limitations of that role, repeatedly refusing honours from the British establishment – he was just too popular, too musical, too direct in his approach to get much critical respect from his peers. Now Kae Tempest is going down a similar route, loved by the masses, all but ignored by poetry critics. It's something we poetry critics probably want to take a look at. I'm as guilty as anyone: I hear Tempest's work on BBC Radio 6 Music and find myself nodding to the beat while glazing over the words, too wrapped up in my own page-centric ways to credit that this, too, is somewhere that contemporary poetry is happening.

And the page–stage ruckus is nothing compared with the other great culture-war hot topic in Poetry Land: Instapoetry. This is an elastic, welcoming term for the kind of poetry that flourishes on social media, though the aesthetic has become synonymous with the work of the subculture's runaway star, Rupi Kaur. Now a mega-selling author with serious industry clout, Kaur started out self-publishing her work using the CreateSpace platform as a way of getting round the traditional poetry gatekeepers. Her poems rocketed to popularity on

Instagram, where they appeared accompanied by Kaur's plaintive illustrations. These hand-drawn images – common subjects include flowers, leaves, kites and the human form – underscore the simplicity of the verse, its unabashed proximity to the literature of mindfulness and self-help.

There are interesting discussions to be had about the quality of Kaur's work, involving knotty ideas to do with self-fashioning, authenticity and gender. More often than not, though, the debate gets boiled down to a more simplistic conundrum: namely, whether this stuff counts as poetry in the first place. To this, at least, we can blow a confident raspberry. Yes, Kaur is a poet. Yes, she makes intentional, and rather original, art objects out of words. Yes, she sells gazillions of copies and appeals to millennial women. Next!

One of the main drawbacks of this whole discourse is the way it flattens our understanding of how contemporary poetry happens on the internet. Poems of all types go viral. Take the rude erotic comedy of Hera Lindsay Bird. This New Zealand poet has won a major audience off the back of work that's allusive, complicated, hip to the tropes of high culture and trash, fourth-wave feminism and '90s sitcoms. In one poem she proudly declares, 'Keats is dead so fuck me from behind.' Here's a new kind of negative capability, administered 'Slowly and with carnal purpose' – the implication being that Keats had been dampening our sex drives all along. Off he pops, then, as the speaker and her addressee get down and dirty, egged on by a veritable death wave of Dead White Poets. 'Coleridge is dead and Auden too,' Bird whoops. 'Shelley died at sea and his heart wouldn't burn / & Wordsworth............................ / They never found his body.'

Wordsworth always gets it in the neck, bless him. Contemporary poetry bridles at the ego on display in a poem like 'I wandered lonely as a cloud', in which his poetic persona (or 'lyric "I"') serenely wafts through the world sniffing daffodils. Contemporary poetry comes at him from serious, theoretical perspectives but also funny, irreverent ones, like those of Bird and Sara Nicholson. In 'What the Lyric Is', Nicholson refers to 'A hoax of golden daffodils', twisting the lovely 'host' at the start of Wordsworth's poem into something tantamount to fraud. Down the years, that kind of easy way with nature has tended to come more readily to people with Wordsworth's chromosomes and skin tone, so contemporary poetry routinely stops to ask the question: who is speaking?

Nicholson answers it by asserting a defiantly large and body-positive – or is it? – female presence. ('I am so big / I mean my ass is so big / I can't fit in this room I'm building,' she announces, punning on the fact that 'stanza' comes from the Italian word for 'room'.) For the Jamaican poet Jason Allen-Paisant – who now lives and works in the north of England, not so far from Wordsworth's old stomping grounds – 'I wandered lonely as a cloud' poses a more basic problem. In 'Those Who Can Afford Time', he relates the strange experience of being taught this poem about wet, leafy England and its flora in a Caribbean school. Such leisurely pursuits seemed completely alien to him:

> somehow I knew
> this wandering was not
> for me
>
>   because
> ours was not the same kind of time
>   our wandering never so accidental
> so entire so free

Contemporary poetry may at a deep level be about permission – but it's keenly aware of the many ways that people lack that liberty, both in daily life and in the life of the imagination.

This mixture of stylistic freedom and ethical commitment finds its deepest expression in poetry of the climate crisis. This is perhaps the key subject of poetry in the twenty-first century, as the First World War was to poets of Eliot's generation. No poet has done more to try to think around, and through, our current catastrophe than Jorie Graham. Her recent work has been a long elegy to the world as it used to be, and in 'Day Off' she specifically compares the burden of living under climate crisis to that of living through a war:

> the pre-war life disappeared, just like that, don't look back you'll
> get stiff-necked – there is exhaust in the air in its
> place – the wilderness (try to think of it) does nothing but point to here, how we
>> got here, says it can't stay
>> a minute longer
>> but that we
>> will have to [. . .]

These are matters of the utmost moral urgency, and it sometimes feels like poetry is the only form of language that can rise to the occasion and lend voice to our collective grief. It can't save the world, or take the place of direct action, but if we're lucky it might help us to think through the value of the world we're left with in the future.

Yet for all its brave new powers and responsibilities, poetry still enjoys some of its old privileges. Ambiguity, metaphor and magical thinking; the ability to hold multiple things in mind at once and glide between the options. This is the quality Keats described all those years ago as 'being in uncertainties, mysteries, doubts, without any irritable reaching after fact and reason' – 'Negative Capability', as he neatly termed it: the place where we started our enquiry, and where we end it, too (albeit after a little detour around Keats's corpse in the poetry of Hera Lindsay Bird).

Contemporary poetry lets us have it both ways, as we dance on Keats's grave and light a candle to his memory. It's the glow from a distant fire crossed with the blue light from a phone screen. It's the lyre and the synthesizer locked in a feral duet. It's whatever you might do next, when you put down this book.

ACKNOWLEDGEMENTS

Thanks go first to my editor, Tomasz Hoskins, who has been a receptive and encouraging presence throughout this project. This may be a book in a series, but Tomasz has allowed it to become something else as well – the work of popular poetry criticism I'd always dreamed of writing. Thanks also to Sarah Jones at Bloomsbury for her unstinting work tracking down permissions and much else besides. Mandy Woods was copyeditor extraordinaire, and spared my blushes on more than one occasion by rooting out factual mistakes as well as grammatical glitches. Needless to say, any remaining errors are my responsibility.

Thanks to my agent Rachel Conway and all at GCA.

Thanks to colleagues and students at the University of Birmingham, where I road-tested some of the ideas (and slide shows) mentioned in the book. Special thanks to Bohdan Piasecki for being a sport and allowing me to write up our conversation on Audre Lorde.

I wrote this book in a feverish year and a half that also involved serious family illness, inter-city moves, and the birth of my first child, Asa. This book is dedicated to him, in the hope that he will lead a life filled with whatever kind of poetry he wants. But I can't let this opportunity go by without thanking all the other loved ones in my life who have made this book possible.

Jasmin, thank you for being the most wonderful partner and mother, and for helping me to burrow away and write, no matter how sleep-deprived we were. Reena and Peter, thank you for pitching in with grandparenting beyond the call of duty.

In many ways, it's been an annus horribilis (or two) for my beloved Welsh family, as we've come to terms with the fallout from the set of strokes my father suffered in September 2022. Mam and Dad, I'm in awe of your grace and resilience. You taught me so much about poetry growing up, and I'm always thankful that ours was a house where I could take for granted that art was a serious calling. Catrin and Hannah, thanks for being the best sisters and keeping the show on the road for all the family. Thanks, finally, to my Nan, Mary Davies, who can still recite more poetry by heart than I can. Love to you all.

PERMISSIONS

Every effort has been made to trace copyright holders and to obtain their permission for the use of copyright material. The publisher apologizes for any errors or omissions and would be grateful for notification of any corrections that should be incorporated in future reprints or editions of this book.

HOMER
The Iliad: Homer, A New Translation by Peter Green, University of California Press, 2016.
Emily Wilson verse published in *The Odyssey* by Homer, translated by Emily Wilson, published by W. W. Norton & Company, 2017.

SAPPHO
Sappho, translated by Mary Barnard, University of California Press, 2012.
If not, Winter, Sappho, translated by Anne Carson, published by Little Brown Book Group Limited. Reproduced with permission of the Licensor through PLSclear
Excerpt from 'Pursuit', published in H. D.'s first collection, *Sea Garden*, published by Carcanet Press (1916).

LI BAI
"Please Drink" from THE BANISHED IMMORTAL: A LIFE OF LI BAI (LI PO) by Ha Jin, copyright © 2019 by Ha Jin. Used by permission of Pantheon Books, an imprint of the Knopf Doubleday Publishing Group, a division of Penguin Random House LLC. All rights reserved.
'Drinking Alone Beneath the Moon' by Li Po, translated by David Hinton in *The Selected Poems of Li Po*, published by Carcanet Press, 1998.
By Li Po, translated by David Hinton, from THE SELECTED POEMS OF LI PO, copyright ©1996 by David Hinton. Reprinted by permission of New Directions Publishing Corp.
Excerpt from 'Taking Leave of a Friend' in *Selected Poems 1908–1969* by Ezra Pound, published by Faber & Faber, 2004.
Excerpt from 'Sea-Fever' by John Masefield, in *Sea-Fever*, published by Carcanet Press, 2023. Printed with Permission of The Society of Authors.
From Wong May's translation of Li Bai's poem 'Climbing the Phoenix Terrace in Jinling' from her anthology *In the Same Light: 200 Tang Poems for our Century*, 2022, printed with the permission of Carcanet Press and The Song Cave.

JALAL AL-DIN RUMI
The Essential Rumi, translated by Coleman Barks with John Moyne (Penguin, 1999). Printed with permission of Coleman Barks.
Haleh Liza Gafori excerpts from *Gold*, published by New York Review Books Classics, 2022. Printed with permission of Haleh Liza Gafori
'Rain' (poem) from *The Voice of Sheila Chandra* by Kazim Ali, Alice James Books, 2020.

DANTE ALIGHIERI
The Portable Dante, edited and translated by Mark Musa, Penguin Books, 1995. Reprinted with permission of Indiana University Press.

PERMISSIONS

INDEX